CONTENTS

MANAGEMENT OF THE ENQUIRY

Organization

The data on postmortems, surgery and anaesthesia are presented in tables which refer to the question number in the relevant questionnaires. The questionnaires (deaths) are reproduced as Appendices C and D.

ANAESTHESIA

A   The NCEPOD Protocol, December 1988

B   Glossary of definitions used by NCEPOD

C   Surgical questionnaire (deaths)

D   Anaesthetic questionnaire (deaths)

E   Participants

F   Local reporters

FOREWORD

This report is the outcome of an immense, voluntary effort on the part of thousands of surgeons and anaesthetists to audit their own practice, to see how it can be improved to provide better care for patients in the future.

To all those who participated by filling in the long and detailed questionnaires; to the panels of specialist advisers; the members of the Steering Group; to Ms Anne Campling and her enthusiastic and hard-working staff - I must here express my admiration and very grateful thanks.

The main result of the Enquiry has been encouraging: the prevailing standard of surgery and anaesthesia is excellent and seems to be improving. Since the last Report there has been a notable increase in the proportion of preoperative consultation by Consultant Surgeons, from 84% to 92%. But the purpose of this audit is not with self-congratulation, but to identify where things can be made better.

A small number of our colleagues have not cooperated with this Enquiry: we can but ask them to reconsider their responsibilities. We were also very concerned to see how seldom the opportunity was taken to verify the diagnosis by postmortem examination.

This Enquiry continues to disclose errors arising from want of resources: these are not new, and were themes in both the previous CEPOD and NCEPOD Reports. Elsewhere we found deficiencies in medical practice, some of which were unexpected.

There are four important shortages of resources.

1   Lack of an operating theatre dedicated to emergencies, so that urgent operations have to wait until the regular operating lists have been completed.

2   Lack of adequate facilities for intensive care, without which some operations in very old and sick people can have little chance of success.

3   Insufficient staff: too many anaesthetics are being given, and too many emergency operations are being performed at night on very old and very sick patients, by doctors in training grades without supervision, and by anaesthetists working alone.

4   Among these doctors were a number classified as *locum tenens*. We continue to be concerned about the standards for these appointments.

Six professional matters give rise to concern.

1   Some operations seem to have been done without any realistic hope of success e.g. amputations in patients destined to die within a few days.

2   Some operations were done with hasty and inadequate preparation of the patient.

3   Postoperative deep vein thrombosis and pulmonary embolism continues to be an important cause of death. Sometimes the conventional precautions were not used - either because the risk was not appreciated - or because it was feared that they would lead to bleeding. Equally often they were used, but failed to prevent thromboembolism i.e. the available precautions do not always work and further research is urgently needed to find better ones. There is no room for complacency.

4   Excessive quantities of fluid were sometimes given during and after the operation in a number of patients.

5   Non-invasive methods of monitoring should be used more often before and during induction of anaesthesia.

6   A few surgeons were tackling operations with which they were not familiar. Peer review and audit ought to put an end to this, but what is to be done about those who participate in neither?

Indeed, the message of this Report must be that we must all take part in audit for there is still much to learn and we need hard data to support our demands for better resources to provide proper care.

J P Blandy

Chairman, Steering Group

The National Confidential Enquiry into Perioperative Deaths

July 1993

INTRODUCTION

The National Confidential Enquiry into Perioperative Deaths was launched in 1988 and commenced data collection on 1 January 1989. It is concerned with the quality of the delivery of anaesthesia and surgery and the perioperative care of the patient: it does not study the causation of death. The protocol is derived from that of the Confidential Enquiry into Perioperative Deaths for which the Report was published in December 1987[1].

The first national Report, on the 1989 data, was published in June 1990[2] and concentrated on the care of children up to the age of 10 years. In April 1992, the 1990 Report was published[3]; the detailed review covered a random sample of one in five of all deaths reported to the Enquiry.

The current (third) national Report is centred on the sample for 1991/92 (1 April to 31 March) which covered specific procedures over all surgical specialties.

We are disappointed at the continuing lack of adequate essential services in some hospitals, the continuing shortfall in data supplied to us, the poor response of some Consultants to us and the persistent problem of locums.

ACKNOWLEDGEMENTS

The Steering Group acknowledges the enormous effort of local reporters and support staff in providing the basic data on deaths and of the anaesthetists, gynaecologists, and surgeons who have completed questionnaires. The advisory groups for anaesthesia, gynaecology, pathology and surgery have devoted many hours to the Enquiry, reviewing questionnaires and drafts of this Report.

The organization of the Enquiry would be impossible without the hard work of the NCEPOD staff; Jennifer Drummond, Linda Friel, Joanne Hawkins, Sharon McGarrity, Michelle Neustroski and Monica Stubbings, and Deputy Administrator Sean Gallimore, who organized the 1991/92 Enquiry and carried out all data analysis.

GENERAL RECOMMENDATIONS

The medical Royal Colleges and the Specialist Societies in Surgery, Gynaecology and Anaesthesia must encourage all Consultants to participate in The National Confidential Enquiry into Perioperative Deaths. Full cooperation would enable the profession to defend itself against charges of falling standards and lack of public accountability. The failure of some Consultants to return questionnaires is unacceptable and a cause for concern.

Surgeons, gynaecologists and anaesthetists need to address the continuing problem of thromboembolism which causes death after surgery. We have emphasised this matter before and we regret that we must again bring the profession's attention to it. Hospitals and clinical directorates should be required to address the issue and develop an agreed local protocol. Every Consultant should then follow this protocol. The research bodies and the Department of Health need to continue actively to encourage and support research in this field.

All grades of surgeons, gynaecologists and anaesthetists must realise the critical importance of fluid balance in elderly patients.

There needs to be a collaborative approach to the matching of surgical and anaesthetic skills to the condition of the patient.

Surgeons, gynaecologists and anaesthetists must have immediate access to essential services (recovery rooms, high dependency and intensive care units) if their patients are to survive. The previous Reports have emphasised the need to have emergency operating and recovery rooms available 24 hours a day.

It is no longer acceptable for basic specialist trainees (Senior House Officers) in some specialties to work alone without suitable supervision and direction by their Consultant. Managers and Consultants must locally achieve these arrangements.

The postmortem rate is too low. At least 49% of postmortems demonstrate, despite clinicians' scepticism, significant, new and unexpected findings which are relevant. Postmortems are an important form of quality control.

The necessary information available within the NHS under the present system is inadequate. Despite our repeated comment about this, we are still unable to obtain basic and timely data about the number of patients who have operations and the number of perioperative deaths. There is a need for an improved method for collection and validation of information on perioperative deaths locally and nationally.

IMPORTANT ISSUES IN MANAGEMENT

Managers must realise that there are resource implications for a service which is increasingly Consultant-based.

Managers should urgently review the storage and retrieval of medical notes (page 28).

Managers should assist local reporters to identify methods of reporting *all* relevant deaths (page 25).

Data on the number of surgical procedures performed and the number of perioperative deaths will be inadequate until a unique patient number is in general use in all medical records (pages 22 and 25).

IMPORTANT ISSUES IN SURGERY

Surgery should be avoided for those whose death is inevitable and imminent. A more humane approach to the care of these patients should be considered; these decisions should be directed by Consultants.

Specialist opinion should be sought before undertaking some procedures (e.g. amputation, page 74, oesophagectomy, page 117, hysterectomy page 141, craniotomy, page 164).

Resuscitation and preparation of patients for surgery should not be inadequate or hasty (e.g. strangulated hernia, page 86).

There is a need for more Consultant involvement in the theatre, particularly for emergency cases (e.g. colorectal resection, pages 96 and 99).

IMPORTANT ISSUES IN ANAESTHESIA

Arrangements whereby anaesthetists could work in teams (with other anaesthetists) should be considered (pages 211 to 213 and Discussion, page 295).

Anaesthetists should review their practice of non-invasive instrumental monitoring at induction of anaesthesia (page 254).

The potential for local protocols or national guidelines for staff-patient matching, the use of anaesthesia teams, the provision of essential services, the transfer of patients and other matters should be realised (Discussion, page 295).

MANAGEMENT OF THE ENQUIRY

MANAGEMENT OF THE ENQUIRY

Protocol

The Enquiry is confidential and does not provide data to any person or organization outside the NCEPOD staff or Steering Group. All questionnaires, reporting forms and other paper records relating to 1991/92 have been shredded. Data linking the patients or clinicians with a questionnaire have been removed from the database.

The protocol for the Enquiry was agreed in December 1988 (see Appendix A).

Corporate structure

The Enquiry is an independent body to which a corporate commitment has been made by the Associations, Colleges and Faculties related to its areas of activity. Each of these bodies nominates members of the Steering Group.

Steering Group

Chairman
Professor J P Blandy
(The Royal College of Surgeons of England)

Secretary
Mr H B Devlin
Consultant Surgeon
(The Royal College of Surgeons of England)

Professor E D Alberman
Emeritus Professor of Clinical Epidemiology
(Faculty of Public Health Medicine)

Dr D C Cumberland
Consultant Radiologist
(Royal College of Radiologists)

Professor T Duckworth
Professor of Orthopaedic Surgery
(The Royal College of Surgeons of England)

Dr N P Halliday
Senior Medical Officer
(Department of Health)

Mr R W Hoile
Consultant Surgeon
(The Royal College of Surgeons of England)

Dr J N Lunn
Reader in Anaesthetics
(Association of Anaesthetists of Great Britain and Ireland)

Dr M Morgan
Consultant Anaesthetist
(Association of Anaesthetists of Great Britain and Ireland)

Dr A R Morley
Consultant Pathologist
(Royal College of Pathologists)

Mr C G Munton
Consultant Ophthalmologist
(College of Ophthalmologists)

Mr W J Owen
Consultant Surgeon
(Association of Surgeons of Great Britain and Ireland)

Dr J C Stoddart
Consultant Anaesthetist
(Royal College of Anaesthetists)

Professor V R Tindall
Professor of Gynaecology
(Royal College of Obstetricians and Gynaecologists)

Mr J Ll Williams
Consultant Maxillofacial Surgeon
(Faculty of Dental Surgery)

Coordinators

Administration	Ms E A Campling
Anaesthesia	Dr J N Lunn
Surgery	Mr H B Devlin
	Mr R W Hoile

The aim of the Enquiry

The Enquiry reviews clinical practice and identifies remediable factors in the practice of anaesthesia and surgery (Protocol, December 1988 - see Appendix A). We consider the *quality* of the delivery of care and do not study specifically causation of death. The commentary in this Report is based on peer review of the data, questionnaires and notes submitted to us: it is not a scientific report based on differences within a control population.

Coverage

All National Health Service and Defence Medical Services hospitals in England, Wales and Northern Ireland, and public hospitals in Guernsey, Jersey and the Isle of Man are included in the Enquiry, as well as hospitals managed by BUPA Hospitals Limited, Compass Healthcare Limited, General Healthcare Group PLC, Nuffield Hospitals and St Martins Limited. Funding is provided by the Department of Health (England), the Welsh Office, the Department of Health and Social Services (Northern Ireland), the relevant authorities in Guernsey, Jersey and the Isle of Man, and by the independent healthcare companies.

Consultant Anaesthetists, Gynaecologists and Surgeons in all specialties are asked to participate.

Reporting of deaths

The Enquiry depends on local reporters (see Appendix F) to provide data on deaths in their hospital(s). The reporters in the public sector are Consultant clinicians, mostly pathologists, who have devised their own methods of obtaining the information; many have delegated the data collection to administrative staff. In the independent sector, hospital or nursing managers provide the data. When incomplete information is received, the NCEPOD staff contact the appropriate Medical Records or Information Officer or secretarial staff.

Deaths of patients *in hospital* within 30 days of a surgical procedure (excluding maternal deaths) are included in the Enquiry. A surgical procedure is defined by NCEPOD as;

"any procedure carried out by a surgeon or gynaecologist, with or without an anaesthetist, involving local, regional or general anaesthesia or sedation"

Reporters provide the following information, which is entered on to the computer database;

Name of authority/trust
Name/sex/hospital number of patients
Name of hospital in which the death occurred (and hospital where surgery took place, if different)
Dates of birth, final operation and death
Surgical procedure performed
Name of Consultant Surgeon
Name of anaesthetist

The data collection year runs from 1 April to 31 March (until 1 April 1991 the data collection year was January to December).

Annual sample - deaths

A sample of the reported deaths is reviewed in more detail. The sample selection varies for each data collection year, and is determined by the Steering Group. The detailed sample for 1991/92 data was a range of specific surgical procedures;

> Amputation of whole or part of lower limb
>
> Surgery for strangulated hernia
>
> Colorectal resection
>
> Breast surgery
>
> Oesophagectomy
>
> Pulmonary resection
>
> Coronary artery bypass graft(s)
>
> Hysterectomy
>
> Prostatectomy
>
> Craniotomy
>
> Primary elective total hip replacement
>
> Surgical management of burns
>
> Any oral/maxillofacial surgery
>
> Any otolaryngological surgery
>
> Any ophthalmic surgery

For each sample case, questionnaires (see Appendices C and D) were sent to the Consultant Surgeon or Gynaecologist and Consultant Anaesthetist. These questionnaires were identified only by a number, allocated in the NCEPOD office. Copies of operation notes, anaesthetic records and postmortem reports were also requested. Surgical questionnaires were sent directly to the Consultant Surgeon or Gynaecologist under whose care the patient was at the time of the final operation before death. When the local reporter had identified the relevant Consultant Anaesthetist, the anaesthetic questionnaire was sent directly to him or her. However, in many cases this was not possible, and the Consultant Surgeon was asked to pass the questionnaire to the appropriate Consultant Anaesthetist, and to inform the Enquiry of his or her name and address.

Advisory groups

Completed questionnaires were reviewed by advisory groups for anaesthesia and surgery (see pages 64 to 66 and page 207). The advisory group in pathology (see page 53) reviewed postmortem data from the surgical questionnaires as well as copies of postmortem reports. All copies of medical notes were rendered anonymous on receipt so that the groups were unable to identify the source of the questionnaires.

These groups were nominated by the relevant Colleges and specialist societies. They were drawn from a variety of hospitals in England, Wales and Northern Ireland, and include academic and non-academic surgeons and anaesthetists.

Annual sample - index cases

Details of a further sample of patients undergoing surgery were requested via the index cases. The sample reflected that chosen for the deaths;

Amputation of whole or part of lower limb

Surgery for strangulated hernia

Colorectal resection

Breast surgery for malignant disease

Oesophagectomy

Pulmonary resection

Coronary artery bypass graft(s)

Hysterectomy

Prostatectomy

Surgery for posterior fossa lesions

Primary elective total hip replacement

Surgical management of burns

Any oral/maxillofacial surgery of more than one hour duration*

Any otolaryngological surgery of more than one hour duration*

Any ophthalmic surgery of more than one hour duration*

* excluding anaesthetic time

The Enquiry requested from all Consultant Surgeons and Gynaecologists information on the number of these procedures performed in 1990. The index case requests for specific procedures were then targeted to the most appropriate Consultants.

The anaesthetic questionnaires were sent via the surgeons, who were asked to select the most recent patient on whom any of the procedures (listed for the relevant specialty) had been performed between 1 April 1991 and 1 February 1992 (the first requests were sent in mid-March 1992). These patients survived for longer than 30 days after surgery.

General surgeons were asked to select the most recent of the first five procedures from the list. Cardiothoracic surgeons were asked to select the most recent of either pulmonary resection or coronary artery bypass grafts.

Survivor cases

The protocol states that "the dead cases sampled will each be compared with similar patients, matched for sex, age, and mode of admission, who underwent similar operations and survived (survivor cases)". The selection of these cases has in previous years proved to be extremely difficult. The Steering Group therefore agreed *not* to attempt selection of these cases for 1991/92.

Consultants

The Enquiry maintains a database, regularly updated, of all Consultant Anaesthetists, Gynaecologists and Surgeons. The names of those Consultants who returned at least one death *or* index questionnaire, and whose names are known to the Enquiry, are listed in Appendix E.

Data analysis

All questionnaires were scrutinised by the Deputy Administrator to identify inconsistencies in the information provided. Data from death and index questionnaires and local reporting forms were entered into the database and analysed to produce the tables and information contained in this Report. Overall data on deaths are aggregated to Regional Health Authority or national level only so that individual hospitals cannot be identified. These aggregated data were then considered by the clinical coordinators with the advisory groups.

Production of the Report

The advisory groups commented on the overall quality of care within their specialty and on any individual cases which deserved particular attention. These comments formed the basis for the anaesthetic, surgical, and postmortem sections of this Report, and all advisory groups contributed to the draft for their specialty. The Report was then reviewed twice and agreed by the Steering Group before it was produced as camera-ready copy in the NCEPOD offices.

THE ENQUIRY 1985 TO 1992

It is very difficult to compare the CEPOD Report of 1987[1] with the three NCEPOD Reports (which cover England, Wales, Northern Ireland, Guernsey, the Isle of Man and Jersey). The CEPOD Report referred to operations carried out in 1985/86 in three English Regions. The first National CEPOD Report[2](1989) concentrated on children aged up to 10 years. The second national Report[3] covered a random selection of deaths in the calendar year 1990; the current Report refers to deaths from 1 April 1991 to 31 March 1992. Over this period Consultant staffing has changed in the National Health Service in England and Wales (see Table M1). Overall Consultant staffing in Anaesthesia, Surgery and Obstetrics and Gynaecology has increased by 6.7% but particular increases relevant to all the CEPOD Reports have occurred in Anaesthetics 10.2%, Orthopaedic Surgery 4.0%, Obstetrics and Gynaecology 5.7%, and General Surgery 2.2%. This increase in the Consultant numbers should be reflected by some increased Consultant input into the management of surgical patients.

Comparing the data from the Reports is somewhat difficult because the questions change slightly over the timespan. However, it is clear that in 1985/86 only 63% of the preoperative decision-making was Consultant-based. In 1990, a Consultant was the most senior surgeon consulted preoperatively in 84% of the patients who died; in the current Report this has increased to 92%. Similarly, the proportion of operations carried out by Consultants has changed. In the 1987 Report only 47% of the patients who died had their operations carried out by a Consultant. In the 1990 Report 52% of patients who died had their operations carried out by a Consultant, whereas in 1991/92 the figure is 55%. It may be that the higher rate of preoperative decision-making by Consultants is accompanied by more appropriate delegation to junior surgeons. However it is a matter of some concern that the management of very sick patients, ASA 3, 4 or 5, who face death, is by relatively junior trainees. This is a particular problem in hernia and colorectal surgery (see pages 86 and 96).

Table M1
Number of Consultants in England and Wales[4,5,6]

	1985*	1989*	1990*	% change 1985 to 1990
Accident and Emergency	166	202	198	+19.2
Anaesthetics	1903	2116	2097	+10.2
Cardiothoracic Surgery	115	119	199	+73.0
General Surgery	1137	1190	1162	+ 2.2
Neurosurgery	92	98	99	+ 7.6
Obstetrics and Gynaecology	759	823	802	+ 5.7
Ophthalmology	423	455	437	+ 3.3
Oral Surgery	289	274	264	- 8.6
Orthopaedic Surgery	704	753	732	+ 4.0
Otolaryngology	386	402	378	- 2.1
Paediatric Surgery	43	47	46	+ 7.0
Plastic Surgery	98	111	112	+14.3
Total	6115	6590	6526	+ 6.7

* as at 31 December

These figures (Table M1) are for England and Wales only. The Consultants participating in NCEPOD include those in Northern Ireland, the Isle of Man, Guernsey and Jersey and the Defence Medical Services. The overall numbers of Consultants involved with NCEPOD are therefore higher than those in this table. In July 1993, the NCEPOD database of Consultants comprised 3976 surgeons, 832 gynaecologists and 2530 anaesthetists (total 7338 Consultants).

UPDATE ON THE 1990 REPORT[3]

We are aware that NCEPOD does not receive reports of *all* the relevant deaths. We do not know, however, *how many* deaths are not reported to us.

The Administrator requested information from the Department of Health on the number of deaths in hospital in England within 30 days of surgery in 1990 (1 January to 31 December). Table M2 compares the number of deaths reported to NCEPOD with the number recorded on the Hospital Episode Statistics (HES) database (1989/90 and 1990/91).

The HES figures, however, must be read in the following context:

1 The Department of Health query was run on a 25% extract of the annual data; the figures were then multiplied by four, but otherwise have not been adjusted for shortfalls or duplication of data (as occurred in North East Thames).

2 The estimated number of deaths within 30 days indicates "the total number of Consultant episodes ... where the episode ended in death within 30 days of an operation".[7]

3 These data do not exclude procedures performed by non-surgeons and non-gynaecologists. They will include *all* coded operative procedures including minor ones such as blood transfusion, removal of urethral catheter, intramuscular injection, which are not included in the NCEPOD data.

Table M2
Deaths in England 1 January to 31 December 1990, in hospital within 30 days of a surgical procedure

Region/Authority	Deaths reported to NCEPOD	Hospital Episode Statistics
Northern	1069	1260
Yorkshire	1395	1512
Trent	1722	3068
East Anglia	768	932
North West Thames	1019	1144
North East Thames	1427	3608
South East Thames	1443	1648
South West Thames	1014	1272
Wessex	913	1064
Oxford	599	612
South Western	1084	1940
West Midlands	1826	2436
Mersey	799	856
North Western	1937	2176
Special Health Authorities		
Hammersmith and Queen Charlotte's	19	108
Moorfields Eye Hospital	1	-
Royal Brompton National Heart and Lung Hospital	15	72
The Hospitals for Sick Children	53	16
The National Hospital for Neurology and Neurosurery	3	12
The Royal Marsden Hospital	17	80
Total	17123	23816

The centrally collected data are held in the form of Consultant episodes; a hospital spell may comprise one or more "concatenated consultant episodes"[7]. These data lack a personal patient identifier and it is therefore impossible to determine either:

1   the number of individual patients on whom a surgical procedure was performed (whether by a surgeon or another medical practitioner)

or

2   the number of patients who died in hospital within 30 days of a surgical procedure, where the patient was transferred to the care of another Consultant before 30 days expired but subsequently died.

We have commented before (page 21, NCEPOD Report 1990[3]) that these data are inadequate and are not useful until the unique patient identifier number is used for all patients. This will not be in general use until at least the 1995/1996 data year.[8]

THE CURRENT ENQUIRY AND THE FUTURE

Funding

The total annual cost of the Enquiry is approximately £400,000. We are pleased to acknowledge the continued support of:

Department of Health (England)

Welsh Office

Department of Health and Social Services (Northern Ireland)

States of Guernsey Board of Health

Jersey Group of Hospitals

Department of Health and Social Security, Isle of Man Government

BUPA Hospitals Limited

General Healthcare Group PLC

Nuffield Hospitals

St Martins Limited

This funding covers the *total* cost of the Enquiry, including administrative, clerical and Clinical Coordinator salaries (13 sessions per week), office rental charges, computer and other equipment as well as travelling and other expenses for the Clinical Coordinators, Steering Group and advisory groups.

1992/1993

The sample for 1 April 1992 to 31 March 1993 covers the largest number of deaths so far considered in detail by the Enquiry. Deaths of patients aged 6 years to 70 years will be included; a maximum of five questionnaires will be sent to each Consultant Surgeon or Gynaecologist. It is estimated that the sample size will be approximately 6000; the total number of surgical questionnaires sent will be approximately 5000. An index case sample was not selected for 1992/93.

1993/1994

Deaths which occur between 1 April 1993 and 31 March 1994 will be selected for the sample by the name of the Consultant Surgeon or Gynaecologist involved; one questionnaire only will be sent to each Consultant in these disciplines.

Distribution of anaesthetic questionnaires

It is clear that a higher percentage of questionnaires are returned to the Enquiry if the request is sent directly to a Consultant Anaesthetist (see Table M27). All questionnaires for 1992/93 and subsequent years will be addressed to a named anaesthetist.

Management of the Enquiry

References see page 300

COMMENTARY ON THE DATA (1 April 1991 to 31 March 1992)

The data for 1991/92 are presented in tabular form on pages 30 to 50.

Local reporting (Tables M4 to M30)

All reports of deaths received by 3 August 1992 were included in the Enquiry; 427 reports were received after this date i.e. at least five months after the date of the death. The local reporters for 487 hospitals were able to provide the data but many experienced difficulties in doing so. In some hospitals, computerised databases are either not yet available or cannot provide adequate or accurate data according to the NCEPOD criteria. However, we are encouraged by reporters for Bloomsbury and Islington, City and Hackney, Wandsworth, Sheffield, Brighton, The Royal Free Hospital and other authorities who have been able to provide data for 1991/92 generated from the patient administration or medical audit databases. We are suggesting a similar approach to other reporters and hope that liaison between them and the medical audit and records departments will increase the accuracy, completeness and timeliness of the data and ease the burden on reporters. The staff in these departments have been very helpful in providing data missing from reporting forms (e.g. name of Consultant, dates, procedure performed).

We are concerned about the continuing difficulties (in July 1993) in obtaining data from the Royal Liverpool University Hospital, the Isle of Wight DHA, Solihull DHA, Westminster Hospital (now Chelsea and Westminster Hospital), St Mary's Hospital (London) and Guy's Hospital (London).

Early notification of deaths to the Enquiry is important so that we can send questionnaires for the sample cases to the Consultants as soon as possible after the death has occurred. Fifty per cent of the reports were received within one month of the deaths and a further 30% within three months.

Regional Health Authorities (RHAs) in England were asked in November 1992 to provide details of the numbers of deaths within the Region which satisfied the NCEPOD criteria (see page 17). The figures for the RHAs which were able to provide data for 1991/92 are shown in Table M3, with the NCEPOD figures. *The figures are not directly comparable.* The RHA figures represent patients whose care was managed by a surgical specialty at the time of their death. Those patients who were treated "under" a non-surgical Consultant will not be included. The surgical procedures will include minor operations not included by NCEPOD, such as blood transfusion, intramuscular injection - in fact any procedure which can be coded under OPCS 4 (Office of Population Censuses and Surveys. Classification of Surgical Operations and Procedures, Fourth Revision).

Table M3
Deaths in England 1 April 1991 to 31 March 1992, in hospital within 30 days of a surgical procedure

Regional Health Authority*	Deaths reported to NCEPOD	Figures provided by RHA
Northern	1141	1436
Yorkshire	1126	1851
Trent	2014	4124
East Anglia	739	443
North West Thames	771	2070
South East Thames	1262	1324
South West Thames	1203	1259
Wessex	874	1058
South Western	973	1709
Mersey	699	1351
North Western	1810	5207
Total	12612	21832

* excluding RHAs from which data were not available

In December 1992, the Information Management Group of the NHS Management Executive published details of its Information Management and Technology Strategy for the NHS in England. Amongst the proposed benefits of the strategy are improvements in the availability of appropriate information for each patient encounter, a reduction in lost patient information and an increase in the ability to analyse and use information to improve performance.

> "*The vision is of an NHS where staff use information to improve continuously the service they provide, where an IM & T environment supports the controlled sharing of information across the Service, and where information is handled and communicated securely, smoothly and efficiently. Through the realisation of this vision, the NHS will see enhanced quality, responsiveness, targeting, and efficiency of its healthcare services*"[9]

We welcome particularly the introduction of a new NHS number (operational April 1995 at the earliest) as a unique patient identifier and the proposed NHS-wide networking within a secure and confidential framework (targeted for 1996).

Commentary on general data

References see page 300

Selecting sample cases (Table M9)

Often, the surgical procedure is described on the local reporting form in an abbreviated form. It was necessary to request further information from Consultant Surgeons, particularly for hernia surgery to establish whether the hernia was *strangulated*, and for total hip replacement since we included only *primary elective* surgery. We are grateful to those clinicians who provided copies of operation notes or detailed replies.

The sample represented 15% of the total number of deaths. Fifty-five of these cases were from the independent sector. A large number of deaths (1696) after colorectal resection were reported; only one in four of these cases were included in the sample. A maximum of five death questionnaires was sent to each Consultant Surgeon or Gynaecologist; 198 cases were thus excluded from the sample.

Questionnaires (Tables M10 to M14 and M26 to M30)

All completed and relevant questionnaires received by 2 November 1992 were included in the analysis. The overall return rates of 68.9% (surgical) and 61.2% (anaesthetic) are disappointing and are lower than for 1990 (73.6% and 65.8% respectively). In 710 cases, no review could take place because neither questionnaire was received.

The Enquiry is already acting to improve the return rates by increasing the number of reminders to non-respondents and encouraging clinicians to contact us with a *reason* for the non-return of a questionnaire. In some cases, the Enquiry may have been given inaccurate information. This effort should be matched by an increased input from Consultant Surgeons, Gynaecologists and Anaesthetists.

We are encouraged to see that in some Regions the return rate is above 70%. Unfortunately, other Regions did not achieve even a 60% return rate.

The highest surgical return rate by specialty (Table M11) was by gynaecologists (82%), the lowest by cardiothoracic surgeons (pulmonary resection 64%, coronary artery bypass grafts 50%) and neurosurgeons (60%).

Table M12 indicates that 331 surgeons or gynaecologists returned *none* of their surgical questionnaires for deaths to the Enquiry. These Consultants must be classed as non-participants. We recommend that the Colleges act to reduce this number as a matter of urgency.

The return rate for index case questionnaires is even lower (Tables M13 and M29 - surgical 48.9%, anaesthetic 41.8%). These low percentages reflect the difficulties in selecting the index case sample. We do not know whether 2312 surgeons or gynaecologists (Table M30) failed to return a questionnaire for a case, or whether these surgeons could not identify a case to fit the NCEPOD criteria (see page 19).

Commentary on general data

References see page 300

Lost medical notes

The loss or difficult retrieval of information and case notes in hospitals in still a major problem for the Enquiry, and there are no signs of improvement. Many hours are wasted by medical and administrative staff in inconclusive searches. Seventy-nine lost case notes resulted in neither the surgical nor the anaesthetic questionnaires being returned to us. In a further 26 cases, the notes were not available for the completion of *one* of the questionnaires (19 anaesthetic, 7 surgical). These problems occurred in at least 70 different hospitals. It is undoubtedly a nationwide problem. These extracts from correspondence illustrate the difficulties:

"I know my potted history above is not at all acceptable for completion of the questionnaire, but unless the notes appear, I am afraid this is all I can give you". (General surgeon)

"Unfortunately none of her notes are available, despite intensive searching. The only documentary evidence ... is the intensive care summary. I have searched theatre records for details of her operation, but to no avail". (Cardiothoracic surgeon)

"We have carried out a thorough search at this hospital and the peripheral hospitals and I very much regret that ... we are unable to trace them. According to our records the case notes were not returned to the Medical Records Department for filing". (from Medical Records Manager to Consultant Orthopaedic Surgeon)

"The only suggestion I can now offer is that I wonder if this is a case of interest for a doctor unknown to us who is undertaking research or who is simply holding on to the records for pure interest". (from Medical Records Manager to Consultant General Surgeon)

"In December last year I had a request for the completion of a CEPOD form on the above lady. To my alarm and amazement, we have found it impossible to retrieve the notes from the system, such that after six months I have now given up trying". (Orthopaedic surgeon, letter dated 30 June 1992)

"The clerk in the appropriate department has told us that she went to look through several sacks of deceased notes waiting for sorting and filing. I am afraid that I, like so many of my Consultant colleagues, cannot cooperate with NCEPOD if the administration and management of the hospital will not organise systems whereby the notes can be retrieved". (General surgeon)

Difficulties in obtaining notes were noted in 187 surgical death questionnaires and 111 surgical index questionnaires (Table M16) and parts of the record were missing in 285 case notes.

Commentary on general data

References see page 300

Urgent action by managers and clinicians is needed to improve the storage and retrieval of medical records. The notes of patients who have died should not be treated as unimportant and of no further use; they are important documents for audit and medicolegal purposes, both local and national.

Local medical audit (Tables M18 and M19)

It is encouraging that 78.9% of the deaths were considered at a local surgical audit meeting. This is an increase of 14% on the figures for 1990 (Table S59, page 157, NCEPOD Report 1990[3]). There is room for improvement and this is commented on in the surgical section by specialty.

It is surprising that 11% of the index case questionnaires from gynaecologists state that local audit meetings are not held.

Out-of-hours operations (Tables M20 and M21)

Surgery took place between 18.01 and 07.59 hours, Monday to Friday, in 244 (13.4%) cases amongst the deaths; a further 222 (12.2%) operations were performed at the weekend. Only 151 (32.4%) of these cases were emergency operations (see the NCEPOD definition in the Glossary, Appendix B). We do not know why the 313 urgent, scheduled or elective operations were done out of hours. It is possible that routine lists were interrupted by emergency cases. We repeat our earlier[3] conclusion that emergency operating theatres should be available 24 hours a day. It is estimated that only one third of acute hospitals currently have this facility.[10]

Grade of the most senior surgeon (Tables M23 to M25)

It is commendable that Consultants made the final decision to operate on 84% of the patients who died and 90% of the index cases. This is an improvement since the 1990 Report[3] when the figures were 74% and 82% respectively. There is a high level of Consultant input in preoperative consultation, decision-making and operating.

Comments on the most senior surgeon who operated are made in the surgical sections.

ANALYSIS OF GENERAL DATA
(1 April 1991 to 31 March 1992)

The commentary on these tables is included in pages 25 to 29.

A total of 18132 deaths were reported to the Enquiry. This figure does not include 60 reports where the data received were incomplete, 427 reports received too late for inclusion in the analysis, and 397 inappropriate reports (see table M5).

Table M4
Deaths reported to NCEPOD

	Reported deaths (n=18132)	Hospitals from which reports received (n=487)
England		
Northern	1141	32
Yorkshire	1126	24
Trent	2014	34
East Anglia	739	13
North West Thames	771	22
North East Thames	1278	31
South East Thames	1262	30
South West Thames	1203	21
Wessex	874	27
Oxford	817	18
South Western	973	24
West Midlands	1578	45
Mersey	699	22
North Western	1810	43
Special Health Authorities	78	4
Wales	1079	26
Northern Ireland	375	17
Other authorities		
Guernsey	18	1
Jersey	25	1
Isle of Man	25	1
Defence Medical Services	75	7
Independent sector	172	44

Table M5
Inappropriate reports received and not included

	(*n*=397)
More than 30 days (day of operation to day of death)	281
No surgical procedure performed	37
Procedure not performed by surgeon	11
"Inappropriate" procedure (according to NCEPOD criteria)	51
Maternal deaths	8
Duplicates	3
Patient still alive (incorrectly coded)	1
Non-participating hospital (independent)	5

Table M6
Days between death and receipt of report by NCEPOD

Number of calendar days	(*n*=18132)
0 to 29	9084
30 to 59	3526
60 to 89	1960
90 to 119	1153
120 to 149	747
150 to 179	528
180+	1134

Table M7
Calendar days from operation to death

	(n=18132)	%	%
0	2087		11.5
1	2233		12.3
2	1427		7.9
3	1153	36.2	6.3
4	951		5.2
5	804		4.4
6	763		4.2
7	793		4.4
8	691	19.3	3.8
9	624		3.4
10	635		3.5
11	541		3.0
12	484		2.7
13	470	12.8	2.6
14	437		2.4
15	394		2.2
16 to 20	1654		9.1
21 to 25	1164		6.4
26 to 30	827		4.6

Figure M1 (see Table M7)
Calendar days from operation to death (all deaths)

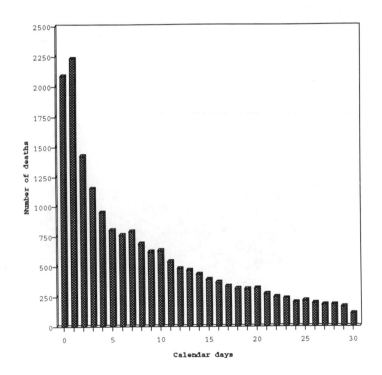

Table M8
Age/sex distribution of reported deaths

	Male	Female	Total
0 to 10 years	144	110	254
11 to 20	81	48	129
21 to 30	136	86	222
31 to 40	161	126	287
41 to 50	342	253	595
51 to 60	839	580	1419
61 to 70	2419	1493	3912
71 to 80	3293	2753	6046
81 to 90	1810	2710	4520
91 to 100	165	565	730
>100	4	14	18
Total	9394	8738	18132

Analysis of general data

References see page 300

Table M9
Deaths selected as sample for further review (see page 20)

	Sampled deaths	% of reported deaths
England		
Northern	151	*13.2*
Yorkshire	165	*14.7*
Trent	305	*15.1*
East Anglia	114	*15.4*
North West Thames	97	*12.6*
North East Thames	175	*13.8*
South East Thames	177	*14.0*
South West Thames	143	*11.9*
Wessex	135	*15.4*
Oxford	125	*15.3*
South Western	150	*15.4*
West Midlands	264	*16.7*
Mersey	128	*18.3*
North Western	302	*16.7*
Special Health Authorities	11	*14.1*
Wales	170	*15.8*
Northern Ireland	53	*14.1*
Other authorities		
Guernsey	5	*27.8*
Jersey	2	*8.0*
Isle of Man	3	*12.0*
Defence Medical Services	9	*12.0*
Independent sector	55	*32.0*
Total	2739*	*15.1*

* Originally, a further 186 cases were selected for further review, but these were excluded from the sample on receipt of correspondence from the surgeon concerned which indicated their exclusion from the sample (e.g. surgery for a non-strangulated hernia). Of these, 122 completed surgical questionnaires and 110 completed anaesthetic questionnaires were received by NCEPOD. These have been excluded from the analysis.

Table M10
Completed surgical questionnaires (deaths) returned to NCEPOD

	Number returned and analysed	(Number of hospitals represented in analysed surgical questionnaires)	% return rate*
England			
Northern	109	(22)	74.8
Yorkshire	128	(17)	79.8
Trent	208	(20)	71.6
East Anglia	84	(12)	73.9
North West Thames	58	(15)	64.8
North East Thames	106	(18)	62.9
South East Thames	106	(20)	62.2
South West Thames	92	(16)	66.7
Wessex	96	(18)	74.3
Oxford	79	(11)	67.2
South Western	91	(15)	65.1
West Midlands	172	(34)	66.2
Mersey	82	(15)	67.4
North Western	206	(24)	70.2
Special Health Authorities	6	(2)	54.5
Wales	116	(20)	69.5
Northern Ireland	32	(10)	61.4
Other authorities			
Guernsey	4	(1)	80.0
Jersey	-		50.0
Isle of Man	3	(1)	100.0
Defence Medical Services	7	(4)	77.8
Independent sector	36	(22)	64.9
Total	1821	317	68.9

* The overall and individual *return rates* include those cases where a questionnaire was received but the case was removed from the sample and not analysed (see footnote to Table M9).

The *return rates* also include those questionnaires that were returned for sample cases but were for some reason excluded from analysis e.g. completion for a previous operation on the correct patient. Thirty-nine surgical questionnaires fell into this category.

The return rate is not therefore a combination of Tables M9 and M10.

Seventy surgical death questionnaires were received after the cut-off date (2 November 1992) and not analysed.

Table M11

Return rates of surgical questionnaires (deaths) by type of operation

	Surgical questionnaires sent	Surgical questionnaires returned	%
Amputation of whole or part of lower limb	696	494	70.9
Surgery for strangulated hernia	100	71	71.0
Colorectal resection	467	356	76.2
Breast surgery	36	23	63.9
Oesophagectomy	103	68	66.0
Pulmonary resection	42	27	64.3
Coronary artery bypass grafts	297	148	49.8
Hysterectomy	83	68	81.9
Prostatectomy	238	175	73.5
Craniotomy	335	200	59.7
Primary elective total hip replacement	134	87	64.9
Surgical management of burns	25	18	72.0
Oral/maxillofacial surgery	42	29	69.0
Otolaryngological surgery	97	63	64.9
Ophthalmic surgery	44	33	75.0

Table M12

Number of individual Consultant Surgeons and Gynaecologists to whom questionnaires (deaths) were sent/returned questionnaires

	Consultants to whom questionnaires sent	All questionnaires returned %		At least one questionnaire returned	No questionnaires returned %	
England						
Northern	85	61	71.8	8	16	18.8
Yorkshire	80	60	75.0	7	13	16.2
Trent	132	83	62.9	20	29	22.0
East Anglia	64	46	71.9	4	14	21.9
North West Thames	54	32	59.2	10	12	22.2
North East Thames	85	51	60.0	8	26	30.6
South East Thames	89	53	59.5	9	27	30.3
South West Thames	69	41	59.4	12	16	23.2
Wessex	65	40	61.5	9	16	24.6
Oxford	61	31	50.8	10	20	32.8
South Western	84	52	61.9	10	22	26.2
West Midlands	130	77	59.2	20	33	25.4
Mersey	53	30	56.6	12	11	20.7
North Western	140	87	62.1	25	28	20.0
Special Health Authorities	6	1	16.7	3	2	33.3
Wales	91	61	67.0	11	19	20.9
Northern Ireland	31	15	48.4	3	13	41.9
Other authorities						
Guernsey	2	1		1	-	
Jersey	2	1		-	-	
Isle of Man	2	2		-	-	
Defence Medical Services	8	5		2	1	
Independent sector	48	35	72.9	1	12	25.0
Total	1381	865	62.6	185	331	24.0

Analysis of general data

References see page 300

Table M13
Surgical questionnaires (index cases) returned and analysed

	Number returned and analysed	% of surgical questionnaires sent
England		
Northern	147	*55.3*
Yorkshire	141	*56.4*
Trent	152	*56.4*
East Anglia	79	*54.0*
North West Thames	115	*48.2*
North East Thames	104	*35.5*
South East Thames	117	*44.4*
South West Thames	89	*42.7*
Wessex	99	*52.3*
Oxford	86	*53.3*
South Western	116	*52.3*
West Midlands	189	*49.5*
Mersey	76	*45.3*
North Western	166	*51.0*
Special Health Authorities	26	*36.2*
Wales	106	*49.1*
Northern Ireland	80	*53.2*
Other authorities		
Guernsey	1	*11.1*
Jersey	6	*60.0*
Isle of Man	4	*62.5*
Defence Medical Services	36	*67.9*
Independent sector	70	*33.1*
Total	2005	*48.9*

A total of 116 surgical index case questionnaires were returned to the Enquiry and did not fit the specified criteria; 132 surgical index questionnaires were received after the cut-off date (11 September 1992) and were not analysed.

The rates of return appear low but many Consultants did not reply; it is possible that some Consultants could not select an appropriate case but did not inform the Enquiry of this fact.

Table M14
Surgical questionnaires (index cases) returned and analysed (by surgical procedure)

	Surgical questionnaires returned and analysed	% of Surgical questionnaires* sent
Amputation of whole or part of lower limb	51	
Surgery for strangulated hernia	8	
Colorectal resection	208	44.9
Breast surgery	126	
Oesophagectomy	30	
Pulmonary resection	21	46.2
Coronary artery bypass grafts	40	
Hysterectomy	468	59.8
Prostatectomy	193	58.8
Craniotomy	43	41.7
Primary elective total hip replacement	357	49.2
Surgical management of burns	38	38.8
Oral/maxillofacial surgery	94	47.5
Otolaryngological surgery	190	46.6
Ophthalmic surgery	138	36.4
Total	2005	48.9

* See notes to Table M13

The percentage return rates for general surgery and for cardiothoracic surgery are grouped, as Consultants in these specialties were asked to select the most recent of several procedures performed (see page 19).

ANALYSIS OF SELECTED DATA FROM SURGICAL QUESTIONNAIRES (see Appendix C)

Table M15 (q 100 deaths, q 86 index)
Who completed this questionnaire?

	Deaths (*n*=1821)	Index (*n*=2005)
House Officer	27	5
Senior House Officer	205	101
Registrar	412	207
Staff Grade	12	6
Senior Registrar	184	114
Associate Specialist	9	15
Consultant	933	1538
Other	13	8
Not stated	26	11

Table M16 (q 101 deaths, q 87 index)
Did you have any problems in obtaining the patient's notes?

	(*n*=1821)	%	(*n*=2005)	%
Yes	187*	*10.3*	111*	*5.5*
No	1596		1879	
Not answered	38		15	

* The length of time that the notes took to reach the surgeon, where there was a problem, ranged from two days to nine months, and in some cases the surgeon was able to complete the questionnaire even though the notes had never been found.

Were all the notes available?

	(*n*=1821)	%	(*n*=2005)	%
Yes	1554		1933	
No	226	*12.4*	59	*2.9*
Not known/not recorded	2		3	
Not answered	39		10	

If no, which part was inadequate/unavailable?

	(*n*=226)	(*n*=59)
Pre-operative notes	15	11
Operation notes	26	10
Postoperative notes	15	5
Death certificate	120	n/a
Other notes	80	25
Not answered	24	18

NB this can be a multiple entry

Table M17
In which type of hospital did the last operation take place?

	Deaths (n=1821)	Index (n=2005)
District General	1200	1263
University/Teaching	459	472
Surgical specialty	96	126
Other Acute/Partly Acute	15	27
Community	1	3
Defence Medical Services	6	36
Independent	44	72
Other	-	5
Not answered	-	1

AUDIT

Table M18 (q 98)
Has this death been considered (or will it be considered) at a local audit/quality control meeting?

	(n=1821)			
	Yes	%	No	Not answered
Amputation of the lower limb	405	83.5	63	17
Surgery for strangulated hernia	63	90.0	6	1
Colorectal resection	315	90.2	28	6
Breast surgery	16	69.6	7	-
Oesophagectomy	52	85.2	9	-
Pulmonary resection	22	95.6	1	-
Coronary artery bypass grafts	132	91.0	8	5
Hysterectomy	37	56.9	24	4
Prostatectomy	135	77.6	36	3
Craniotomy	128	64.6	62	8
Total hip replacement	58	68.2	23	4
Surgical management of burns	16	88.9	1	1
Oral/maxillofacial surgery	17	58.6	10	2
Otolaryngological surgery	32	50.8	22	9
Ophthalmic surgery	8	24.2	21	4
Total	1436	78.9	321	64

These data appear in the surgical section, by specialty.

Table M19 (q 83)

Does your hospital/unit hold local audit/quality control meetings (index cases)?

	Yes (*n*=1829)	No (*n*=86)	Not answered (*n*=19)
	(n=1934*)		
Amputation of whole or part of lower limb	49	-	1
Surgery for strangulated hernia	8	-	-
Colorectal resections	204	1	1
Breast surgery	120	-	-
Oesophagectomy	30	-	-
Pulmonary resection	19	-	1
Coronary artery bypass grafts	34	2	-
Hysterectomy	391	48	2
Prostatectomy	177	3	2
Craniotomy	41	-	2
Primary elective total hip replacement	329	9	8
Surgical management of burns	35	3	-
Any oral/maxillofacial surgery	84	5	2
Any otolaryngological surgery	180	8	-
Any ophthalmic surgery	128	7	-

* excludes independent hospitals

If yes, what is the duration of the meetings?

	(n=1829)
Less than 1 hour	256
1 to 2 hours	956
More than 2 hours	612
Not answered/not known	5

How frequent are the meetings**?

	(n=1829)
Weekly	225
Fortnightly	91
Monthly	1305
Other	201
Not answered/not known	1

** where more than one frequency was answered, the smallest time interval was chosen

THE OPERATION

Table M20 (q 53)
Day and time of start of operation

	Deaths (n=1821)	%	Index (n=2005)	%
Weekday 08.00 to 18.00	1281	70.3	1866	93.1
Weekday, outside these hours	244	13.4	40	2.0
Weekday, time not given	74	4.1	60	3.0
Weekend	222	12.2	35	1.7

Table M21 (qs 53 and 62)
Classification of operation where operation took place at a weekend or outside 08.00 - 18.00 during the week

	Deaths (n=466)
Emergency	151
Urgent	273
Scheduled	31
Elective	9
Not answered	2

Analysis of general data
References see page 300

THE SURGEONS

Table M22 (q 1)
Stated specialty of Consultant Surgeon in charge at time of final operation before death

	(*n*=1821*)
General	188
General/Paediatric/Gastroenterology	3
General/Paediatric	8
General/Paediatric/Urology	1
General/Paediatric/Vascular	5
General/Urology	70
General/Urology/Vascular	7
General/Urology/Vascular/Gastroenterology	1
General/Urology/Gastroenterology	3
General/Urology/Breast surgery	2
General/Vascular	417
General/Vascular/Gastroenterology	5
General/Vascular/Endocrinology	1
General/Vascular/Colorectal	4
General/Vascular/Breast surgery	2
General/Vascular/Laparoscopic surgery	1
General/Vascular/Transplantation	4
General/Gastroenterology	216
General/Gastroenterology/Endocrinology	8
General/Gastroenterology/Breast surgery	9
General/Gastroenterology/Oncology	1
General/Gastroenterology/Hepatobiliary	1
General/Gastroenterology/Laparoscopic surgery	1
General/Endocrinology	9
General/Endocrinology/Breast surgery	2
General/Endocrinology/Oesophageal surgery	1
General/Breast surgery	19
General/Colorectal	10
General/Transplantation	7
General/Hepatobiliary	4
General/Oncology	3
General/Thoracic	2
General/Head and Neck surgery	1
General/Upper gastrointestinal surgery	1

continued on next page

Table M22 continued

Cardiac - Paediatric	2
Cardiac - Adult	85
Cardiac - Mixed	14
Cardiac/Transplantation	1
Cardiothoracic - Mixed	13
Cardiothoracic - Adult	33
Cardiothoracic/Transplantation	7
Thoracic	24
Gynaecology	49
Neurosurgery	193
Paediatric **Neurosurgery**	1
Ophthalmology	33
Oral/Maxillofacial	24
Orthopaedic	110
Otolaryngology	58
Otolaryngology/Head and Neck surgery	1
Plastic	18
Plastic/Burns	1
Transplantation/Urology	1
Urology	123
Vascular	13

* the total number refers to the number of questionnaires, not the number of individual surgeons

Table M23 (q 40)

What was the grade of the most senior surgeon consulted before the operation?

	Deaths (*n*=1821)	%	Index (*n*=2005)	%
Senior House Officer	4	0.2	6	0.3
Registrar	63	3.4	18	0.9
Senior Registrar	61	3.3	39	1.9
Consultant	1668	91.6	1915	95.5
Staff Grade	2		1	
Clinical Assistant	1		2	
Associate Specialist	9		4	
Other	1		2	
Not known/not recorded	1		1	
Not answered	11		17	

Table M24 (q 39)

Which grade of surgeon made the final decision to operate?

	Deaths (*n*=1821)	%	Index (*n*=2005)	%
Senior House Officer	13	0.7	11	0.5
Registrar	134	7.3	68	3.4
Senior Registrar	112	6.1	87	4.3
Consultant	1534	84.2	1811	90.3
Staff Grade	6		9	
Clinical Assistant	5		5	
Associate Specialist	10		5	
Other	1		3	
Not known/not recorded	1		1	
Not answered	5		5	

There is a high level of input from Consultant Surgeons and Gynaecologists.

Table M25 (q 54)

What was the grade of the most senior operating surgeon?

	Deaths (*n*=1821)	%	Index (*n*=2005)	%
Senior House Officer	59	3.2	26	1.3
Registrar	471	25.9	268	13.4
Senior Registrar	240	13.2	180	9.0
Consultant	994	54.6	1470	73.3
Staff Grade	18	1.0	18	0.9
Clinical Assistant	10	0.5	6	0.3
Associate Specialist	22	1.2	23	1.1
Other	3		6	
Not answered	4		8	

Table M26
Completed anaesthetic questionnaires (deaths) returned to NCEPOD

	Number returned and analysed	(Number of hospitals represented in analysed anaesthetic questionnaires)	% return rate*
England			
Northern	97	(22)	65.8
Yorkshire	114	(17)	71.3
Trent	183	(20)	62.3
East Anglia	74	(12)	67.0
North West Thames	56	(16)	61.0
North East Thames	98	(19)	58.3
South East Thames	81	(18)	43.3
South West Thames	72	(16)	53.4
Wessex	86	(12)	66.9
Oxford	79	(13)	65.4
South Western	88	(16)	61.8
West Midlands	163	(29)	64.2
Mersey	65	(13)	50.8
North Western	190	(23)	63.8
Special Health Authorities	4	(1)	36.4
Wales	93	(18)	58.1
Northern Ireland	33	(12)	64.3
Other authorities			
Guernsey	3	(1)	60.0
Jersey	2	(1)	100.0
Isle of Man	1	(1)	33.3
Defence Medical Services	5	(4)	55.6
Independent sector	29	(22)	52.6
Total	1616	306	61.2

* Completion of the anaesthetic questionnaire was not appropriate in 29 cases where local anaesthesia or sedation was administered by the surgeon.

The overall and individual return *rates* include those cases where a questionnaire was received but the case was removed from the sample and not analysed (see footnote to Table M9).

The *return* rates also include those questionnaires that were returned for sample cases but were for some reason excluded from analysis e.g. completion for a previous operation on the correct patient. Seventeen anaesthetic questionnaires fell into this category.

The return rate is therefore not a combination of Tables M9 and M26.

Ninety-nine anaesthetic questionnaires were received after the cut-off date (2 November 1992) and not analysed.

Analysis of general data
References see page 300

Table M27
Return rates of anaesthetic questionnaires (deaths) by method of distribution

	Number returned*	%
Anaesthetic questionnaire sent via surgeon (*n* = 2169)	1187	54.7
Anaesthetic questionnaire sent directly to named anaesthetist (*n* = 570)	446	78.2

* includes 17 questionnaires returned and not analysed

Table M28
Completed questionnaires (deaths) returned to NCEPOD (surgical and anaesthetic)

Questionnaires received		%
Both surgical and anaesthetic*	1489	54.4
Surgical only	371	6.2
Anaesthetic only	169	13.5
Neither received**	710	25.9

* includes 25 cases where an anaesthetic questionnaire was not required

** includes 4 cases where an anaesthetic questionnaire was not required and the surgical questionnaire was not returned

This table *includes* 39 surgical and 17 anaesthetic questionnaires which were received but not analysed (see footnotes, Tables M10 and M26).

This table *does not include* questionnaires which were received but found not to be part of the sample (see footnote, Table M9).

Table M29
Completed anaesthetic questionnaires returned and analysed (index cases)

	Number returned	% return rate
England		
Northern	130	*50.2*
Yorkshire	114	*47.3*
Trent	133	*48.8*
East Anglia	69	*45.4*
North West Thames	92	*41.1*
North East Thames	82	*29.0*
South East Thames	89	*35.7*
South West Thames	73	*36.6*
Wessex	92	*48.2*
Oxford	78	*47.9*
South Western	99	*46.4*
West Midlands	162	*43.6*
Mersey	63	*37.6*
North Western	135	*42.1*
Special Health Authorities	21	*33.3*
Wales	92	*42.5*
Northern Ireland	71	*47.4*
Other authorities		
Guernsey	1	*11.1*
Jersey	6	*60.0*
Isle of Man	3	*50.0*
Defence Medical Services	30	*56.6*
Independent sector	54	*25.2*
Total	1689	*41.8*

An anaesthetic questionnaire was not required in two cases where the local anaesthesia was administered by the surgeon.

A total of 108 anaesthetic index questionnaires were received after the cut-off date (11 September 1992) and were not analysed.

Table M30
Completed questionnaires (index cases) returned to NCEPOD (surgical and anaesthetic)

Questionnaires received		%
Both surgical and anaesthetic*	1740	39.3
Surgical only	342	0.8
Anaesthetic only	37	7.7
Neither received	2312	52.2

* includes two cases for which the anaesthetic questionnaire was not required as local anaesthesia was administered by the surgeon

The table excludes invalid questionnaires received e.g. inappropriate procedure.

PATHOLOGY

Blank page
References see page 300

POSTMORTEM EXAMINATIONS

ADVISERS

Dr P J Gallagher	Southampton
Dr C E Keen	London
Dr R J Kellett	Abergavenny
Dr S Love	Bristol
Dr J H McCarthy	South Shields
Dr A R Morley (Chairman)	Newcastle upon Tyne
Professor P G Toner	Belfast
Dr K P West	Leicester

KEY ISSUES

1   Postmortem examination can produce new and clinically valuable information. The number of postmortems should be increased.

2   Confirmation of surgical findings is a valuable form of audit.

3   Better communication between pathologists and other clinicians is needed.

4   Although the overall quality of postmortem examination is good, more frequent use of clinical/pathological commentaries and greater precision in the statement of causes of death are desirable.

5   The Enquiry deplores the action of some Coroners in refusing to supply the postmortem report to the surgical team.

SAMPLE

1821 surgical questionnaires (deaths) were included in the analysis of postmortem data.

   820 postmortems were performed out of this total, of which

   628 were *Coroners'* and

   192 were *hospital* postmortems

Postmortem reports

419 postmortem reports were reviewed by the advisers

Fifty-six per cent of the deaths were initially reported to the Coroner. A hospital postmortem was requested in 33% of those cases (excluding non-responses) where the death was not referred to the Coroner. This means that in 67% of all possible hospital postmortems a clinical judgement was made that examination was not needed.

Table P1
Did a postmortem take place?

	(n=1821)	%
Yes: Coroner's postmortem	628	34.5
Yes: hospital postmortem	192	10.5
No: relative's refusal	178	9.8
No: not requested	759	41.7
Not recorded/not answered	64	3.5

Reporting deaths to Coroners

Previous NCEPOD reports[2, 3] have hinted at failures to recognise reportable deaths. All doctors should be aware of the various categories of death which require referral to the Coroner and should revise their knowledge from time to time. This applies in particular to senior clinicians who may, by default of postgraduate education, have less understanding than their juniors of the coronial system[11]. A brief guide is given below, describing those cases which should be referred to the Coroner. In addition to this brief guide, clinicians are encouraged to request a postmortem examination in all cases about which they are uncertain. It may be wise for hospital pathologists to report to the Coroner any death where there is an allegation of medical mismanagement or where there are any unusual or disturbing features. Advice is always available from the Coroner, Coroner's Officers, or senior pathologists.

Deaths reportable to the Coroner: a brief guide (adapted from reference 11)

Any death should be referred to a Coroner if the Medical Practitioner cannot readily certify death as being due to natural causes within the terms of regulation 41 of the "Registration of Births and Deaths Regulations 1987". Some of the major categories of death which should be reported are when:

- there is any element of suspicious circumstances or history of violence;
- the death may be linked to an unnatural event (whenever it occurred);
- the death may be due to industrial disease or related in any way to the deceased's occupation ;
- the death is linked with an abortion;
- the death occurred during an operation or before full recovery from the effects of anaesthesia or was in any way related to the anaesthesia;

- the death may be related to a medical procedure or treatment;
- the actions of the deceased may have contributed to his or her own death - for example suicide, self-neglect, drugs or solvent abuse;
- the death occurred in police or prison custody (includes death from an illness or injury which arose during detention);
- the death was within 24 hours of admission to hospital (not statutory);
- the deceased was detained on a criminal charge under the Mental Health Act.

Table P2 (q88)
If a hospital postmortem was not requested, why not?

	(*n*=759)	%
Cause of death assumed to be known	461	60.7
Coroner's case (Coroner did not order a postmortem)	19	2.5
Relative-related	18	2.4
Death on medical ward	9	1.2
Death not in hospital	7	0.9
Oversight/forgot	7	0.9
Shortage of resources (e.g. staff, facilities)	5	0.7
Organ donor/body donated to medical science	2	0.3
Not stated/not recorded	231	30.4

Surgeons were given the opportunity to give reasons why a postmortem had not been requested. The main reason given was that the cause of death was already known.

Table P3 (q 95)
Was the pathological information given useful i.e. did it contribute additional information to the understanding of the patient's illness?

	(*n*=659*)	%
Yes	454	69
No	192	29
Not answered	13	2

* number of surgical teams who received a copy of the postmortem report.

Surgeons and anaesthetists need to be reminded that postmortems can produce new information. When diagnosis had been confirmed at operation or by other methods, surgeons felt that the postmortem reports did not contribute additional information. Postmortem examination failed to confirm the clinical diagnosis or to explain the clinical observations in 10% of the cases where reports were received by the surgical team.

The procedure of requesting postmortem permission from relatives is one of the most difficult that is required of medical staff. A previous study[2] has shown that the success in obtaining permission is related to the seniority of the doctor involved. The high proportion of requests undertaken by the most junior staff (65% by Registrars, Senior House Officers or House Officers) may be in part responsible for the low rate of permissions (52%) granted for hospital postmortems. Other factors such as poor public perception of the value of postmortem examination, and the sometimes over-dramatic exposure in the media must also be taken into account.

Table P4 (q91)
Which members of the surgical team attended the postmortem?

	(*n*=318*)
House Officer	61
Senior House Officer	50
Registrar	57
Senior Registrar	21
Associate Specialist	2
Consultant	32
Other	6
None	129
Not known/not recorded/not answered	9

NB this can be a multiple entry

* number of postmortems for which the surgical team were informed of the date and time.

When the surgical team was informed of the date and time of the postmortem, the percentage of postmortems attended by at least one surgeon, (excluding non-responses) is 57% (180/318). The postmortem examination serves both as a legal and clinical audit. If clinicians are not aware of the date and time of the examination they cannot be expected to attend. Unfortunately the clinician was not able to attend because this information was lacking in more than half of our sample . The extent to which this reflects on organization in pathology departments cannot be determined. It is recommended that the date and time of postmortems should be routinely supplied to surgeons, and that surgeons should request this information from pathologists.

The time taken to transmit written information about a postmortem is a measure of communication between pathologist and surgeon. The data received by NCEPOD are likely to be a minimum standard since valuable telephone and personal contact is not reported on NCEPOD questionnaires. A communication was received in 63% of cases within seven days, but it is not possible to determine the nature of this from the questionnaire.

An element of clinical care is lost if the postmortem report does not reach the clinical team. Unfortunately nearly one in six reports did not reach the surgeon (16% of cases, when non-responses are excluded). There is evidence that in part this may be due to restriction of circulation of reports to clinicians by some Coroners. Proceeding litigation may be a factor but this is unlikely to involve most cases of perioperative death. NCEPOD deplores this failure of Coroners to send evidence from Coroners' postmortem examinations to clinicians. How are clinicians to survey and improve their work if audit continues to be obstructed in this way?

A 65-year-old woman died following a right hemicolectomy complicated by an anastomotic leak. The patient died four days after surgery and the case was referred to the Coroner who ordered a postmortem examination. The surgeon wrote to the Enquiry stating that the Coroner would not release the full report of the postmortem and that he was therefore unable to notify us of the cause of death.

An 88-year-old woman died after a subtotal colectomy. As the death was within 24 hours of surgery, it was reported to the Coroner, who did not order a postmortem examination. The surgeon wrote stating that he was unable to give a cause of death.

COMMENTARY ON POSTMORTEM REPORTS

The Consultant Pathologists on the advisory group met on five occasions and reviewed the 419 postmortem reports received.

The Royal College of Pathologists has recently published guidelines for postmortem reports[12]. These state that a postmortem report will normally include;

1 Demographic details

2 History

3 External examination

4 Internal examination

5 Summary of findings

6 Histology report

7 Commentary/conclusions

8 Cause of death (Office of Population Censuses and Surveys format)

The presence of a clinical history is a clear indication that the pathologist is in command of the available facts. References to letters, a history from the Coroner's officer or documents not part of the report are less persuasive. A history was present in 77% of reports, with more histories in hospital postmortems (86%) than in Coroner's postmortems (75%). The quality of the history was generally good with only eight per cent being poor or unacceptable. Ninety-two per cent were judged to be good or satisfactory. Some one-page proformas did not contain sufficient space for a history. Only three of the 419 reports were handwritten.

The gross description was adequate in 88% and measurements were made of scars and incisions in 79% of the reports. The organs were described in a systematic manner in 96% of cases. In the remainder, there was no clear approach or method. In eight per cent of cases there was no evidence that the skull and the brain had been examined. In none of these cases was there an indication that a limited examination had been requested.

The significance of fluid collections (effusions, ascites) depends greatly on the volume. Unless such measurements are made surgeons cannot begin to judge the importance of the finding. In 62% of all reports these measurements were made, with fewer measurements in the Coroners' postmortems than in hospital.

While the importance of *individual* organ weights may be debatable, few would contest the need for *major* organ weights. Most pathologists weigh five to six organs. It is hard to justify the 39 cases in which no organ weights are given. Where only one or two organ weights are given, these are usually of the heart and lungs. There was no difference between hospital and Coroners' cases.

Figure P1
Number of organs weighed

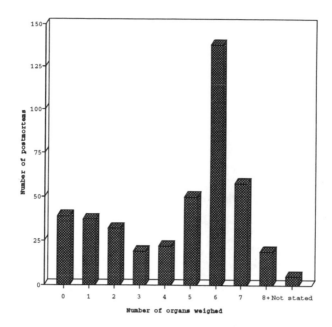

The examination of histological tissue is an integral part of all hospital postmortems. Twenty-six per cent of reports mentioned retention of material mainly for histology. Minor modification of postmortem report forms would allow this useful information to be recorded.

A histology report was present in 15% of postmortems. There was a higher proportion of histology reports in the hospital, (24%) than in the Coroners' (12%) postmortems. Despite legal and financial complexities a histology report is highly desirable in Coroners' postmortems as audit of the macroscopic examination and confirmation of the cause of death. Issue of the histology report combined with the macroscopic findings is desirable and increasingly easy with information technology.

The examination should seek to answer questions arising from the clinical history. There was evidence of this approach in 89% of the postmortem reports.

A summary of lesions was present in 27% of reports. There were fewer summaries in Coroners' cases (21%) than in hospital postmortems (51%).

Correlation of the clinical and pathological findings is one of the most important elements, ideally undertaken when all the evidence, both macroscopic and microscopic, is present. A clinical/pathological correlation was present in 51% of reports, and was regarded by the group as adequate in 86% of these.

In 86% of reports the cause of death was given in the format prescribed by the Office of Population Censuses and Surveys (OPCS). This format is reproduced in the Glossary (Appendix B). It was present in 94% of Coroners' and 60% of hospital postmortems. The OPCS cause of death, where present, was not consistent with the findings in 11% of these.

Pathology
References see page 300

Table P5
Classification of the overall performance of postmortems

	Total (n=419) %	Coroner's Postmortems (n=334) %	Hospital Postmortems (n=85) %
Excellent	16.5	15.6	20.0
Good/satisfactory	66.0	65.8	67.0
Poor	13.1	14.1	9.4
Unacceptable	4.4	4.5	3.6

Table P6
What is the value of the information provided by the postmortem?

	Total (n=419) %	Coroner's Postmortems (n=334) %	Hospital Postmortems (n=85) %
New information	49	47	57
Confirmation of surgical observations	51	53	43

Confirmation of surgical findings should not be under-valued.

SURGERY

This section of the report deals with the surgical replies received. The information relating to each procedure has been abstracted from the questionnaires and is presented as a commentary. Comments below tables refer to those patients who died, unless otherwise indicated.

Information concerning index cases is presented alongside that of the patients who died. It must be stressed that index cases are *not* controls as in a trial.

Blank page
References see page 300

CONTENTS - SURGERY

The data are presented in tables which refer to the question number in the surgical questionnaire (reproduced as Appendix C).

There has been nationwide cooperation from surgeons and gynaecologists in providing details of patients. It is a pleasure to record that this Report provides evidence of *a prevailing high standard of good practice*. We must stress that *the great majority of patients reviewed in this Report received safe surgery of a high quality.*

Generations of surgeons and anaesthetists have promoted quality by self-scrutiny and peer review. We should all try to learn. Participation in audit and NCEPOD are ways of sharing knowledge and experience with others. There is a need for more local audit to enable care and resources to be better matched.[13]

Many of the cases reported concern elderly, ill patients with advanced malignancy and co-existing diseases. Inevitably, some procedures for fatal disorders are followed by deaths and the surgeon often has difficulty in deciding when some chance of benefit justifies an operation when death is inevitable without the intervention.

The commentary in this Report is based on *peer review* of the questionnaires and notes submitted to us: it is *not* a scientific Report based on differences with a control population.

ADVISORY GROUPS

Specialist advisers for each procedure were invited to review the data. We are grateful to these advisers for their help and especially for their agreement and guidance in drawing up comments relative to their specialties. The advisers wrote brief accounts of each case and it is these accounts which form the basis for the clinical vignettes. The advisers were nominated by relevant Colleges and Specialist Associations.

Amputations of the lower limb
nominated by the Vascular Surgical Society

A D B Chant	Southampton
L de Cossart	Chester
B P Bliss	Plymouth
J H N Wolfe	London

Surgical management of strangulated hernia
nominated by the Association of Surgeons of Great Britain and Ireland

E A Benson	Leeds
R E C Collins	Canterbury
D N L Ralphs	Norwich
C M S Royston	Hull

Colorectal resection
nominated by The Association of Coloproctology of Great Britain and Ireland

A Gunn	Ashington
M M Henry	London
N J Mortensen	Oxford
J Stamatakis	Bridgend
H L Young	Cardiff

Breast Surgery
nominated by the Breast Group of The British Association of Surgical Oncology

T J Archer	Ipswich
A T Stotter	Leicester

Oesophagectomy
nominated by The British Society of Gastroenterology Surgical Committee

R J Donnelly	Liverpool
H R Matthews	Birmingham
J Spencer	London
C J Stoddard	Sheffield
J H Wyllie	London

Pulmonary resection
nominated by the Society of Cardiothoracic Surgeons of Great Britain and Ireland

D C T Watson	Birmingham
E Townsend	Harefield
B A Ross	Norwich
J E Dussek	London
R E Lea	Southampton

Coronary artery bypass grafts
nominated by the Society of Cardiothoracic Surgeons of Great Britain and Ireland

C Hilton	Newcastle upon Tyne
M D Rosin	Coventry
J R Pepper	London

Hysterectomy
nominated by the Royal College of Obstetricians and Gynaecologists

P J Bolton	Romford
A C Dunbar	Croydon
J D Hamlett	Wrexham
G D Ward	Walsall
P F Whiteley	Banbury

Prostatectomy
nominated by the British Association of Urological Surgeons

C G Fowler	London
D A Griffiths	Yeovil
D E Neal	Newcastle upon Tyne
R G Notley	Guildford
P Whelan	Leeds
C R J Woodhouse	London
F J Bramble	Bournemouth

Craniotomy
nominated by the Society of British Neurological Surgeons

T T King	London
G Neil-Dwyer	Southampton
R P Sengupta	Newcastle upon Tyne
M D M Shaw	Liverpool

Total hip replacement
nominated by the British Orthopaedic Association

J G Bradley	Scarborough
A T Cross	Sunderland
P Gregg	Leicester
B J Main	Bury St Edmunds
J D Spencer	London

Surgical management of burns
nominated by the British Association of Plastic Surgeons

F B Bailie	Nottingham
J A Clarke	London
J P Gowar	Birmingham
R Millar	Belfast

Oral and maxillofacial surgery
nominated by the British Association of Oral and Maxillofacial Surgeons

A M Corrigan	Leeds
J D Langdon	London
K M Lavery	Wolverhampton
P G McAndrew	Rotherham
D W Patton	Swansea

Otolaryngological surgery
nominated by the British Association of Otolaryngologists

D A Adams	Belfast
P Beasley	Exeter
R Ramsden	Manchester

Ophthalmic surgery
nominated by the College of Ophthalmologists

R H C Markham	Bristol
B A Noble	Leeds

INDEX CASES

Details of a further sample of patients undergoing surgery were requested via the index cases. The sample reflected that chosen for the deaths (see page 19). These patients survived for longer than 30 days after surgery.

VENOUS THROMBOEMBOLISM

Pulmonary embolism was given as the cause of death in 1244 cases recorded in England and Wales in 1991[14]. This figure, while significant, is probably an underestimate of the true incidence of fatal pulmonary embolism and a considerable underestimate of the total incidence of pulmonary embolism which is associated with deep vein thrombosis. Deep vein thrombosis can be minimized by adequate prophylaxis and, when it occurs, treatment. There have been numerous calls for the more widespread adoption of preventive measures in previous CEPOD and NCEPOD Reports[1, 3] and in the medical literature in recent years[15]. Indeed one leading article in a major journal suggests it might be construed as medical negligence not to have a protocol[16].

Surgery is the main causal factor. Patients over the age of 40 years and undergoing anaesthesia and surgery lasting more than 30 minutes carry a 25% risk of developing a deep vein thrombosis.[17] This risk increases in the presence of obesity, pregnancy, previous deep vein thrombosis or pulmonary embolism, malignancy, deep pelvic surgery and hip surgery. Immobility due to co-existing medical disorders is another additional risk factor in many surgical patients.

Several sets of 'guidelines' help surgeons to assess the risk of deep vein thrombosis, and various prophylactic treatment regimens for deep vein thrombosis have been worked out. The key paper is that of the THRIFT Consensus Group reported in the British Medical Journal in 1992.[17] There are many similar documents.[18, 19,20] All these documents have been widely distributed to surgeons. Prophylaxis is known to reduce the incidence of deep vein thrombosis but a consequent reduction of cases of fatal pulmonary embolism is more difficult to quantify.

It is against this background of a barrage of information that this year's NCEPOD report must be read. In the sample of 1821 deaths reviewed from the surgical questionnaires there were 119 proven fatal cases of pulmonary embolism (see table S1). As the rate of ventilation/perfusion scanning and postmortem is relatively low this suggests that the true rate of fatal pulmonary embolism may be much higher. The problem exists particularly in total hip replacement, hysterectomy and prostatectomy where the incidence of pulmonary emboli amongst those who died was 42.4%, 20.0% and 16.15% respectively based on both clinical investigations and confirmatory postmortem information when available. NCEPOD cannot be certain about the role or non-role of prophylaxis because the only question asked of surgeons was question 49 (y) on DVT prophylaxis and question 50, "If no prophylaxis was used, is this your normal policy?".

Table S1
Occurrence of pulmonary embolism in those cases where a postmortem was performed

(*n*=820)

	DVT prophylaxis			No DVT prophylaxis		
	All	Pulmonary embolism	No pulmonary embolism	All	Pulmonary embolism	No pulmonary embolism
Amputations of the lower limb	55	12	43	90	14	76
Surgical management of strangulated hernia	15	2	13	14	2	12
Colorectal resection	104	15	89	45	3	42
Breast surgery	7	-	7	6	1	5
Oesophagectomy	21	2	19	7	-	7
Pulmonary resection	7	1	6	1	-	1
Coronary artery bypass grafts	30	-	30	60	-	60
Hysterectomy	13	4	9	13	6	7
Prostatectomy	22	4	18	71	15	56
Craniotomy	22	2	20	85	2	83
Primary elective total hip replacement	36	18	18	21	12	9
Surgical management of burns	2	-	2	15	-	15
Oral/maxillofacial surgery	3	1	2	12	-	12
Otolaryngological surgery	6	1	5	22	-	22
Ophthalmic surgery	1	1	-	14	1	13

Table S2
Method of prophylaxis used

(*n*=344)

Heparin	191
Dextran infusion	8
Leg stockings	124
Calf compression/stimulation	16
Warfarin	11
Other	11
Not specified on questionnaire	40

NB this can be a multiple entry

We note the high number of pulmonary emboli (119); this continues to be a complication of surgery and is a cause for concern.

NCEPOD has not investigated whether the prophylaxis was of adequate duration or whether the drugs were in therapeutically effective dosages. We set out the methods employed but note that often more than one was used in any patient.

We therefore recommend that every hospital (and every directorate) should have an agreed policy for the prophylaxis and management of venous thrombosis and pulmonary embolism and this should be regularly scrutinized by directors and clinicians to ensure that it is being routinely followed. Every surgeon and gynaecologist should be aware of the problem and be signed up to the locally agreed policy. This is an aspect of risk management.

There is a need for further large scale research into new and better methods of mechanical and drug prophylaxis.

Selected references

Office of Population Censuses and Surveys. Mortality Statistics 1991 - cause. England and Wales. HMSO 1993.

Parker-Williams J, Vickers R. Major orthopaedic surgery on the leg and thromboembolism. BMJ 1991;303:531-532.

Thromboembolic Risk Factors (THRIFT) Consensus Group. Risk of and prophylaxis for venous thromboembolism in hospital patients. BMJ 1992;305:567-574.

Venous Thromboembolism. A continuing challenge. A symposium organized by the Association of Surgeons of Great Britain and Ireland and The Thrombosis Research Institute. St Helier, Jersey. 3 April 1992.

NB Readers should also refer to the main list of references on page 300.

AMPUTATIONS OF THE LOWER LIMB

SURGICAL PROCEDURE

Amputation of whole or part of lower limb.

KEY ISSUES

1   There were a large number of deaths following amputation.

2   Arterial thrombosis is the most common cause of acute limb ischaemia. Clinical management requires the provision of vascular surgeons, emergency radiology and thrombolysis. Primary arterial embolism is a rare cause of acute ischaemia in elderly patients.

3   An opinion from a Consultant with vascular expertise should be obtained before proceeding to a major amputation for ischaemia.

4   Amputation surgery should be supported by the best possible postoperative care, including the provision of intensive care and high dependency services.

5   Major amputation should be avoided for those whose death is inevitable within a short time.

SAMPLE

Deaths

696   surgical death questionnaires sent out

494   returned (return rate 71%)

485   death questionnaires suitable for analysis

Index Cases

51 index case questionnaires returned (see page 19).

AUDIT

Table S3 (q 98)

Has this death been considered (or will it be considered) at a local audit/quality control meeting?

	Deaths (n=485)	%
Yes	405	84
No	63	
Not answered	17	

This is a good figure and shows an increase in audit from that found in the previous NCEPOD Reports.

PATIENT PROFILE

The patients who died were elderly, 377 (78%) being over 70 years of age and 188 (39%) over 80 years of age. In addition 389 (80%) of those who died were in ASA classes 3, 4 or 5, many had extensive comorbidity, at least 118 (24%) were diabetics and the majority were urgent or emergency admissions (416, 86%). Thus many patients presenting for amputation were terminally ill and many deaths were inevitable whatever the standard of delivery of care.

Table S4 (q 4)

Age at final operation

	Deaths (n=485)	Index (n=51)
<10 years	1	-
10 - 19	-	-
20 - 29	-	1
30 - 39	1	1
40 - 49	5	1
50 - 59	17	4
60 - 69	84	17
70 - 79	189	14
80 - 89	161	12
90 - 99	26	1
100+	1	-

Table S5 (q 24)
Was there any delay in referral (urgent or emergency admissions)?

	Deaths (*n*=416)		Index (*n*=23)
Yes	42		4
No	360		19
Not known/not recorded	1		-
Not answered	13		-
If yes, the delay was			
Doctor-related	18		3
Patient-related	25		1
Organizational	1		-

NB this can be a multiple entry

Referrals were delayed by the patient as well as for "doctor-related" reasons. In one case a patient's referral was delayed for 13 days because a letter was lost in the Christmas post. Following referral seven admissions were delayed. These were due to reluctance on behalf of the patient and to lack of beds.

Table S6 (q 12 Deaths, q 11 Index)
Initial admission intention for the last operation performed (all cases)

	Deaths (*n*=485)		Index (*n*=51)
Elective	69		28
Urgent	138		11
Emergency	278		12

Table S7 (q 16A)
Admissions

	Deaths (*n*=485)		Index (*n*=51)
Weekday	414		49
Weekend	66		2
Public holiday/extra-statutory holiday	3		-
Not answered	2		-

Amongst the 69 elective admissions who subsequently died one cancellation occurred, due to a lack of beds. The same reason was given for the cancellation of an index case.

Most patients were admitted to surgical wards (66%) but referrals within hospitals also came from medical wards (18%) and geriatric units (9%).

Table S8 (q 47)
ASA Class

	Deaths (n=485)	Index (n=51)
1	3	4
2	76	25
3	201	17
4	175	3
5	13	-
Not answered	17	2

There was a high percentage (80%) of ill patients with ASA grades 3, 4, or 5 and extensive comorbidities. Our vascular surgery advisers questioned whether patients of ASA class 4 or 5 should have amputation surgery under any circumstances. Decision-making here will require good judgement and it is essential that the experience of the surgeon should match the ASA class of the patient.

THE SURGICAL TEAM

Table S9 (q 1)
Specialty of Consultant Surgeon in charge at time of final operation

	Deaths (n=485)	Index (n=51)
Vascular	13	3
General with vascular interest	333	40
General	117	8
Orthopaedic	22	-

Vascular surgeons, or those in general surgery who expressed a vascular interest, performed the majority of the amputations (346 cases, 71%).

Vascular opinion needed for amputation

Whatever the specialty of the Consultant in charge, the advisers suggested that it is in the best interest of patients that the opinion of a Consultant with vascular expertise is obtained prior to embarking on all amputations for ischaemia. This ensures that opportunities to perform reconstructive surgery are not missed and gives an opportunity for helpful and supportive discussion regarding the appropriateness and level of amputation. This does not imply that vascular surgeons and their teams should do all amputations.

Should orthopaedic surgeons manage diabetic gangrene?

The general orthopaedic surgeons in the above list were mainly doing amputations for diabetic gangrene. The advisers queried whether it is advisable for general orthopaedic surgeons, other than those with a special interest, to manage patients when there may be a need to consider other methods of treatment and to offer vascular reconstruction in addition to amputation. The ideal situation would be to manage diabetic patients with a combined input from disciplines such as diabetic physicians, vascular and orthopaedic surgeons and prosthetists.

The following vignettes illustrate cases where the advisers considered that a vascular opinion might have altered the clinical course or offered a better standard of care.

> *Whilst on call for emergencies, a Consultant Surgeon with an interest in breast surgery was called to treat an 81-year-old man (ASA 4) with a ruptured iliac aneurysm. This was repaired but the leg became ischaemic. There was then a delay of six days before an embolectomy was attempted, and another four days before an above-knee amputation was done. The patient died in renal failure.*

There was time to obtain a vascular opinion which might have avoided the inappropriate embolectomy. A vascular surgeon might have felt that he could reconstruct the vasculature to the ischaemic leg.

> *A Consultant general surgeon with an interest in gastroenterology in a Teaching Hospital supervised the treatment of a 71-year-old diabetic woman (ASA 3). Several gangrenous toes had already been amputated and, without consultation, the Senior Registrar decided to amputate another toe. The operation was finally done by a Registrar. The patient died following a myocardial infarct.*

While the outcome might not have been different, was the choice of specialist appropriate for a teaching hospital?[21]

Table S10 (q 40)
What was the grade of the most senior surgeon consulted before the operation?

	Deaths (*n*=485)	(Locum)	Index (*n*=51)	(Locum)
Senior House Officer	1		-	
Registrar	7	(1)	-	
Senior Registrar	14	(2)	-	
Consultant	456	(8)	51	(2)
Clinical Assistant	1		-	
Associate Specialist	3		-	
Not answered	3		-	

There was an extremely high level of discussion with Consultant staff prior to surgery (456 cases, 94%). This figure is a great improvement on the 1987 CEPOD Report.[1] Clearly the Senior House Officer and the seven Registrars should not have been undertaking an amputation without discussion with a more senior surgeon. Despite this comment this table demonstrates commendable behaviour on behalf of those surgeons undertaking amputation surgery and is an example of excellent practice.

Table S11 (q 54)
What was the grade of the most senior operating surgeon?

	Deaths (*n=485*)	(Locum)		Index (*n=51*)	(Locum)
Senior House Officer	39	(1)		7	
Registrar	202	(1)		16	(1)
Staff Grade	7	(1)		-	
Senior Registrar	78	(5)		8	
Clinical Assistant	5			1	
Associate Specialist	5			-	
Consultant	147	(8)		18	
Not answered	2			1	

Table S12 (q 57)
When the most senior operating surgeon was not a Consultant, was a more senior surgeon immediately available, i.e. in the operating room/suite?

	Deaths (*n=485*)		Index (*n=33*)
Yes	135		15
No	192		17
Not known/not recorded	2		-
Not answered	9		1

Consultant Surgeons did 147 (30%) of the amputations on those who died, whilst Registrars did 42%. Senior supervision was available for 104 of the 241 cases when a junior trainee was operating. Where Senior House Officers are doing an operation as important and irrevocable as an amputation, supervision should be available.

TIME OF SURGERY

Table S13 (q 53)
Day of and time of operation

	Deaths (*n=485*)		Index (*n=51*)
Weekday, between 08.00 and 18.00	318		40
Weekday, outside these hours	69		1
Weekday, time not given	25		3
Weekend	73		7

Amputations were done throughout the week although few index cases were done at weekends. At least 29% of the patients who died had their surgery "out of hours" or at the weekend. This suggests that amputations take a low priority on elective lists and are often left to be done "out of hours".

RESOURCES

Table S14(q 62)
Classify the final operation

	Deaths (n=485)	Index (n=51)
Emergency	15	-
Urgent	249	16
Scheduled	202	32
Elective	16	2
Not answered	3	1

Delays in operation due to factors other than clinical were reported in 15 (3%) deaths, and in three (6%) index cases . For both deaths and index cases, the delays were due to a lack of theatre provision or to the patient refusing surgery.

Table S15 (q 2)
In which type of hospital did the last operation take place?

	Deaths (n=485)	Index (n=51)
District General	384	31
University/Teaching	91	17
Single Specialty Hospital	1	-
Other Acute/Partly Acute	3	-
Community	1	-
Defence Medical Services	2	2
Independent	3	1

Table S16 (q 71)
Which of the following are available in the hospital in which the final operation took place?

	Deaths (n=485)	Index (n=51)
Theatre recovery area	462	50
Adult intensive care unit	403	42
Adult high dependency unit	101	8
None of the above	6	-
Not answered	2	1

Table S17 (q 74)

Were you at any time unable to transfer the patient into an ICU/HDU within the hospital in which the surgery took place?

	Deaths (*n=485*)		Index (*n=51*)
Yes	8		-
No	445		48
Not answered	32		3

Eighty-two patients who died had amputations in units without an intensive care unit (see Appendix B). Although an ICU may be available problems arise when these units are full. In eight cases (2%) the surgeon and anaesthetist wanted to admit the patient to an ICU/HDU but were unable to do so; this was because the unit was full (six cases) or did not exist on site (two cases).

Many reports quote perioperative mortality of 10 to 20%. An aggressive policy towards preparation together with high dependency or intensive care postoperatively can reduce mortality to 0.9%.[22, 23] A team approach lowers perioperative mortality and increases the chances of successful rehabilitation.

> *An 82-year-old diabetic woman developed a gangrenous foot. She was managed well by a vascular surgical team collaborating with a medical diabetic specialist. Initially her amputation was delayed because of problems with excessive anticoagulation. When she was finally ready for surgery there was no available theatre space. In all, her surgery was delayed for six days; she was finally operated on in the evening. She died 16 days later with bronchopneumonia.*

Whilst the delay may not have been directly related to the patient's death the advisers commented that it was inappropriate to be operating out of hours on an ill patient who required very careful management and the availability of all support services.

> *A 70-year-old woman had critical ischaemia of a leg for which an ilio-popliteal bypass graft was attempted. This failed and an above-knee amputation became necessary. The patient subsequently died of bronchopneumonia. The surgeon wrote to the Enquiry stating "There is no ICU in this hospital and yet I am expected to provide a vascular surgery service in a hospital where adequate facilities do not exist".*

This is an acute District General Hospital.

COMPLICATIONS

Table S18

Most common complications of amputation surgery (deaths)

	(n=485)
Bronchopneumonia	140
Myocardial infarction	127
Cerebrovascular accident	62
Renal failure	52
Septicaemia	45
Pulmonary embolism	42
Wound infection	16
Skin flap necrosis	14
Loss of diabetic control	8
Stress ulcer	6
Mesenteric ischaemia	6
Perforated duodenal ulcer	3

NB this can be a multiple entry

This list of complications reflects the type of comorbidity present in arteriopathic and/or diabetic patients and is a pattern recognised by vascular surgeons. Many of these complications are not preventable. There was a high incidence of pulmonary emboli (42 cases), of which 26 were proved at postmortem (see table S1, page 69). Not all cases had postmortem examinations and the remaining diagnoses of pulmonary embolism were clinical, supported by ventilation-perfusion scans etc.

A toxic 78-year-old diabetic woman with a gangrenous foot was admitted to a District General Hospital. An urgent above-knee amputation was planned although there was clearly a risk (ASA 4). Surgery was delayed due to electrolyte disturbances and it was midnight before these were satisfactorily corrected. No thromboembolic prophylaxis was given. A successful operation was done. Twelve days later the patient suffered a massive pulmonary embolism and died.

Prophylaxis of some kind was given against deep venous thrombosis in 202 (42%) patients of those who died; however we do not have any information as to the duration and effectiveness of the prophylaxis.

Table S19 (q 49)
Was DVT prophylaxis used?

	Deaths (*n=485*)
Yes	202
No	283

If yes, which method was used?

	(*n=202*)
Heparin	134
Heparin/stockings	9
Heparin/stockings/other	1
Heparin/other	5
Stockings	17
Stockings/other	1
Warfarin	9
Other	7
Not stated	19

NB this can be a multiple entry

There is evidence that prophylaxis against iliofemoral venous thrombosis should be used when undertaking above-knee amputation as this is known to have a high incidence of thromboembolic complications. This does not seem to be happening, and 110 surgeons reporting a death stated that it was not their policy to give DVT prophylaxis. The advisers suggest that all units undertaking amputation surgery should draw up a protocol of locally agreed measures to combat thromboembolic disease and abide by it.

ISSUES IN AMPUTATION SURGERY

Vascular surgical opinion before major amputation

Major amputations are carried out by a variety of specialist surgeons, some of whom do not have a vascular interest. Advances in femoro-distal bypass grafting have allowed vascular surgeons to salvage many limbs which in the past would have been amputated. Patients who have vascular disease deserve the opinion of a Consultant surgeon with vascular expertise.

Pain relief services

The provision of good pain relief services, enabling the use of all methods of pain relief, might help to avoid inhumane surgery.

> *It was a Sunday when a geriatrician referred an 87-year-old man with a gangrenous leg. He had undergone a failed embolectomy four days previously. The Consultant Surgeon had an interest in vascular surgery. The patient also suffered from Alzheimer's disease, ulcerative proctitis and mitral valve disease (for which he was anticoagulated) and an established chest infection. A locum Senior Registrar did an above-knee amputation at 18.30 on the day of referral. The patient died in respiratory failure within 24 hours.*

> *An 81-year-old man had disseminated colorectal cancer, cardiac and renal failure. He underwent a failed embolectomy, followed three days later by an above-knee amputation. The operation was done as an urgent case by a Registrar at 22.15. The patient died the same night at 03.35. Cause of death was myocardial infarction and carcinomatosis.*

> *A 51-year-old woman was dying with carcinomatosis when she developed bilateral venous gangrene of the legs. Initially below-knee amputations were done and eventually she had bilateral high above-knee amputations, this last operation being done just days before she died.*

The provision of essential services

The Enquiry confirms that amputees who die are elderly and suffer from serious co-existing disease. If a major amputation is indicated, the patient is entitled to expect the best possible postoperative care, including the availability of a high dependency or intensive care bed. Some acute hospitals still have no high dependency or intensive care facilities (see Glossary, Appendix B).

Pulmonary embolism and the use of prophylaxis (see also pages 68 to 70)

Ilio-femoral venous thrombosis after above-knee amputation is common, and prophylaxis has been advocated. No comment may be made on the usefulness of DVT prophylaxis from the figures given in this Report.

Amputations of the Lower Limb
References see page 300

Inappropriate amputations in the terminally ill

Major limb gangrene is a common final event for the aged chronic sick and in the terminally ill. Major amputation may relieve pain and aid nursing management, but many of these patients could be more properly treated conservatively with other pain-relieving measures, avoiding distressing decisions and operations at a sensitive time for patients and relatives. Major amputation should be avoided for those whose death is inevitable within a short time. Surgeons need support to resist the temptation to "do something" for these patients, and to resist demands from well-meaning but misguided carers or relatives.

A general surgeon with a vascular interest was caring for an 82-year-old woman in a University Hospital because she had a gangrenous right foot. She was a diabetic with dementia, classed as ASA 4 and there had been a previous left above-knee amputation. The Consultant Surgeon obviously had a good relationship with the patient's relatives and after lengthy discussion with them he agreed to amputate the leg "more in hope than expectation". The patient died 16 days after surgery, following a stroke.

Inappropriate "embolectomy"

Acute arterial thrombosis has replaced arterial embolism as the most common cause of acute ischaemia of the lower limb. The operation of emergency embolectomy is inappropriate for acute arterial thrombosis. It is usually unsuccessful and commonly ends with a major amputation. Many of these amputations can be avoided by emergency vascular imaging followed by thrombolysis and/or bypass grafting. No patient admitted with acute ischaemia of a lower limb should be subject to an emergency operation without the prior opinion of a trained vascular surgeon.

An 80-year-old woman was under the care of a vascular surgeon in a District General Hospital. Two left femoral "embolectomies" were done on consecutive days. These procedures failed and an above-knee amputation was done ten days later. The patient died with bronchopneumonia.

Following a laparotomy and repair of a strangulated inguinal hernia a 72-year-old man developed an ischaemic left leg. A Registrar did a femoral embolectomy and a fasciotomy. Three days later an above-knee amputation was done. The patient died in renal failure.

SURGICAL MANAGEMENT OF STRANGULATED HERNIA

SURGICAL PROCEDURE

The surgical management of strangulated hernia. The advisers took as a definition that a strangulated hernia was one in which the contents of the sac had an interrupted blood supply leading to impaired viability of the contents.

In NHS hospitals in England, approximately 53,000 primary inguinal hernia repairs and 5,000 primary femoral hernia repairs are performed on adults over the age of 16 years annually. In 1990, 210 English residents died as a result of complications of inguinal hernias and a further 120 died following femoral hernia complications.[24] There are wide variations in the standardized hernia repair rates and morbidity rates between English districts.

KEY ISSUES

1   Both the specialties of the surgeon and the sites at which surgery was performed were appropriate.

2   Despite the fact that these patients were elderly and ill, resuscitation was often inadequate and surgery hasty.

3   Forty-four per cent of cases were done out of hours; this was often because theatre space was not available during the normal working day rather than for clinical reasons.

4   Consultant Surgeons were rarely involved in the management and surgery of strangulated hernias.

SAMPLE

Deaths

100 surgical death questionnaires sent out

71 returned (return rate 71%)

70 death questionnaires were suitable for analysis

Index Cases

Presentation of index case details has been omitted from this section as only eight questionnaires for this procedure were returned (see page 19).

AUDIT

Table S20 (q 98)
Has this death been considered (or will it be considered) at a local audit/quality control meeting?

	(*n*=70)
Yes	63
No	6
Not answered	1

PATIENT PROFILE

The patients were all over 60 years of age and 65 (93%) were over 70 years of age. Forty-nine patients (70%) were ASA classes 3, 4 or 5 and 62 (89%) were admitted as emergencies. The female to male ratio was 1.6:1.

Table S21 (q 4)
Age at final operation

60 - 69 years	5
70 - 79	16
80 - 89	45
90 - 99	4

Table S22 (q 12 Deaths and q 11 Index)
Initial admission intention for the last operation performed

Elective	1
Urgent	7
Emergency	62

Table S23 (q 16A Deaths and q 16 Index)
Admission

Weekday	54
Weekend	16

Delays in referral occurred in 18 (26%) cases where the patient subsequently died. These delays were "doctor-related" in eight cases, and "patient-related" in ten. There were examples of delay in referral within hospitals.

> *An 85-year-old man was transferred from a geriatric ward to a surgical ward. He had had a strangulated inguinal hernia for some time but referral had been delayed due to failure to recognise the diagnosis. At the time of transfer to a surgical service the patient was classified as ASA 3. A surgical Registrar operated on the strangulated inguinal hernia and resected strangulated small bowel. The patient died 11 days after surgery with a myocardial infarction.*

It is possible, had the patient been referred immediately the strangulated hernia was noticed, that the small bowel might not have been gangrenous and that the outcome might have been different.

Table S24 (q 47)
ASA Class

	(n=70)
1	2
2	17
3	24
4	21
5	4
Not answered	2

Table S25
Sites of strangulated hernia

Femoral	39
Inguinal	14
Umbilical	7
Incisional	5
Femoral and incisional	1
Obturator	1
Spigelian	1
Epigastric	1
Internal	1

THE SURGICAL TEAM

Table S26 (q 1)
Specialty of Consultant Surgeon in charge at time of final operation

General	47
General with special interest in gastroenterology	21
Urology	2

Only 54% of cases were discussed preoperatively with Consultants. These patients were elderly and sick, and their problems should not be underestimated. Discussion with a Consultant Surgeon is mandatory.

Table S27 (q 54)
What was the grade of the most senior operating surgeon?

		(Locum)
Senior House Officer	4	
Registrar	35	(5)
Staff Grade	2	
Senior Registrar	16	(2)
Consultant	13	

Table S28 (q 57)
Where the most senior operating surgeon was not a Consultant, was a more senior surgeon immediately available, i.e. in the operating room/suite?

	(*n=57*)
Yes	4
No	53

Consultants operated on 19% of all patients. When a Consultant was not operating, but had been consulted about the case, there was little practical supervision of an operating trainee. The advisers felt that in many cases the surgeons who operated in the absence of adequate supervision were too junior for these elderly sick patients.

TIME OF SURGERY

Table S29 (q 53)
Day and time of start of operation

	(*n=70*)
Weekday between 08.00 and 18.00	15
Weekday outside these hours	31
Weekday, time not given	4
Weekend	20

Twenty-nine per cent of operations were done at weekends and 44% (31 cases) were done out of hours. This was often stated to be due to the lack of day-time emergency theatres.

Haste and lack of resuscitation

Patients were often rushed to theatre at night, apparently in order to clear the emergency workload, without adequate resuscitation. This meant that trainee surgeons were operating on elderly, dehydrated patients. This occurred in six out of 70 (9%) cases. The following vignettes are examples.

An 86-year-old man with a large strangulated recurrent left inguinal hernia was in the operating theatre within 90 minutes of admission. The case was managed throughout by a Registrar with five months' experience. After only one litre of fluid and no central venous pressure measurements the patient was anaesthetised by an Associate Specialist. After surgery the patient was hypotensive but was not nursed in an intensive care unit. He died of hypotension and renal failure 20 hours after surgery.

A 77-year-old man (ASA 4) presented with a strangulated hernia. A locum Registrar managed the case throughout. The patient was suffering from severe chronic obstructive airways disease and a hiatus hernia. He was anaemic, dehydrated and uraemic, yet surgery was done within three hours of admission. At surgery there was a strangulated small intestine and a Meckel's diverticulum in the hernial sac. The bowel was resected and the hernia repaired. The patient died the same day.

An 85-year-old woman presented as an emergency with a strangulated femoral hernia. She was dehydrated and moribund. Without consultation or apparent attempts at resuscitation, a surgical Registrar operated within 15 minutes of admission on a Sunday evening. A resection of the small intestine and hernia repair were done. The patient aspirated gastric contents and died seven hours after the surgery.

The advisers felt that the management of these cases was disastrous. No consultation took place at any time. Where was Consultant responsibility? There were several other cases where it appeared that nasogastric aspiration was not used in patients with intestinal obstruction, and respiratory complications arose as a result of aspiration of vomit.

These points have all been made in previous CEPOD and NCEPOD Reports. It is unacceptable that these practices persist.

RESOURCES

Table S30 (q 2)
In which type of hospital did the last operation take place?

	(*n*=70)
District General	55
University/Teaching	14
Other Acute/Partly Acute	1

An 88-year-old woman was admitted to a medical ward in a University Hospital. She had a duodenal ulcer that was bleeding. She was also known to suffer from epilepsy, ischaemic heart disease and osteoarthritis. It was noticed that she became confused and eventually it was realised that she had intestinal obstruction. She was resuscitated carefully, until an optimum time was reached for surgery. There was then no emergency theatre available and a further eight hours passed until the theatre became available. A strangulated obturator hernia was found which required resection of small bowel. The patient died seven days later with bronchopneumonia.

It is debatable whether this woman should have had an operation at all but having made the decision and having appropriately prepared her it was unfortunate that there were not adequate facilities to allow her to have a timely operation.

Table S31 (q 71)

Which of the following are available in the hospital in which the final operation took place?

	(n=70)
Theatre recovery area	65
Adult intensive care unit	58
Adult high dependency unit	7
None of the above	1
Not answered	1

Twelve patients (17%) were operated on in units without an intensive care unit. Three patients could not be admitted to an ICU because there were no vacant beds when problems arose.

A 73-year-old man delayed admission for his strangulated left inguinal hernia for four days. On arrival at the hospital he was septicaemic and in renal failure (ASA 5). He was poorly resuscitated preoperatively with only 1 litre of fluid, before a Consultant Surgeon operated and resected gangrenous small intestine and repaired the hernia. The patient could not be transferred to the intensive care unit because it was full. The patient's lungs were ventilated for 24 hours on the ward until a bed in ICU could be found. He died three days after surgery. There was no postmortem examination.

An 81-year-old man was known to suffer from chronic obstructive airways disease, heart failure and a hiatus hernia. When his recurrent left inguinal hernia strangulated he presented to his local District General Hospital at which there was no intensive care unit. He was seen by a Consultant Surgeon who decided to operate, and as the patient represented a high risk a Consultant Anaesthetist assessed the patient and classed him as ASA 4. Surgery was done under spinal anaesthesia by a Consultant Surgeon (see page 278 of Anaesthesia). The patient died 30 minutes after surgery due to a myocardial infarction.

This death was probably inevitable but the surgeon should not be required to manage desperately ill patients such as this in a hospital without appropriate intensive care services.

Table S32
Complications after surgery for strangulated hernia (deaths)

	(*n*=70)
Respiratory infection	20
Myocardial infarction	18
Septicaemia	13
Heart failure	12
Renal failure	11
Cerebrovascular accident	5
Pulmonary embolism	5
Anastomotic leak	2
Aspiration pneumonia	2
Miscellaneous (wound infection, haemorrhage and perforated duodenal ulcer)	3

NB this can be a multiple entry

The number of pulmonary emboli is derived from both clinical and postmortem information.

IMPORTANT ISSUES IN SURGERY FOR STRANGULATED HERNIA

Inappropriate operations

There were instances when the advisers felt that the patients should not have received surgery at all, and other instances where the decisions taken at operation by trainee surgeons were erroneous. The vignette below is one example of such a case.

> *A 74-year-old man was admitted with a strangulated, left femoral hernia. The hernia was found to contain sigmoid colon. This was not resected but returned to the abdominal cavity. The patient died 48 hours later. A postmortem revealed an infarcted sigmoid colon. This patient was never seen by a surgeon above the grade of Registrar.*

Areas of concern in surgery for strangulated hernia

1   It is not surprising that elderly people with strangulated hernias die. If a decision is made to operate on these high risk patients then at least consultation with a senior anaesthetist and surgeon should take place. The experience of the anaesthetist and surgeon attending the patient should then be matched to the ASA class of the patient.

2   There is too much haste and lack of resuscitation in preparing these patients for surgery.

3   There is an inadequate provision of emergency operating theatres.

4   There is an inadequate provision of intensive care and high dependency units and when these are provided they often cannot be used.

5   Some patients may be too ill for surgery and a more humane approach to their care should be considered. This should be a Consultant decision.

Blank page
References see page 300

COLORECTAL RESECTION

SURGICAL PROCEDURE

Colorectal resection.

The Enquiry received reports of 1696 deaths following a colorectal resection. In order to reduce this to a manageable number, questionnaires were sent out for 467 cases, randomly selected.

KEY ISSUES

1   The patients were predominantly elderly and frail, presenting as emergencies. A substantial proportion of the deaths were inevitable.

2   The need for more Consultant presence in the operating theatre, particularly for urgent and emergency surgery.

3   A requirement to match the experience of the surgeon and anaesthetist to the severity of the pathology and the illness of the patient.

4   The provision of emergency theatres during the day to reduce "out-of-hours" operating.

5   The continuing issue of prophylaxis for thromboembolic phenomena. Can we afford to be complacent about this problem?

6   Colorectal surgery must be supported by adequate essential services.

SAMPLE

Deaths

467 surgical death questionnaires sent out

356 returned (return rate 76%)

349 death questionnaires suitable for analysis

Index Cases

208 questionnaires returned (see page 19).

AUDIT

Table S33 (q 98)
Has this death been considered, (or will it be considered) at a local audit/quality control meeting?

	(n=349)
Yes	315
No	28
Not known/not recorded	1
Not answered	5

Ninety per cent of these deaths have been subjected to the audit process. This is a commendable figure and compares well with the rates from other procedures reviewed in this report.

PATIENT PROFILE

Table S34 (q 4)
Age at final operation

	Deaths (n=349)		Index (n=208)
10 - 19 years	-		1
20 - 29	-		11
30 - 39	2		10
40 - 49	5		8
50 - 59	15		23
60 - 69	68		54
70 - 79	128		73
80 - 89	114		27
90 - 99	16		1
100+	1		-

Table S35 (q 12 Deaths and 11 Index)
Initial admission intention for the last operation performed

	Deaths (n=349)		Index (n=208)
Elective	72		168
Urgent	60		13
Emergency	217		27

There were a large number (217, 62%) of emergency admissions amongst the patients who died. This reflects the severity of their presenting illness. The index cases show a much smaller number (13%) of emergencies and this may be due in part to the method of selection (page 19).

Colorectal Resection
References see page 300

Table S36 (q 16)
Admission

	Deaths (n=349)		Index (n=208)
Weekday	281		177
Weekend	62		30
Public Holiday	4		-
Not answered	2		1

Amongst the 72 elective admissions who died there were no cancellations as a result of a lack of resources.

Table S37 (q 24)
Was there any delay in referral (urgent and emergency admissions)?

	Deaths (n=277)		Index (n=40)
Yes	34		7
No	241		32
Not answered	2		1

If yes, the delay was

	Deaths (n=34)		Index (n=7)
Doctor-related	12		5
Patient-related	20		2
Other	3		1

NB this can be a multiple entry

It is worth noting that delays in urgent and emergency admissions were more often related to the patient's wishes and behaviour than to delays by medical attendants. Delays in admission for emergency cases were only quoted as occurring in four cases; the delay affected the outcome in only two of these.

Patients were generally admitted to surgical wards (69%) but referrals came from a wide variety of sites including medical wards (12%), geriatric wards (9%), admission wards (2%), and accident and emergency holding areas (5%).

Table S38 (q 47)
ASA Class

	Deaths (*n*=349)		Index (*n*=208)
1	12		85
2	85		98
3	120		22
4	104		1
5	17		-
Not answered	11		2

There is a marked contrast between the good ASA classes of the index cases, the majority of whom (168 out of 208, 81%) were elective cases, compared with the ASA classes of the patients who died. In this latter group, not only were 62% emergency admissions but 70% were also in ASA classes 3, 4 and 5. Given this workload of elderly, frail patients presenting as emergencies, there is a need to assess and note the ASA grade more carefully.

Figure S1 (qs 53 and 81)
Number of days between operation and death

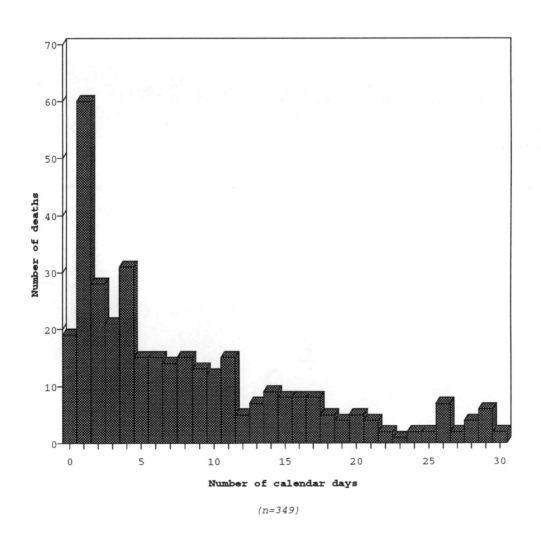

(n=349)

Colorectal Resection
References see page 300

THE SURGICAL TEAM

Table S39 (q 1)

Specialty of Consultant Surgeon in charge at time of final operation before death (in charge at time of operation specified, for index cases)

	Deaths (n=349)		Index (n=208)
General Surgery	111		53
General with special interest in gastroenterology/colorectal surgery	141		115
Vascular surgery	70		32
Urology	25		3
Surgical oncology	2		5

There was a range of surgical interest amongst the surgeons who performed a colorectal resection where a patient subsequently died. In addition to 111 (32%) general surgeons, 141 (40%) surgeons had a special interest in gastroenterology or colorectal surgery.

Decision-making

Table S40 (q 40)

What was the grade of the most senior surgeon consulted before the operation?

	Deaths (n=349)	(Locum)	Index (n=208)	(Locum)
Registrar	21	(2)	-	
Senior Registrar	23		2	
Consultant	302	(4)	205	(1)
Not answered	3		1	

Consultant discussion took place prior to surgery in 87% of cases (deaths). This is very encouraging and matches the figure of 85% quoted in the 1990 NCEPOD Report[3]. However, there is still room for improvement.

Table S41 (q 54)
What was the grade of the most senior operating surgeon?

	Deaths (n=349)	(Locum)	Index (n=208)	(Locum)
Senior House Officer	3		1	
Registrar	112	(8)	21	(2)
Staff Grade	4	(1)	-	
Senior Registrar	54	(3)	16	
Clinical Assistant	1		-	
Associate Specialist	1		-	
Consultant	174	(6)	170	

Was a more senior surgeon immediately available, i.e. in the operating room/suite?

	Deaths (n=349)	Index (n=208)
Yes	42	22
No	131	16
Not applicable (Consultant operating)	174	169
Not answered	2	1

Grade of the operating surgeon

Consultant Surgeons did 174 (50%) of the operations in those who died, whilst Senior House Officers and Registrars did 115 (33%) and Senior Registrars 54 (15%) cases. The advisers expressed their concern that in 72% of the cases operated on by junior trainees no Consultant was available to supervise. This is in sharp contrast to the index cases where a Consultant was available or operating in 92% of cases. This may be related to the lack of daytime operating room facilities.

> *A 62-year-old woman underwent an anterior resection of the rectum for a carcinoma. Six days later she developed peritonitis. A locum Registrar was then delegated to operate and sort out the problem. A laparotomy was done and the anastomosis taken down and resutured. The patient died two days later from septicaemia and multi-system failure.*

The advisers felt that it was inappropriate to leave an unsupervised locum Registrar to deal with this problem.

> *A 78-year-old woman developed a pericolic abscess adjacent to a carcinoma of the desending colon. The Consultant in charge resected the tumour and all went well initially. Ten days later, on a Saturday afternoon, a Senior House Officer was left to do a second-look laparotomy because the anastomosis had broken down. He performed a new anastomosis with staples and added a caecostomy; all without senior assistance. The patient suffered a fatal stroke 15 days later.*

The advisers felt that this case was an even worse example of inappropriate delegation and substandard care in that a Senior House Officer was left to perform this difficult revisional surgery.

Colorectal Resection
References see page 300

A 70-year-old woman (ASA 3) was operated on by a Registrar when she presented with a perforation of the sigmoid colon secondary to diverticular disease. The operation took place at 20.00 hours, and a Hartmann's procedure was done. At no time did the Registrar discuss the case with his Consultant. The patient died of septicaemia in the intensive care unit three days later.

Criticism of this case is levelled at the trainee who did not ask for help.

An 80-year-old man (ASA 4) died 20 days after a Hartmann's procedure. The operation was done at 01.40 hours by a surgical Registrar operating alone and a locum Senior House Officer anaesthetist, with no higher qualification, who sought help from a Registrar. A carcinoma of the sigmoid colon with hepatic metastases was found.

The grades of both anaesthetist and surgeon, together with the timing of the surgery on this ASA 4 patient were inappropriate. This is not an acceptable standard of care.

There were several cases in colorectal surgery where the assessors felt that the grade of anaesthetist was inappropriate. This is commented on further in the Anaesthesia section (pages 277 and 294).

Table S42
Who anaesthetised and who operated on ASA class 3, 4 and 5 patients?

	ASA class (surgical questionnaires)*		
	3	4	5
Grade of most senior operating surgeon	(*n*=120)	(*n*=104)	(*n*=17)
Senior House Officer	-	-	1
Registrar	35	42	5
Staff Grade	-	3	-
Senior Registrar	17	25	4
Consultant	68	34	7
Grade of most senior anaesthetist			
Senior House Officer	20	13	4
Registrar	18	20	5
Senior Registrar	9	10	4
Consultant	51	30	2
Staff Grade	-	3	-
Associate Specialist	2	3	-
Clinical Assistant	3	1	2
Not answered	1	-	-

* NB 40 anaesthetic questionnaires not received for these cases

Colorectal Resection
References see page 300

Elderly patients should be treated as if they were ASA 4 and the experience of the surgeon and anaesthetist should match the severity of the pathology and the illness of the patient.

> *A 76-year-old man (ASA 2) presented to a District General Hospital with large bowel obstruction. He had suffered from previous myocardial infarctions and was a known high-risk case. A Consultant Surgeon operated appropriately but the anaesthetic was conducted by a locum Senior House Officer. The patient required ventilation of the lungs postoperatively and was managed in the intensive care unit. The patient died after transfer to a surgical ward. The fluid charts from the ward were poor but the cause of death appeared to be pulmonary oedema secondary to intravenous fluid overloading.*

This case reflects the dangers of intravenous fluid overload in elderly patients or in those whose cardiopulmonary function is compromised. More importantly however is the failure to anticipate problems in the elderly and apply the necessary precautions highlighted by a high ASA class. The advisers were concerned at the discrepancy between the grades of anaesthetist and surgeon. They felt that it was inappropriate to have an anaesthetist who was not only of a junior grade but probably also of low skill, for such a high risk patient. Criticism must be levelled at the anaesthetic department for allowing this inferior provision. The surgeon may have had no option but to proceed. However, should he not have demanded a more senior anaesthetist?

TIME OF SURGERY

Table S43 (q 53 C)
Time of start of operation

	Deaths (*n*=349)		Index (*n*=208)
Weekday between 08.00 to 18.00	187		194
Weekday outside these hours	84		5
Weekday time not given	10		5
Weekend	68		4

Colorectal resections were done throughout the week although few of the index cases reported were done at weekends. Eighty-four (24%) of those patients who died had their surgery "out of hours" and 68 (19%) at weekends; compared with five (2%) "out of hours" and four (2%) at the weekend in the index cases. Given the high number of emergency admissions this is not surprising. However many of the out-of-hours operations were done purely because of the failure to provide emergency theatre services during the working day. It is acknowledged that organizational problems may arise for Consultants if emergency theatres are available for the day after 24 hours "on-take". Consultants may be committed elsewhere and the lack of Consultant availability may affect the type of cases which can be done in an emergency theatre. A review of working practice may be needed to free Consultants in order that emergency theatres can be used successfully.

A gastroenterological surgeon operated appropriately on an 86-year-old man who presented as an emergency with a left-sided colonic tumour causing intestinal obstruction and minor rectal bleeding. There was no need to hurry but due to the lack of theatre space during the day the operation took place out of hours. The patient died following a cardiac arrest on the third postoperative day.

The availability of an emergency theatre may not have altered the outcome in these cases but did impose tiring night-time surgery on the staff. The availability of other services such as pathology, radiology, physiotherapy and expert nursing are all better during the daytime and thus a more favourable outcome is likely for patients if surgery is done during the traditional working day.

A 47-year-old man presented with intestinal obstruction due to a carcinoma of the colon. He was admitted urgently following outpatient consultation, and prepared for surgery. It was planned to operate on an elective list, but these plans had to be cancelled and eventually, due to the lack of operating space, he was operated on at 23.30 hours by a locum Registrar. A right hemicolectomy was done for a tumour in the ascending colon. It was noted that he had intraperitoneal secondaries. He died two days later with carcinomatosis.

This case stresses the need for Consultant involvement in theatre. There can be no justification for a locum Registrar operating on this patient. The advisers were alarmed by the lack of available daytime theatre provision for a case like this. This lack of operating space meant that there was inadequate Consultant supervision. A colorectal Consultant Surgeon would have dealt with this patient differently when he was found to have widespread intraperitoneal malignancy.

RESOURCES

Table S44 (q 2)
In which type of hospital did the last operation take place?

	Deaths (n=349)	Index (n=208)
District General	270	140
University/Teaching	71	58
Single Specialty	-	1
Other Acute/Partly Acute	1	-
Community	-	1
Defence Medical Services	2	6
Independent	5	2

Table S45 (q 71)
Which of the following are available in the hospital in which the final operation took place?

	Deaths (n=349)	Index (n=208)
Theatre recovery area	312	200
Adult intensive care unit	312	178
Adult high dependency unit	58	42
None of the above	1	1
Not answered	2	-

Delays in operations due to factors other than clinical were reported in 11 (3%) instances where patients died and 19 (9%) of the index cases. Where patients died the problems were: lack of emergency theatre availability (6), patient-imposed delays (3), Consultant on holiday (1) and preoperative medical complications (1). The delays in the 19 index patients were due to: Christmas theatre closures (4), lack of availability of operating theatres (5), delay in radiological diagnoses (3), patient-imposed delays (3), long waiting lists (2), delays with histology (1) and delay in referral (1).

The sites where surgery took place were appropriate for the nature of the pathology. However there were problems with major surgery being done in private hospitals which did not have any intensive care facilities.

> *A 64-year-old man had a recurrent carcinoma of the colon. He was treated in an independent hospital and at laparotomy a total colectomy and an ileostomy were performed. There was evidence of tumour spread at laparotomy, but it was not likely that this would produce a rapid decline. Following the surgery the patient was hypovolaemic and the surgeon wrote that he thought that, ideally, the patient should have been treated in an intensive care unit and that this would have improved his chance of recovery. Intensive care facilities were not available in this hospital and the patient was therefore "specialled" in a private room. The patient died on the twelfth postoperative day following a cardiac arrest, and resuscitation was not attempted. No cause of death was given.*

The advisers considered that the surgeon and anaesthetist should not have taken on this case without having confirmed the availability of intensive care facilities or having made arrangements for transfer should this have become necessary. Colorectal resection, especially for recurrent disease, should not be carried out in hospitals without adequate intensive care provision whether in the NHS or the independent sector.

Thirty-seven patients who died were operated on in hospitals without a recovery room and an identical number were operated on in hospitals which did not have an adult intensive care unit. In 16 cases where the patient subsequently died, the surgeon commented that he had been unable to admit the patient to an ICU/HDU within the hospital where surgery took place. The reasons given were: no vacant bed in ICU (9), no ICU available in the hospital (5) and death in transit to ICU (2).

Answers to questions about the adequacy of intensive care facilities made it obvious that there are still units with an underprovision of services despite a heavy workload of sick patients. Typical comments were:

"The unit has too few beds for the size of the district population."

"There is an inadequate number of ICU beds here, patients frequently cannot be admitted. We have no HDU which compounds the problem."

"Our ICU is part of recovery, not a separate department. It is busy and noisy for the patients."

Previous CEPOD and NCEPOD reports have been critical of the provision of essential services.[1,2,3] It appears that there has been little change.

COMPLICATIONS

Complications of colorectal resection

Although there were 349 deaths following colorectal resection, only 198 of these were reported to have complications. However, problems could be identified by the advisers when reading the questionnaires. These undeclared complications have been included in the table below.

Table S46
Most common surgical complications of colorectal resection (deaths)

	(n=349)
Wound complications	
Wound infections	10
Burst abdomen	2
Superficial dehiscence of wound	1
Respiratory complications	
Respiratory failure	65
Pulmonary infections	46
Pulmonary embolism*	28
Adult respiratory distress syndrome/shock lung	8
Aspiration pneumonia	4
Pulmonary oedema	4
Pneumothorax	2
Upper respiratory obstruction	1
Pleural effusion	1
Cardiovascular complications	
Cardiac failure	52
Myocardial infarction	38
Cerebrovascular accident	21
Life-threatening arrhythmia	5
Ischaemic gangrene of limb	1
Mesenteric ischaemia	1

continued overleaf

Colorectal Resection
References see page 300

Table S46 continued

Gastrointestinal complications

Anastomotic leak	25
Intraperitoneal abscess	6
Gastrointestinal bleeding (including "stress" ulcer)	7
Generalized peritonitis/septicaemia	4
Hepatorenal failure	3
Pancreatitis	3
Prolonged ileus	2
Stoma-related complications	2
Perforated duodenal ulcer	2

Genito-urinary

Renal failure	44
Urinary retention	3
Urinary tract infection	2

Metabolic

Hypoalbuminaemia	7
Uncontrolled diabetes mellitus	4
Endocrine problems	2
Acid base disorder	1

Miscellaneous

Septicaemia	78
Haemorrhage	11
Carcinomatosis	12

NB this can be a multiple entry

*The diagnosis of pulmonary embolism is based on clinical investigations and postmortem confirmation, where available.

Anastomotic failure

Anastomotic failure following colorectal resection occurred in only 25 (7%) patients. However the advisers felt that there was a need for a high index of suspicion with respect to an anastomotic leakage since the diagnosis was often delayed. Once diagnosed, appropriate action should be taken by adequately experienced staff.

Postoperative fluid balance

> *A 76-year-old man had an elective sigmoid colectomy. He was operated on by a Consultant and, despite his chronic obstructive airways disease, all was going well. Forty-eight hours after surgery he became breathless and confused. For an unexplained reason he was given increased fluids intravenously which produced pulmonary oedema, deterioration and death. The Consultant Surgeon wrote, "I felt that there was a casualness by the locum Registrar about the postoperative care of this patient which was reprehensible and not enough notice was taken of the postoperative problems".*

There are other examples in this report of over-enthusiasm for postoperative intravenous fluids.

Pulmonary emboli (see also pages 68 to 70)

There were 28 cases of pulmonary emboli in the patients who died. Deep venous thrombosis prophylaxis of some kind was given in 247 (71%) patients of those who died and 187 (90%) of the index cases. This difference can be accounted for by the higher number of emergencies amongst those who died; prophylaxis may be forgotten for acute emergencies and protocols are often perceived as only applying to elective admissions.

Table S47 (qs 12 and 49)
DVT prophylaxis/admission category (deaths)

	All cases (n=349)	Emergency admissions (n=217)	%	Other admissions (n=132)	%
DVT prophylaxis given	247	139	64	108	82
No DVT prophylaxis	102	78	36	24	18

If DVT prophylaxis was used, which method was employed?

	(n=247)
Heparin	126
Heparin/stockings	38
Heparin/other	4
Stockings	34
Stockings/other	3
Other	8
Not stated	34

NB this can be a multiple entry

The timing of administration of prophylaxis for the prevention of deep venous thrombosis and pulmonary emboli can pose a problem.

A 92-year-old patient (ASA 3) was on a geriatric unit for 14 days prior to transfer to a surgical unit. Surgery in the form of a left hemicolectomy was done for a carcinoma of the descending colon, which had caused an intestinal obstruction. At the time of transfer to the surgical unit this woman received subcutaneous heparin but had not had any prophylaxis for the previous 13 days. Seven days postoperatively she died from a pulmonary embolism.

The advisers stated that, when patients have been in hospital for several weeks prior to transfer and surgery, it is often impossible for the surgeon to prevent fatal pulmonary emboli, especially when there are other high-risk factors as in the above case.

Inappropriate procedures

A 44-year-old woman was diagnosed as having carcinoma of the stomach. However, at laparotomy, an extensive linitis plastica was found, invading the transverse colon. The tumour was also involving the pancreas. A Senior Registrar performed a total gastrectomy and an extended right hemicolectomy. The patient died seven days later with bronchopneumonia.

This was called a palliative operation but in fact it was badly conceived and only succeeded in shortening the patient's life.

An 82-year-old woman presented with intestinal obstruction. Laparotomy revealed extensive carcinomatosis yet a sigmoid colectomy was done. The patient died six days later with carcinomatosis.

A 39-year-old woman was admitted under the care of a general surgeon with an interest in paediatric surgery. She had peritonitis and after preparation, a decision was made to perform a laparotomy. At laparotomy, by a Registrar, there was considerable small bowel infarction and the abdomen was closed. Following discussion with a Consultant, a second operation was planned. At this operation, it was found that there had been infarction from the proximal jejunum to the ileo-colic junction. The gall bladder was also infarcted and the stomach looked ischaemic. The whole ileum and jejunum were resected and a cholecystectomy was done. At the end of this operation, the duodenum looked to be ischaemic and the colon also was unhealthy and therefore a right hemicolectomy was done. The proposition was to manage this patient with permanent parenteral nutrition. The patient died six days later with gangrene of the stomach.

This was not a survivable condition and, although heroic, the second operation was quite inappropriate.

Quality of the information submitted to NCEPOD

The advisers were disappointed with the poor quality of some of the information which hindered their ability to analyse cases and make meaningful comment.

> *A questionnaire was submitted from a general surgeon concerning a death after a colorectal resection. A Registrar had completed the form without discussion with a Consultant. Large parts of the questionnaire were unanswered; there was no cause of death given and an operation note was not submitted. The form was therefore returned to the Consultant for his comment and in the hope that further information would be submitted. The Consultant returned the form with no additions and no comment.*

Unhelpful behaviour such as this makes it difficult for audit to be meaningful.

IMPORTANT ISSUES IN COLORECTAL RESECTION

Although Consultant involvement in decision-making was very good, Consultant involvement in operative surgery has not increased in this area; however audit is widely used. There are many issues to be addressed by surgeons who perform colorectal resections, including;

1   The incidence of inappropriate operations being performed by inappropriate grades and inappropriate specialties. This applies particularly to out-of-hours surgery.

2   Lack of availability of theatre space during daytime hours to avoid out-of-hours emergency work.

3   Consultant Surgeons are operating on poor-risk patients with junior grade anaesthetists who often have little in the way of higher qualifications.

4   Pulmonary embolism and the use of prophylaxis continue to present problems.

5   There should be a high index of suspicion with respect to anastomotic leakage, which was a common technical problem. Unsupervised trainees should not be expected to perform laparotomies to correct these postoperative complications.

6   The availability of intensive care and high dependency beds is less than desirable and the location of services is not always appropriate.

7   Secretarial services should be available to provide legible typewritten records of operations. (NCEPOD has commented previously on the inadequacy of operation records[3]).

References see page 300

BREAST SURGERY

SURGICAL PROCEDURE

Any breast surgery.

For index cases, surgeons were requested to complete questionnaires on breast surgery for malignancy.

KEY ISSUES

1   Ideally, breast cancer patients should be managed by multi-disciplinary teams.

2   Significant bleeding during or after breast surgery may precipitate events leading to a poor outcome.

3   Aggressive ablative surgery is often futile and inappropriate in the elderly with advanced breast cancer.

SAMPLE

Deaths

36 surgical death questionnaires sent out

23 returned (return rate 64%)

23 death questionnaires suitable for analysis

Index Cases

126 questionnaires returned (see page 19)

AUDIT
Table S48 (q 98)
Has this death been considered, (or will it be considered) at a local audit/quality control meeting?

	(n=23)
Yes	16
No	7

PATIENT PROFILE

The patients were elderly and infirm. All suffered with breast cancer and many were having a "toilet" mastectomy due to locally advanced disease rather than any possibly curative surgery. Detailed comment on the care of these patients before breast surgery was often hampered by a lack of information within the questionnaire on their clinical history.

Table S49 (q 4)
Age at final operation

	Deaths (n=23)	Index (n=126)
20 - 29 years	-	2
30 - 39	-	10
40 - 49	-	28
50 - 59	-	31
60 - 69	5	28
70 - 79	8	16
80 - 89	8	11
90 - 99	2	-

Table S50 (q 12 deaths, q 11 index)
Initial admission intention for the last operation performed

	Deaths (n=23)	Index (n=126)
Elective	14	121
Urgent	3	4
Emergency	6	1

Table S51 (q 16)
Admission

	Deaths (n=23)	Index (n=126)
Weekday	20	115
Weekend	3	8
Public holiday	-	1
Not answered	-	2

Table S52 (q 47)
ASA Class

	Deaths (n=23)		Index (n=126)
1	4		85
2	8		30
3	3		4
4	4		1
5	-		-
Not answered	4		6

Table S53 (q 2)
In which type of hospital did the last operation take place?

	Deaths (n=23)		Index (n=126)
District General	18		92
University/Teaching	4		23
Other Acute/Partly Acute	-		3
Defence Medical Services	-		2
Independent	1		6

THE SURGICAL TEAM

Table S54 (q 1)
Specialty of Consultant Surgeon in charge at time of final operation

	Deaths (n=23)		Index (n=126)
General surgery	15		87
General with special interest in breast surgery	7		35
Oncology	1		4

Only 35% of surgeons treating the patients who died declared a special interest in breast surgery or oncology. However if it is assumed that breast surgery falls within the range of conditions dealt with by general surgeons then the number rises to 100%.

Only six patients were managed on a formal shared basis with another specialty. There was rarely a mention of joint management with radiotherapists or oncologists. Ideally patients with breast cancer should be managed under a formal joint arrangement between the surgeon and a radiotherapist or oncologist.[25] This care should be supported by nurses specialised in breast care and counselling, expert radiology, cytology and histopathology. Adequate consultation time should be available, preferably in a combined clinic, to enable balanced decisions to be made.

A 93-year-old woman was referred from a medical ward to a general surgeon with an interest in breast surgery. She was suffering with ischaemic heart disease, atrial fibrillation, chronic obstructive airways disease, leg ulcers and a fungating carcinoma of the breast. She was classed as ASA 2 by the surgeon and ASA 4 by the anaesthetist. A Registrar performed a "toilet" mastectomy as the lesion was offensive. The patient died 22 days later with a chest infection.

The advisers felt that sympathetic care and symptom control might have been more appropriate.

An 83-year-old woman had an elective mastectomy and axillary clearance for a fungating carcinoma of the breast. The anaesthetists classed her as ASA 4, the surgeon as ASA 1. She died four days later in respiratory distress due to a chest infection.

It is difficult to assess whether this treatment was appropriate or not as no indication was given as to any previous treatment and whether or not a radiotherapist or oncologist had been involved in her care.

Table S55 (q 40)
What was the grade of the most senior surgeon consulted before the operation?

	Deaths (n=23)	Index (n=126)	(Locum)
Consultant	22	124	(1)
Associate Specialist	1	-	
Not answered	-	2	

Table S56 (q 54)
What was the grade of the most senior operating surgeon?

	Deaths (n=23)	(Locum)	Index (n=126)	(Locum)
Senior House Officer	2		2	
Registrar	5		31	
Staff Grade	-		3	
Senior Registrar	2	(1)	7	(1)
Associate Specialist	2		-	
Consultant	12		82	
Not answered	-		1	

In six of the eleven cases where a Consultant was not operating there was supervision available close at hand.

Table S57 (q 59)
Final operation (deaths)

	(*n*=23)
Mastectomy and axillary clearance	5
Simple mastectomy	5
Wide lumpectomy	2
"Toilet" mastectomy	2
Open biopsy of breast lesion	2
Quadrantectomy and axillary clearance	1
"Toilet" mastectomy, axillary node biopsy and biopsy of humeral shaft	1
Mastectomy, axillary clearance and split skin grafting to chest wall	1
Wide excision of breast carcinoma and insertion of prosthesis	1
Axillary clearance only	1
Trucut needle biopsy	1
Drainage of haematoma	1

No deaths were reported following surgery for benign disease of the breast.

COMPLICATIONS

Table S58 (q 79)
Were there any postoperative complications?

	Deaths (*n*=23)		Index (*n*=126)
Yes	14		14
No	8		109
Not answered	1		3

In eight cases the surgeons reported no complications but problems could be identified by the advisers when reading the questionnaires. These undeclared complications have been included in the table below.

Table S59
Complications after surgery (deaths)

	(*n*=23)
Myocardial infarction	9
Respiratory infections	8
Heart failure	7
Major wound infections/septicaemia	4
Pulmonary embolism*	3
Complications of carcinomatosis	3
Primary operative haemorrhage	2
Uncontrolled diabetes mellitus	2
Renal failure	2

NB this can be a multiple entry

* One case of pulmonary embolism was proven at post mortem. The other two cases were diagnosed clinically, but postmortems were not done.

Postoperative bleeding

Bleeding after surgery is low down in the list of complications notified to the Enquiry. However, on close reading of the questionnaires, the advisers detected a common theme of considerable operative bleeding in elderly, frail, cachectic women. Subsequent postoperative progress was then a struggle against decreasing myocardial function and eventual death.

> *A 78-year-old woman died four days after a simple mastectomy for persistent breast cancer which was enlarging despite tamoxifen therapy. There was considerable bleeding at surgery and the patient died within three days in heart failure.*

> *An 81-year-old woman was known to have disseminated breast cancer which was not controlled with tamoxifen. She also had mitral valve disease, heart failure and was taking warfarin. She was under the care of a general surgeon with an interest in urology who performed a mastectomy and axillary clearance after withdrawing the warfarin. During the operation there were cardiac arrhythmias. Postoperatively the patient was given heparin immediately which caused bleeding and a massive wound haematoma. The patient died in heart failure.*

The advisers questioned the need to perform such a radical procedure; was this the appropriate specialist to make this decision? The decision to restart anticoagulants is a difficult one and the timing can be critical.

ISSUES IN BREAST SURGERY

Inappropriate procedures

There were a number of cases where elderly patients with advanced disease were subjected to mastectomy. Information was often scanty but had these patients been jointly managed a better perception of the risks might have resulted in alternative modalities of treatment being considered. Given proper, caring counselling, many patients, their carers and relatives will accept the limitations and risks of aggressive but futile treatment and adopt a more pragmatic approach to the disease. One problem appears to be that having adopted a conservative approach earlier in the history of the disease because of the patient's general health, the surgeon is then faced with difficult choices when the tumour growth breaks through the inhibiting effect of drugs such as tamoxifen. The surgeon is then often under pressure to operate. Some operations appeared to be inappropriate.

A general surgeon with an interest in paediatric surgery was treating a patient with disseminated breast cancer and an ulcerated primary tumour. In addition there was ascites and intestinal obstruction. Her care was shared with a radiotherapist. She was admitted in a moribund state but a Senior House Officer felt it was necessary to obtain a biopsy. This was done on the ward under local anaesthesia. She died four days later.

An elderly woman concealed her fungating cancer of the breast from her relatives. When she was finally admitted with a pleural effusion she was terminally ill. An incision biopsy of the breast lesion was done under local anaesthetic. She died seven days later.

Was it really necessary to subject these women to the biopsy procedures? If there was any possibility of a therapeutic advantage in obtaining histology, why was a needle biopsy not considered?

And finally.....

A Senior Registrar working for a general surgeon with an interest in oncology did a wide excision of a breast carcinoma in a 78-year-old woman in a University/Teaching hospital. The tumour was enlarging despite tamoxifen treatment. Following the excision of the tumour a breast prosthesis was inserted. No thromboembolic prophylaxis whatsoever was given at any stage. She died on the sixth day after surgery following a pulmonary embolism. The consent form was sent to the Enquiry. It contained no mention of consent for reconstruction or the insertion of a prosthesis.

Blank page
References see page 300

OESOPHAGECTOMY

SURGICAL PROCEDURE

Partial or complete oesophagectomy

KEY ISSUES

1   Oesophagectomy is not an operation for the occasional surgeon. A degree of specialism is required, and complex cases should be referred to an appropriate specialist.[26]

2   The provision of adequate intensive care services is vital to the practice of oesophagectomy.

3   There is under-reporting to the Enquiry of deaths following oesophagectomy.

SAMPLE

Deaths

103 surgical death questionnaires sent out

   68 returned (return rate 66%)

   61 death questionnaires suitable for analysis

There were fewer deaths reported than expected. We cannot understand why, when other independent sources suggest more.[27] We are surprised that so few cases were operated on by thoracic surgeons compared to general surgeons; there may be an organizational reason for this.

Index Cases

30 questionnaires returned (see page 19).

AUDIT

Table S60 (q 98)
Has this death been considered, (or will it be considered) at a local audit/quality control meeting?

	(*n*=61)
Yes	52
No	9

It is commendable that 85% of these cases were considered at audit meetings.

PATIENT PROFILE

Fifty-seven per cent (35) of the patients who died were over 70 years of age and only 21 (34%) patients were in ASA classes 3, 4 or 5. Seventy-two per cent were elective admissions. The male to female ratio was 2.4:1.

Table S61 (q 4)
Age at final operation

	Deaths (*n*=61)		Index (*n*=30)
30 - 39 years	1		-
40 - 49	-		2
50 - 59	5		6
60 - 69	20		16
70 - 79	26		5
80 - 89	9		1

Table S62 (q 12 Deaths, q 11 Index)
Initial admission intention for the last operation performed

	Deaths (*n*=61)		Index (*n*=30)
Elective	44		29
Urgent	8		-
Emergency	9		1

Table S63 (q 47)
ASA Class

ASA Class	Deaths (*n*=61)		Index (*n*=30)
1	7		11
2	29		12
3	14		4
4	6		2
5	1		-
Not answered	4		1

Oesophagectomy
References see page 300

THE SURGICAL TEAM

Table S64 (q 1)
Specialty of Consultant Surgeon in charge at time of final operation

	Deaths (n=61)		Index (n=30)
Thoracic	8		-
Cardiothoracic	1		-
General surgery	11		9
General surgery with special interest in gastroenterology	39		20
Oesophageal surgery	1		1
Head and neck surgery	1		-

Consultant Surgeons were consulted prior to surgery and made the decision to operate in all cases.

Table S65 (q 54)
What was the grade of the most senior operating surgeon?

	Deaths (n=61)	(Locum)		Index (n=30)
Registrar	2			-
Consultant	59	(1)		30

Table S66 (qs 1 and 54)
Specialty of Consultant Surgeon in charge at time of final operation/ number of similar procedures performed by the most senior operating surgeon in the previous year

	Deaths (n=61) Specialty		
Number of similar procedures performed in the previous year	Thoracic/ Cardiothoracic		General
0-9	-		29 (9)
10 - 19	3 (1)		13 (2)
20 - 29	2 (-)		8 (1)
30 - 39	2 (-)		-
40 - 49	1 (-)		-
50 - 59	-		-
100+	1 (1)		2 (-)

The figures in brackets refer to the number of deaths that occurred within two days of operation.

There is a growing awareness that oesophagectomy is a difficult procedure with identifiable risks and a mortality worse than that of transplantation and cardiac surgery. Although NCEPOD does not have comprehensive data it is noticeable that 29 (48%) of the deaths followed operations by "low volume" operators. These cases should be concentrated in specialised centres or referred to local teams with adequate experience, regular throughput and the best possible back-up.[26]

Oesophagectomy
References see page 300

Both cases where a Registrar was operating raised questions despite the fact that Consultants were present in the operating theatre.

> *A woman of 87 years of age (ASA 1) had a squamous carcinoma of the oesophagus treated in a District General Hospital by a team consisting of both a locum Consultant and a locum Registrar. At the initial rigid oesophagoscopy the Consultant perforated the oesophagus. This was recognised and the Registrar then resected the tumour and the perforated oesophagus, assisted by the Consultant. The anaesthetist was a Senior House Officer who sought advice from a Senior Registrar. The patient died two days later following a cardiac arrest.*

The advisers felt that the surgical team (both locums) and the grade of anaesthetist were inappropriate.

> *A Registrar took six and a half hours to resect an oesophageal tumour in a severely anaemic malnourished woman of 63 years. Preoperatively a bleeding diathesis had been diagnosed and it was noticed that her anaemia was probably not due to the tumour alone. A Consultant Surgeon was available in theatre but did not assist. According to the operation note the surgery was potentially curative. The patient died from a generalised bleeding disorder.*

The preoperative assessment and preparation of this woman failed to take adequate note of her coagulation disorder. Given the anticipated complexity, this case was not suitable for a trainee surgeon.

TIME OF SURGERY

Table S67 (q 53)
Day and time of start of operation

	Deaths (*n*=61)		Index (*n*=30)
Weekday 08.00 - 18.00	56		28
Weekday outside these hours	1		1
Weekday time not given	1		-
Weekend	3		1

Most operations (56, 92%) were done on weekdays and during the working day.

Oesophagectomy
References see page 300

RESOURCES

Table S68 (q 2)
In which type of hospital did the last operation take place?

	Deaths (n=61)	Index (n=30)
District General	42	20
University/Teaching	15	10
Single Specialty Hospital	1	-
Defence Medical Services	3	-

Table S69 (q 62)
Classify the final operation

	Deaths (n=61)	Index (n=30)
Emergency	5	-
Urgent	3	3
Scheduled	41	24
Elective	12	3

Table S70 (q63)
In view of your answer to q 62, was there any delay due to factors other than clinical?

	Deaths (n=61)	Index (n=30)
Yes	3	4
No	53	24
Not answered	5	2

When delays did occur in patients who died, these were due to delay in diagnosis (1), no bed in ICU (1) and holidays for both the surgeon and the patient (1). Amongst the index cases, delays were due to theatre shortages (2), no bed in ICU (1) and a patient-imposed delay (1).

Table S71 (q 71)
Which of the following are available in the hospital in which the final operation took place?

	Deaths (n=61)	Index (n=30)
Theatre recovery area	51	28
Adult intensive care unit	56	28
Adult high dependency unit	13	6

Oesophagectomy should not be done in units where an intensive care bed is not available on the day of operation (whether or not it is subsequently used).

> *A general surgeon in a District General Hospital operated on a 66-year-old woman with carcinoma of the oesophagus. She was known to have existing respiratory, renal and cardiac problems. In addition she was taking warfarin for previous deep venous thrombosis and a pulmonary embolism, four years prior to the surgery. She was classed as ASA 3 and was considered to be unfit for a thoracotomy. A transhiatal "pull-through" operation was done, but it was then discovered that there was no bed in the intensive care unit. The patient's lungs were ventilated in the recovery room for three hours whilst a bed was cleared on the ICU. The patient died two days later with respiratory and cardiac problems.*

The advisers questioned whether or not the procedure was appropriate for this woman. They also felt that the surgeon should have checked whether a bed was available in the ICU, and in the absence of a bed the operation should not have proceeded.

Table S72 (q 80)
Was mechanical ventilation employed postoperatively?

	Deaths (n=59*)	Index (n=30)
Yes	43	19
No	14	9
Not answered	2	2

* two patients died in theatre

Table S73 (q 80A)
Is this your usual practice in this type of procedure?

	Deaths (n=59)	Index (n=30)
Yes	46	25
No	7	2
Not answered	6	3

A 69-year-old man had an Ivor Lewis procedure to resect an oesophageal carcinoma. Care was of a high standard and the site and specialty of the surgeon appropriate. However, there was no bed available in the intensive care unit for postoperative ventilation which was the surgeon's usual practice. The surgeon was therefore forced to manage the patient without ventilatory support. The patient died following an attack of pancreatitis and an anastomotic leak.

The availability of the bed in the ICU probably made no difference to the outcome, but the surgeon should not have embarked on the case knowing that he would have to compromise his usual standard of postoperative management.

A 69-year-old man had established respiratory problems. An experienced surgeon performed an oesophagectomy in a unit where an intensive care bed and long-term pulmonary ventilation were not available. The patient died with pulmonary complications twenty-four hours later.

The implications of this patient's pre-existing respiratory disease and the potential need for pulmonary ventilation postoperatively appear to have been ignored. This poor patient selection had fatal consequences.

COMPLICATIONS

Table S74
Complications after oesophagectomy (deaths)

	(n=61)
Respiratory infection	19
Septicaemia	14
Anastomotic leak	13
Myocardial infarction	9
Haemorrhage	7
Renal failure	7
Pulmonary embolism*	4
Heart failure	4
Adult respiratory distress syndrome/shock lung	3
Pancreatitis	3
Mesenteric ischaemia	2
Cerebrovascular accident	2
Miscellaneous (pneumothorax, life-threatening arrhythmia, hepatorenal failure and subphrenic abscess)	4

NB this can be a multiple entry

* Two pulmonary emboli were found at postmortem. Two others were diagnosed by clinical investigations.

IMPORTANT ISSUES IN OESOPHAGEAL SURGERY

Referral of complex cases

> *A 66-year-old man underwent a left thoraco-abdominal resection of an oesophageal tumour. Some years before this surgery he had undergone a right upper lobectomy for a carcinoma of the bronchus. In the postoperative period the patient was transferred to the intensive care unit with the intention of giving ventilatory support but this was not given. The patient died five days later with respiratory failure.*

This case was clearly complicated by another factor, in that there had been a previous pulmonary resection. Even when a unit has good experience with "routine" cases, the advisers felt that there was a need to refer such complex cases to a more specialised tertiary referral centre.

Inappropriate procedures

> *A 76-year-old diabetic man had a transhiatal "pull-through" procedure for a carcimona of the middle third of the oesophagus. He died fifteen days later with septicaemia and a chylothorax.*

> *An attempted transhiatal resection of an oesophageal tumour resulted in the death of a 58-year-old man. The azygos vein was torn and he bled to death on the operating table.*

The advisers felt that neither of these two cases had an appropriate procedure and that the difficulties encountered might have been avoided by the use of a different operative technique. There were also other cases where it was clear that the patients should not have had surgery at all. Benefits of surgery must outweigh the disadvantages. If the balance appears to be shifted then consideration should be given as to whether or not surgery should be withheld or reconsidered.

A combination of problems

A 72-year-old diabetic man had an adenocarcinoma of the lower end of the oesophagus. He also suffered with metastatic carcinoma of the prostate which was well controlled. A three-stage oesophagectomy was done by an experienced gastrointestinal surgeon in a District General Hospital. The operation was done on a Saturday and there were no beds in the intensive care unit. During the surgery there was profuse bleeding from the splenic pedicle. This was not initially noticed until unexplained hypotension occurred during the thoracic stage of the operation. The abdomen was then re-opened and the bleeding stopped. However a bleeding diathesis then developed and clotting factors were difficult to obtain as there was a local shortage of fresh frozen plasma. The problem with blood transfusion services was compounded by the fact that it was a weekend. The patient died from continuing generalised bleeding as a consequence of the coagulopathy.

This case contains elements of many of the problems mentioned throughout this Report; the lack of intensive care facilities, a surgeon who proceeds despite this lack, difficulties in obtaining blood products at weekends and the overall burden of selecting the best mode of treatment in a patient with co-existing widespread malignancy.

Blank page
References see page 300

PULMONARY RESECTION

SURGICAL PROCEDURE

Pneumonectomy or lobectomy

KEY ISSUES

1   There was a very high degree of Consultant involvement.

2   Pulmonary infection was the most common mode of death.

3   No patient should have a major pulmonary resection without confirmatory pre- or perioperative histology.

SAMPLE

Deaths

42 surgical death questionnaires sent out

27 returned (return rate 64%)

23 death questionnaires suitable for analysis

Index Cases

21 questionnaires returned (see page 19)

AUDIT

All cases had been considered at an audit meeting, apart from one case where the respondent failed to reply to the question.

PATIENT PROFILE

The mean age of the patients was 63 years with a preponderance of men (3.6:1). The majority of the patients who died (70%) were classed as ASA 1 or 2. However most of the surgery was major, for malignancy, and as such represented a high-risk undertaking.

Table S75 (q 4)
Age at final operation

	Deaths (n=23)		Index (n=21)
0 - 9 years	1		1
30 - 39	1		1
40 - 49	-		1
50 - 59	1		4
60 - 69	12		8
70 - 79	8		6

This table accurately reflects the age distribution of patients undergoing thoracic surgery in general.[27]

Table S76 (q 12 Deaths, q 11 Index)
Initial admission intention for the last operation performed

	Deaths (n=23)		Index (n=21)
Elective	20		20
Urgent	3		1
Emergency	-		-

Table S77 (q 47)
ASA Class

	Deaths (n=23)		Index (n=21)
1	4		2
2	12		16
3	4		3
4	1		-
5	-		-
Not answered	2		-

THE SURGICAL TEAM
Table S78 (q 1)
Specialty of Consultant Surgeon in charge at time of final operation

	Deaths (n=23)		Index (n=21)
Thoracic	12		16
Cardiac	2		2
Cardiothoracic	9		3

Decision-making and timing of surgery

There was discussion with a Consultant about the management of all but one case. Many of these cases were considered to be at risk as a result of the magnitude of the surgery so the involvement of Consultants is especially gratifying.

All operations were done on weekdays during the hours of 09.00 to 18.00.

Grade of surgeon
Table S79 (q 54)
What was the grade of the most senior operating surgeon?

	Deaths (Locums) (n=23)			Index (n=21)
Registrar	6			-
Senior Registrar	2			1
Associate Specialist	1	(1)		-
Consultant	14	(1)		20

Consultants and Senior Registrars operated on 16 (70%) of those patients who subsequently died.

Table S80 (q 57)
Was a more senior surgeon immediately available, i.e. in the operating room/suite?

	Deaths (n=23)		Index (n=21)
Yes	8		-
No	1		1
Not applicable (Consultant operating	14		20

RESOURCES

Table S81 (q 2)
In which type of hospital did the last operation take place?

	Deaths (*n*=23)		Index (*n*=21)
District General	9		6
University/Teaching	10		9
Single Specialty Hospital	4		5
Independent	-		1

Table S82 (q 71)
Which of the following are available in the hospital in which the final operation took place?

	Deaths (*n*=23)		Index (*n*=21)
Theatre recovery area	19		20
Adult intensive care unit	21		19
Adult high dependency unit	12		12
Paediatric ICU/HDU	7		9

COMPLICATIONS

Table S83
Postoperative complications (deaths)

	(*n*=23)
Respiratory infection/failure	14
Cardiac problems	8
Adult respiratory distress syndrome/shock lung	3
Pulmonary oedema	3
Neurological problems	3
Renal failure	3
Septicaemia	3
Bronchopleural fistula	2
Primary haemorrhage	2
Miscellaneous (pulmonary embolism, perforated duodenal ulcer, uncontrolled diabetes mellitus and reactionary haemorrhage)	4

NB this can be a multiple entry

Pulmonary infections

The most common mode of death was pulmonary infection. In particular, following a pneumonectomy, infection in the remaining lung has a very bad prognosis.

ISSUES IN PULMONARY RESECTION

Fluid balance management

A 71-year-old man had a right pneumonectomy for a carcinoma of bronchus. This was appropriately done by an experienced specialist. The patient was managed in an HDU where he died on the fourth postoperative day. Death was due to pulmonary oedema. Careful scrutiny of the fluid balance charts revealed a fluid overload of three litres.

The problem of fluid overload in the elderly is highlighted elsewhere (see page 297). There is a need for continued awareness when intravenous fluids are given to frail people in the absence of major fluid losses.

Non-steroidal anti-inflammatory drugs

A 61-year-old man was treated at a University Hospital by a thoracic surgeon. An upper lobectomy was done for a carcinoma of the bronchus. An anti-inflammatory drug was used for postoperative analgesia. On the fifth day the patient developed a perforated duodenal ulcer. This was accurately diagnosed but the patient could not be adequately resuscitated to enable surgery to take place. The patient died with peritonitis and pulmonary oedema.

Non-steroidal anti-inflammatory drugs (NSAID) are frequently used during the postoperative period but are not without their risks;[28] and the use of an NSAID in this case may have contributed to the perforated duodenal ulcer. However the use of non-steroidal anti-inflammatory drugs has dramatically reduced the amount of postoperative analgesia, especially opiates, and the advisers opined that thoracic surgeons may feel that the benefits tend to outweigh the risks, especially in patients with poor respiratory function.

Specific problems

Preoperative histological diagnosis

> *A surgeon was treating a 39-year-old man who was thought to have either a carcinoma or a metastatic melanoma of the right lung. He was classed as ASA 1. Despite bronchoscopy and mediastinoscopy, no histological diagnosis could be made. At thoracotomy a large mass was found in the apex of the lower lobe extending across the fissure onto the right upper lobe. There were widespread nodules throughout the right lung and enlarged lymph nodes in front of the trachea and below the carina. A right pneumonectomy was performed. There appears to have been no attempt to obtain preoperative histology. On the third postoperative day the patient's condition began to deteriorate and he was admitted to the intensive care unit. He died on the 19th postoperative day and the postmortem showed a confluent bronchopneumonia of the left lung. Histology of the resected lung showed tuberculosis and no malignancy.*

It was the advisers' opinion that the management of this case was inappropriate. Had the surgeon obtained histology a pneumonectomy might have been avoided.

> *A working diagnosis of "pulmonary artery sarcoma" and associated Eaton Lambert syndrome was made in a 62-year-old woman. A pneumonectomy was done without prior mediastinoscopy or histology of any kind. The patient returned to the ward after a brief stay in a high dependency unit, developed adult respiratory distress syndrome and was admitted to the intensive care unit where she died. The final histology was an oat cell carcinoma.*

The fact that this patient had a myasthenic syndrome should have made the surgeon more aware of the possible diagnosis of a small cell carcinoma. Had histology been obtained, this patient would not have been submitted to a pneumonectomy since chemotherapy might have been more appropriate.

No patient should have a high-risk major resection of an organ for malignancy without confirmatory histology being obtained either pre- or per-operatively.[29]

CORONARY ARTERY BYPASS GRAFTS

SURGICAL PROCEDURE

Coronary artery bypass graft(s).

KEY ISSUES

1   There was a high degree of Consultant involvement in patients undergoing coronary artery bypass grafting.

2   The returned cardiac physiological data and typed operating notes were most impressive.

3   Cardiothoracic surgeons show a low level of cooperation with National CEPOD.

SAMPLE

Deaths

297 surgical death questionnaires sent out

148 returned (return rate 50%)

145 death questionnaires suitable for analysis

This is a low level of cooperation from cardiothoracic surgeons. The 1991 Register for The Society of Cardiothoracic Surgeons[27] reports 457 deaths out of a total number of operations of 15,127. This suggests that in addition to a poor response to the questionnaires on reported deaths there may also be some under-reporting to NCEPOD.

Index Cases

40 questionnaires returned (see page 19).

AUDIT

Table S84 (q S8)

Has this death been considered, (or will it be considered) at a local audit/quality control meeting?

	Deaths (*n*=145)
Yes	132
No	8
Not answered	5

PATIENT PROFILE

The mean age of the patients was 62.6, and 97 (67%) were ASA classes 3, 4 or 5. The male to female ratio was 2.5:1. The majority of the patients were treated following elective admissions (87 cases, 60%).

The finding of a male to female ratio of 2.5:1 is contrary to the reported incidence of coronary artery surgery which shows a higher male to female ratio of between 4:1 and 5:1. This appears to suggest as far as this small sample can be interpreted that females do worse after surgery than males. This would confirm the findings of several large studies of coronary artery surgery [30,31,32] which have attributed the increased mortality in women to their higher average age, increased incidence of unstable angina and poorer status according to the NYHA classification.

Table S85 (q 4)

Age at final operation

	Deaths (*n*=145)	Index (*n*=40)
30 - 39 years	1	-
40 - 49	13	8
50 - 59	28	16
60 - 69	73	13
70 - 79	27	1
80 - 89	3	2

Table S86 (q 47)

ASA Class

	Deaths (*n*=145)	Index (*n*=40)
1	1	6
2	42	16
3	50	13
4	39	3
5	8	-
Not answered	5	2

133

Table S87 (q 12 Deaths and q 11 Index)
Initial admission intention for the last operation performed

	Deaths (*n*=145)		Index (*n*=40)
Elective	87		32
Urgent	28		7
Emergency	29		1
Not answered	1		-

Table S88 (q 16)
Admission

	Deaths (*n*=145)		Index (*n*=40)
Weekday	127		34
Weekend	16		6
Public Holiday	1		-
Not answered	1		-

Delays and cancellations

Delayed admissions were reported in three out of 87 elective admissions. These were due exclusively to the non-availability of intensive care beds which caused the surgeon, appropriately, to defer the operation. Similar reasons were given for two index cases.

THE SURGICAL TEAM

Table S89 (q 1)
Specialty of Consultant Surgeon in charge at time of final operation

	Deaths (*n*=145)		Index (*n*=40)
Cardiac	98		30
Cardiothoracic	44		10
Thoracic	3		-

Decision-making

Table S90 (q 40)
What was the grade of the most senior surgeon consulted before the operation?

	Deaths (Locums) (*n*=145)		Index (*n*=40)
Senior Registrar	1		-
Consultant	138	(3)	40
Staff Grade	1		-
Associate Specialist	3		-
Other	1		-
Not answered	1		-

Table S91 (q 54)
What was the grade of the most senior operating surgeon?

	Deaths (Locums) (*n*=145)		Index (*n*=40)
Registrar	4		4
Senior Registrar	11		7
Associate Specialist	3		-
Consultant	124	(3)	29
Other	3		-

Table S92 (q 57)
Was a more senior surgeon immediately available, ie in the operating room/suite?

	Deaths (*n*=145)	Index (*n*=40)
Yes	12	11
No	8	-
Not applicable (Consultant operating)	124	29
Not answered	1	-

TIME OF SURGERY

Table S93 (q 53C)
Day and time of start of operation

	Deaths (*n*=145)	Index (*n*=40)
Between 08.00 and 18.00	122	35
Weekday outside these hours	13	1
Weekday (time not given)	3	-
Weekend	7	4

RESOURCES

Table S94 (q 2)
In which type of hospital did the last operation take place?

	Deaths (n=145)	Index (n=40)
District General	32	4
University/Teaching	69	21
Single Specialty Hospital	34	11
Other Acute/Partly Acute	2	-
Independent	8	4

Amongst the cases who subsequently died, Consultants reported that there were 15 incidences of delay in operation due to resource problems. These were lack of intensive care beds (5) and long waiting lists (10) which produced a deterioration in the patients' condition during the waiting time. In the index cases there were eight cases of delay due to long waiting lists.

A 63-year-old woman required an urgent coronary artery bypass graft for unstable angina. This was delayed until a bed in the intensive care unit became available. The surgery was done by a newly appointed thoracic surgeon in a University Hospital. During surgery the patient developed a myocardial infarct, biventricular failure, and died.

It is uncertain whether the lack of an ICU bed and the subsequent delay caused a problem here. The advisers pointed out that if this surgeon was a "thoracic surgeon" rather than a "cardiac" surgeon he may not have been provided with the full services and with a surgical team familiar with cardiac surgery. Unfortunately no further information was available to the Enquiry.

Apart from one case, no problems were reported with the quality of intensive care/high dependency facilities provided for coronary care surgery.

A 64-year-old man had a routine coronary artery bypass graft done by a Consultant. The patient progressed well and was extubated early. Due to pressure on the intensive care beds the patient was transferred to a high dependency unit where it was acknowledged that monitoring was less than comprehensive. On the third postoperative day he became hypoxic, developed bradycardia and could not be resuscitated despite the insertion of an intra-aortic balloon pump and full resuscitative measures. The surgeon and anaesthetist commented in their questionnaires that the deficiencies in the HDU have now been remedied.

The advisers postulated that this patient might have survived had he not been transferred out of the intensive care unit.

Blank page
References see page 300

HYSTERECTOMY

SURGICAL PROCEDURE

Hysterectomy

KEY ISSUES

1   One of the higher incidences of pulmonary embolism occurred in women who had hysterectomy operations and especially when other operative procedures were carried out at the same time. The incidence of fatal pulmonary embolism at the time of the collection of the NCEPOD data was of the order of 13 out of 75,000 hysterectomy operations (all indications). That is approximately 1 in 5,700 hysterectomies. The risk, however, increases dramatically with age, the presence of obesity and malignancy. Gynaecologists cannot therefore afford to be complacent about this problem and each Department of Gynaecology should produce a protocol regarding thromboembolic prophylaxis for patients undergoing hysterectomy.

2   Cases which represent a high risk must be done in an appropriate unit offering a full range of services for postoperative care.

3   Some general surgeons sometimes failed to consult their gynaecological colleagues when they encountered gynaecological pathology.

SAMPLE

Deaths

83 surgical death questionnaires sent

68 returned (return rate 82%)

65 death questionnaires suitable for analysis

Index Cases

468 index case questionnaires returned (see page 19).

Table S95 (q 45)
Diagnoses (deaths)

	(*n*=65)
Malignant ovarian tumours	17
Carcinoma of the endometrium	13
Carcinoma of the colon/rectum	7
Uterine prolapse	6
Carcinoma of the cervix	5
Uterine fibroids	4
Metastatic tumours from breast/stomach	3
Leiomyosarcoma of the uterus	3
Menorrhagia (no macroscopic pathology)	3
Pyometra	2
Miscellaneous (diverticular disease and benign ovarian tumour)	2

Forty-eight out of the 65 cases (73.8%) in which hysterectomy was carried out had malignancy of the genital tract, colon/rectum, or metastatic tumours.

Table S96
Surgical procedures undertaken

	(*n*=64*)
Total abdominal hysterectomy and bilateral salpingo-oophorectomy ($^+/_-$ omentectomy)	31
Total abdominal hysterectomy	5
Hartmann's procedure, total abdominal hysterectomy and bilateral salpingo-oophorectomy	4
Vaginal hysterectomy, anterior and posterior vaginal repairs	4
Anterior resection of rectum and hysterectomy	3
Subtotal hysterectomy	3
Subtotal hysterectomy and bilateral salpingo-oophorectomy	3
Anterior resection of rectum, partial cystectomy and hysterectomy	2
Sigmoid colectomy and hysterectomy	2
Wertheim's hysterectomy	1
Cystectomy, ileal conduit and hysterectomy	1
Vagotomy and pyloroplasty + total abdominal hysterectomy	1
Resection of gastric tumour + total abdominal hysterectomy with bilateral salpingo-oophorectomy	1
Vaginal hysterectomy	1
Vaginal hysterectomy and posterior repair	1
Hysterectomy and colostomy	1

* one patient died on induction of anaesthesia

Forty-nine out of 64 (76.7%) had a hysterectomy operation with or without removal of the appendages, or with or without omentectomy: procedures expected to be carried out by all competent gynaecologists.

AUDIT

Table S97 (q 98)
Has this death been considered, (or will it be considered) at a local audit/quality control meeting?

	All (n=65)	Gynaecologists (n=49)	General surgeons (n=16)
Yes	37	22	15
No	24	23	1
Not answered	4	4	-

Thirty-seven per cent of deaths after hysterectomy were not submitted to local audit. Fifteen per cent (68/468) of respondents who submitted index cases work in units with no audit or quality control meetings.

A gynaecologist with an interest in oncology performed a total abdominal hysterectomy and bilateral salpingo-oophorectomy in a 71-year-old woman (ASA 3). It was also necessary to resect some small and large bowel. The patient died unexpectedly 10 days postoperatively. No cause of death was established as no postmortem examination was done. The surgeon wrote "... it is not our routine to do postmortems on oncology patients". The case was not discussed at an audit meeting.

This practice is unacceptable.

PATIENT PROFILE

Table S98 (q 4)
Age at final operation

	Deaths (n=65)	%	Index (n=468)	%
20 - 29 years	-		12	2.6
30 - 39	4	6.2	126	27.0
40 - 49	4	6.2	212	45.3
50 - 59	7	10.8	61	13.1
60 - 69	17	26.2	31	6.6
70 - 79	24	36.9	24	5.1
80 - 89	9	13.8	1	0.2
Date of birth not given	-		1	0.2

The median age of the patients who died was 70 years; 77% were over 60 years of age with many co-existing medical problems. It will be noted that the number of deaths increases from 50 years of age onwards.

Table S99 (q 12)
Initial admission intention for the last operation performed

	Deaths (n=65)	Index (n=468)
Elective	37	455
Urgent	10	4
Emergency	18	9

Delays

The few delays commented on in those patients who died were: long waiting lists, lack of operating time, lack of provision of diagnostic services and patient-imposed delay for social reasons.

Amongst the index cases 10% of surgeons quoted delays due to factors other than clinical; these factors included: long waiting lists (18), patient-imposed delays (13), lack of theatre space (5), bed shortages (4), District financial difficulties (4), Christmas closures (1) and difficulties with cross-matching blood (1).

Table S100 (q 47)
ASA Class

	Deaths (n=65)	Index (n=468)
1	17	351
2	21	75
3	10	6
4	11	1
5	2	-
Not answered	4	35

Table S101 (q 48)
What was the anticipated risk of death related to the proposed operation?

	Deaths (n=65)	Index (n=468)
Not expected	15	377
Small but significant risk	17	18
Definite risk	23	2
Expected	1	-
Not answered	9	71

At least two patients were moribund (ASA 5) and 32% (21/65) were ASA classes 3 and 4. Occasionally the case selection seemed questionable.

Hysterectomy
References see page 300

THE SURGICAL TEAM

Table S102 (q 1)
Specialty of Consultant Surgeon in charge at time of final operation

	Deaths (n=65)	Index (n=468)
Gynaecology	49	468
General surgery	2	-
General surgery with special interest in		
Gastroenterology	11	-
Urology	1	-
Vascular	2	-

Twenty-five per cent of the cases (16/65) were done by non-gynaecologists. Where a general surgical team was involved these cases were usually those in which a hysterectomy was needed as part of a radical resection for carcinoma of the colon and rectum. Occasionally however a highly inappropriate procedure was done by a meddlesome general surgeon.

A Senior Registrar in general surgery was operating on an 80-year-old woman with a perforated duodenal ulcer. A fibroid uterus was found incidentally. After a vagotomy and pyloroplasty, the surgeon went on to perform a hysterectomy. The patient died following a myocardial infarction.

There was no justification whatsoever for this hysterectomy.

Collaborative management

In eleven cases, there was shared care with physicians, radiotherapists or oncologists. Given the high incidence of co-existing diseases and malignancy in patients undergoing hysterectomy this is a practice to be encouraged.

Decision-making

Table S103 (q 40)
What was the grade of the most senior surgeon consulted before the operation?

	Deaths (n=65)	(Locum)		Index (n=468)	(Locum)
Senior House Officer	-			1	
Registrar	2			6	
Senior Registrar	3			17	(2)
Consultant	60	(1)		437	(8)
Staff Grade	-			1	
Not known/not recorded	-			1	
Not answered	-			5	

There was discussion with a Consultant in 92% (60/65) of cases where the patient died and in 93% (437/468) of the index cases. There were seven index cases where the decision to operate was made by junior trainees; this is unacceptable.

Table S104 (q 54)
What was the grade of the most senior operating surgeon?

	Deaths (n=65)	(Locum)		Index (n=468)	(Locum)
Senior House Officer	-			7	(1)
Registrar	7			97	(5)
Staff Grade	-			4	
Senior Registrar	8			44	(1)
Clinical Assistant	1			2	
Associate Specialist	-			6	
Consultant	49	(3)		306	(10)
Other	-			1	
Not answered	-			1	

In the index cases there was a high level of senior support (junior trainees operated in 104 cases and in 79 of these senior help was at hand).

When a Registrar was operating on patients who died (seven cases) help was close at hand in only two cases.

A 70-year-old woman presented to a general surgeon with intestinal obstruction. She had had a previous cerebrovascular accident, was taking warfarin and was classed as ASA 4. At laparotomy a general surgical Registrar found widespread carcinomatous deposits from an ovarian tumour. A Hartmann's procedure, total abdominal hysterectomy and salpingo-oophorectomy were done. There was considerable blood loss and the patient suffered a cardiac arrest. She was resuscitated but died two days later in the intensive care unit.

A 36-year-old woman was dying with an obstructed uropathy from an advanced carcinoma of the cervix. She presented as an emergency when her uterus ruptured. At 21.40 on a Friday, without consulting a Consultant, a gynaecological Registrar performed a radical procedure involving a hysterectomy and several bowel resections. The patient died within five days from renal failure.

These operations seem inappropriate. A more senior person might have managed these cases more humanely.

During an urgent laparotomy, a general surgical Registrar encountered a perforated uterus due to a pyometra in a 76-year-old woman with peritonitis. The sigmoid colon was adherent to the uterus. A hysterectomy and sigmoid colectomy were done; no Consultant general surgeon was involved or gynaecologist consulted. The patient died in renal failure.

A Consultant Surgeon or Gynaecologist should have been consulted.

TIME OF SURGERY

Table S105 (q53)
Day and time of start of operation

	Deaths (*n*=65)		Index (*n*=468)
Weekday 08.00 to 18.00	58		440
Weekday outside these hours	3		5
Weekday, time not given	2		20
Weekend	2		3

RESOURCES

Table S106 (q 2)
In which type of hospital did the last operation take place?

	Deaths (*n*=65)		Index (*n*=468)
District General	50		304
University/Teaching	12		114
Single Specialty Hospital	1		6
Other Acute/Partly Acute	1		10
Community	-		2
Defence Medical Services	-		5
Independent	1		27

Hysterectomy
References see page 300

Essential services

Table S107 (q 71)
Which of the following are available in the hospital in which the final operation took place?

	Deaths (*n*=65)		Index (*n*=468)
Theatre recovery area	64		454
Adult intensive care unit	51		293
Adult high dependency unit	11		117
None of the above	-		7
Not answered	-		3

Reference to table S95 (deaths) shows that most of the surgery was done for major pathology. In that context, 14 (22%) of these patients were operated on in hospitals without intensive care facilities.

Table S108 (q 72)
Was the patient admitted immediately to an ICU or HDU postoperatively?

	Deaths (*n*=65)		Index (*n*=468)
Intensive care unit	15		1
High dependency unit	2		11
Neither of the above	48		452
Not answered	-		4

Table S109 (q 73)
If neither, was the patient admitted to an ICU/HDU after an initial period on a routine postoperative ward?

	Deaths (*n*=48)		Index (*n*=452)
Yes	5		1
No	42		443
Not answered	1		9

If yes, after how many days postoperatively?

	Deaths		Index
Same day	1		-
First postoperative day	2		-
Second postoperative day	1		-
Not stated	1		1

Twenty-two of the patients who subsequently died were admitted to an intensive care or high dependency unit; 17 immediately and five at a later date during the postoperative period.

Table S110 (q 74)
Were you at any time unable to transfer the patient into an ICU/HDU within the hospital in which the surgery took place?

	Deaths (n=65)		Index (n=468)
Yes	2		17
No	62		409
Not known/not recorded	1		1
Not answered	-		41

An elderly woman presented with intestinal obstruction. At laparotomy there was a large ovarian tumour with widespread peritoneal metastases. A total abdominal hysterectomy and bilateral salpingo-oophorectomy and a small bowel resection were done. A decision was made at this time not to resuscitate the patient. Notwithstanding this decision the patient was nursed in an intensive care unit for eleven days until she died of bronchopneumonia.

It was inappropriate to nurse this dying patient in an intensive care unit when a decision not to resuscitate her had been taken.

Cases which represent a high risk must be done in an appropriate unit offering full support and able to offer a full range of essential services.

A 78-year-old woman had an obvious pelvic mass. She suffered with generalized vascular disease and was classified as ASA 3. A Consultant Gynaecologist performed an hysterectomy in a specialist hospital without an intensive care unit. When surgical difficulties were encountered, uncontrollable haemorrhage occurred and the patient died despite transfer to an ICU in a neighbouring hospital.

Might not the presence of an intensive care unit on site together with the involvement of an appropriate colleague such as a general or vascular surgeon have produced a different outcome?

A 52-year-old woman with menorrhagia and a large fibroid uterus underwent a total abdominal hysterectomy and bilateral salpingo-oophorectomy in an independent hospital with no intensive care unit. She had had a deep venous thrombosis sixteen years previously. She was not given heparin prophylaxis preoperatively; the gynaecologist's explanation was fear of haemorrhage. When this patient suffered a fatal pulmonary embolism on the ninth postoperative day there was only one doctor (and no anaesthetist) available to attempt resuscitation.

The management of this case and the choice of site for operation were inappropriate bearing in mind the anticipated risks.

A 62-year-old woman was admitted as an emergency to a specialist hospital by a gynaecological Registrar. There was no intensive care unit at the hospital, so, after a telephone discussion with the Consultant, the patient was transferred to a general hospital where there was an ICU, but no bed was actually available. The patient was then found to have a perforated viscus. Twenty-four hours after resuscitation a general surgical Registrar did a laparotomy and found a pyometra. A Consultant Gynaecologist was then called in. He performed a total abdominal hysterectomy and bilateral salpingo-oophorectomy at 03.30 on a Sunday. The patient's postoperative course was stormy and she died from septicaemia 13 days after operation.

Again, this vignette emphasises the importance of providing essential services on sites where emergency admissions are accepted.

COMPLICATIONS

Table S111
Complications associated with hysterectomy (deaths)

	(n=65)
Cardiovascular problems (eg heart failure, myocardial infarction and arrhythmia)	27
Pulmonary embolism*	13
Respiratory infections	12
Renal failure	10
Carcinomatosis	8
Primary haemorrhage	6
Neurological complications	5
Septicaemia	4
Coagulopathy	2
Uncontrolled diabetes mellitus	2
Prolonged ileus	2
Gastrointestinal haemorrhage	2
Miscellaneous (one each: wound infection, ischaemic gangrene of limb, anastomotic leak)	3

NB this can be a multiple entry.

* The majority of pulmonary emboli (10/13) were found at postmortem examination. Three were diagnosed clinically.

Complications and deaths from embolism, thrombophlebitis, pneumonia, ileus and infection are recognised problems after hysterectomy and the postoperative mortality within 30 days of admission for hysterectomy is quoted as 16.1 per 10,000 head of population.[33]

Thromboembolic prophylaxis (see also pages 68 to 70)

Deep vein thrombosis and pulmonary embolism are significant causes of postoperative morbidity and mortality following gynaecological surgery.[34] The incidence of deep venous thrombosis after gynaecological surgery is said to be comparable to that in general surgery. The risk in gynaecology is highest in operations for malignancy and all such patients should receive some form of prophylaxis. In the group of patients reported here, many of them (74%) suffered with pelvic malignancy and as such were in a high-risk group for pulmonary embolism. There is evidence that some gynaecologists do not commence prophylaxis until the postoperative period. This is too late. This is a subject which gynaecological surgeons must address urgently.

IMPORTANT ISSUES IN HYSTERECTOMY

Overall, hysterectomy is a safe operation when performed for the right indications.

> *An 83-year-old woman was offered surgery for a uterovaginal prolapse. There was a history of a previous myocardial infarct and she suffered with angina. The gynaecologists classed her as ASA 2. The patient died during induction of anaesthesia (see page 294, anaesthesia section).*

Clearly surgery in this woman's case carried a risk, but surgeons must use their judgement and experience in case selection.

> *A Consultant's clinical notes concerning a lady with a sarcoma of the uterus stated, ".... she is not a good surgical risk. I firmly believe an abdominal hysterectomy is too risky. Therefore refer for radiotherapy and hormone treatment." The patient in question was 69-years-old, a known arteriopath and an amputee. She was also bed-ridden as a consequence of a previous stroke. However, due to pressure from relatives and the patient's General Practitioner the gynaecologist eventually gave in and did a total hysterectomy and bilateral salpingo-oophorectomy. The patient died eight days later when gangrene of her remaining leg occurred.*

Surgeons must resist pressure to operate when they feel that it is inappropriate to do so.

Surgery in the presence of metastatic non-gynaecological malignancy

A 69-year-old woman underwent a total abdominal hysterectomy and bilateral salpingo-oophorectomy for an assumed ovarian tumour in the presence of advanced carcinoma of the bronchus. The histology was consistent with a metastatic carcinoma of the bronchus and she died from carcinomatosis.

An 87-year-old woman with an advanced carcinoma of the breast had a vaginal hysterectomy and pelvic floor repair. She died from carcinomatosis one month after this surgery.

Was an operation justifiable in either of these cases?

An inexplicable death?

A 48-year-old woman suffered with severe menorrhagia due to large fibroids. An abdominal hysterectomy was done. Some time between ten and sixteen hours after surgery she died. She was found "collapsed" in bed and resuscitation was attempted but was unsuccessful. Apparently no cause for the death was identified at postmortem but the possibility of a cardiac arryhthmia was suggested. The evidence for this is unknown.

The anaesthetic questionnaire and the postmortem report were not returned to the Enquiry.

PROSTATECTOMY

SURGICAL PROCEDURE

Prostatectomy

Prostatectomy is the hallmark operation of urologists. In England, 45,106 prostatectomies were carried out within the NHS in 1989-90. NHS data shows that during this period 93% of all prostatectomies were transurethral resections. The majority of prostatectomies in the UK are in men aged 65-74 years.[35]

KEY ISSUES

This Enquiry shows an encouraging improvement in the proportion of operations performed or supervised by Consultants, and in the increased use of clinical audit. It draws attention to three important issues which should be addressed by surgeons performing prostatectomy:

1   The continuing risk of pulmonary embolism.

2   The risk of unexpected major operative haemorrhage which means that no prostatectomy should be done in hospitals without a full range of essential services.

3   The threat of fluid overload is ever present, especially in the elderly and should be anticipated. Again, a full range of essential services is necessary.

SAMPLE

Deaths

238 surgical death questionnaires sent

175 returned (return rate 74%)

174 death questionnaires suitable for analysis

Index Cases

193 index case questionnaires returned (see page 19).

AUDIT

Table S112 (q 98)
Has this death been considered, (or will it be considered) at a local audit/quality control meeting?

	Deaths (n=174)
Yes	135
No	36
Not answered	2
Not known/not recorded	1

There was a high level of activity in audit, 78% of cases being considered at audit meetings. However many surgeons complained about difficulties in obtaining notes (one set took six months to reach a surgeon) and the difficulties in obtaining information from Coroners and pathologists. One surgeon wrote to the Enquiry from a University teaching hospital to say that attendance at postmortems was actively discouraged by the pathologists at his hospital. The whole thrust of audit will be a waste of time if there is such a low level of support for the medical records department and from our pathologists.

PATIENT PROFILE

The majority of the deaths (147, 84%) were of patients over 70 years of age and in both these and the index cases, few patients were in ASA class 4 and none were in ASA class 5.

Table S113 (q 4)
Age at final operation

	Deaths (n=174)	Index (n=193)
50 - 59 years	2	19
60 - 69	25	68
70 - 79	75	87
80 - 89	67	18
90 - 99	5	1

Table S114 (q12 deaths, q11 Index)
Initial admission intention for the last operation performed

	Deaths (*n*=174)		Index (*n*=193)
Elective	91		152
Urgent	15		13
Emergency	68		28

Thirty-nine per cent of patients who died were admitted as emergencies, i.e. immediately following referral. The reasons for emergency admission may have been varied and may have been unrelated to a urological problem e.g. patients admitted initially with a cerebrovascular accident. This highlights the extra risks of prostatectomy in patients admitted as an emergency, possibly but not always because they develop acute on chronic urinary retention.

Table S115 (q 47)
ASA Class

	Deaths (*n*=174)		Index (*n*=193)
1	16		81
2	88		90
3	50		16
4	14		1
Not answered	6		5

The majority of patients who died were in ASA classes 1 to 2 (60%) and only 38 (22%) patients were identified as being at definite risk of death after surgery (question 48).

Table S116 (q 7)
Final operation performed

	Deaths (*n*=174)
Transurethral resection	146
Retropubic prostatectomy	15
Other/method not specified	13

THE SURGICAL TEAM

Table S117 (q 1)
Specialty of Consultant Surgeon in charge at time of final operation

	Deaths (*n*=174)		Index (*n*=193)
Urology	122		135
General surgery with special interest in urology	40		52
General surgery	12		6

The majority of surgeons caring for patients who died (162, 93%) were either urologists or declared a special interest in urology within the overall umbrella of general surgery.

Table S118 (q 40)
What was the grade of the most senior surgeon consulted before the operation?

	Deaths (*n*=174)	(Locum)	Index (*n*=193)	(Locum)
Senior House Officer	1	(1)	1	
Registrar	2		2	
Senior Registrar	2		6	(1)
Consultant	168	(3)	183	(2)
Not answered	1		1	

There was substantial Consultant involvement (96.5%) in the care of those undergoing prostatectomy with 97% of cases being discussed with a Consultant prior to surgery. It is worrying, however, that a locum Senior House Officer was managing a case on his own. (The 1990 NCEPOD Report[3] showed 88.2% urology patients who died were reviewed by a Consultant prior to surgery. However, there was no specific breakdown of prostatectomy deaths in that Report).

Table S119 (q 54)
What was the grade of the most senior operating surgeon?

	Deaths (*n*=174)	(Locum)	Index (*n*=193)	(Locum)
House Officer	-		-	
Senior House Officer	3	(1)	1	
Registrar	17	(1)	22	
Staff Grade	1		1	
Senior Registrar	10	(1)	18	
Clinical Assistant	1		-	
Associate Specialist	3		3	
Consultant	139	(5)	148	(1)

Table S120 (q 57)

Was a more senior surgeon immediately **available, i.e. in the operating room/suite?**

	Deaths (n=174)	Index (n=193)
Yes	31	37
No	4	8
Not applicable (Consultant operating)	139	148

Consultants and Senior Registrars operated on 149 (86%) patients who died. In the 20 cases operated on by Senior House Officers or Registrars, supervision was available in all but one case. We are encouraged to see such a small number of cases being done by unsupervised, and possibly inexperienced, trainees. However, there were sometimes breakdowns in supervision.

> *A very junior trainee, who had previously done only four transurethral resections of the prostate, operated on a 79-year-old man in urinary retention. The patient was classed as ASA 3. Surgery was unsupervised and took one hour. The patient suffered a cardiac arrest 24 hours later and died.*

The advisers considered that to delegate this case to a trainee was a bad decision. The patient represented a moderately poor risk, and the grade of surgeon was inappropriate.

TIME OF SURGERY

Table S121 (q53)
Day and time of start of operation

	Deaths (n=174)	Index (n=193)
Weekday 08.00-18.00	188	179
Weekday outside these hours	2	3
Weekday, time not given	3	9
Weekend	1	2

Only one patient who died was operated on at a weekend and only two were operated on out of hours. Even in acute retention, relief is provided by a catheter and it is difficult to see why any prostatectomy should have to be done out of hours, unless this was simply due to shortage of theatre time.

RESOURCES

Table S122 (q 62)
Classify the final operation

	Deaths (n=174)	Index (n=193)
Emergency	4	-
Urgent	12	2
Scheduled	85	59
Elective	72	132
Not answered	1	-

The majority of operations were elective or scheduled (157, 90%). One-hundred-and-three of these cases went to theatre with an indwelling catheter suggesting that the original presentation was for urinary retention (whether acute or chronic). The presence of a catheter represents an increased risk of postoperative urinary tract infection.

Table S123 (q 63)
In view of your answer to question 62, was there any delay due to factors other than clinical?

	Deaths (n=174)	Index (n=193)
Yes	7	36
No	162	148
Not answered	5	9

Delays amongst those who died were due to long waiting lists (3), lack of theatre space (3) and a lost referral letter (1). The index sample produced the following reasons for delay: lengthy waiting lists (21), theatre closure (1), Christmas ward closures (4), lack of operating theatre space (three), lack of beds (3) and patient-imposed delay (4).

Table S124 (q 2)
In which type of hospital did the last operation take place?

	Deaths (n=174)	Index (n=193)
District General	131	142
University/Teaching	27	34
Single Specialty Hospital	1	-
Other Acute/Partly Acute	4	3
Community	-	1
Defence Medical Services	1	2
Independent	10	11

Table S125 (q 71)
Which of the following are available in the hospital in which the final operation took place?

	Deaths (n=174)	Index (n=193)
Theatre recovery area	167	190
Adult intensive care unit	127	137
Adult high dependency unit	46	41
None of the above	2	4
Not answered	1	-

Forty-seven cases (27%) were operated on in hospitals without an intensive care unit. As patients undergoing prostatectomy are usually elderly, and can develop severe complications, such as urosepsis and the TUR syndrome, they should not have a prostatectomy in a unit unless fully staffed essential services are available.[36]

Table S126
Problems associated with prostatectomy (deaths)

	(n=174)
Cardiac problems	72
Respiratory problems	37
Pulmonary embolism*	28
Cerebrovascular accident	19
Carcinomatosis	18
Renal failure	14
Reactionary haemorrhage	12
Primary haemorrhage	9
Diabetes mellitus (uncontrolled)	7
Septicaemia	6
Urinary tract infection with catheter in situ	5
Urinary retention	3
Clot retention	3
Haematuria	3
Gastrointestinal haemorrhage	3
Deep venous thrombosis	3
Urinary tract infection without catheter	3
Intestinal obstruction	2
Miscellaneous (gangrene of limbs, arterial graft occlusion, pancreatitis, TUR syndrome, secondary haemorrhage, mesenteric infarction and multi-system failure)	7

NB this can be a multiple entry

* Nineteen of the pulmonary emboli were found at postmortem. The remaining cases (9) were diagnosed clinically and by the use of ventilation/perfusion scanning.

Primary operative haemorrhage is a risk of prostatectomy.

> *A Consultant Urologist operated on a 66-year-old man (ASA 1) in a hospital which did not take emergencies, had no emergency radiology and no intensive care or high dependency beds. He performed a retropubic prostatectomy during which there was copious bleeding leading to a cardiac arrest. The patient was resuscitated and transferred to another hospital where he developed a coagulopathy and died 24 hours later. The patient's death was not considered at an audit meeting.*

> *An elective transurethral prostatectomy was done in an 81-year-old man. The operation (done by a Consultant) was swift, a 60 gram prostate being resected in 35 minutes. There was considerable haemorrhage with a decrease of 5G/dl in the haemoglobin level on the day of operation. Postoperatively the haemorrhage continued and despite transfusion the patient died on the second postoperative day due to myocardial infarction.*

The ideal time to achieve haemostasis is at the initial operation. When haemorrhage as serious as this continues, another operation should have been done in order to obtain haemostasis.

> *During a transurethral resection of prostate on an 81-year-old man the prostatic capsule was perforated. This was seen and noted. Fourteen units of blood were transfused in the immediate postoperative period and the patient died as a result of a myocardial infarction related to the acute blood loss.*

The advisers found the management of this case unacceptable.

The ability to deal with the consequences of major blood loss becomes even more important when patients refuse blood transfusion.

> *A urologist in a District General Hospital did a transurethral resection of prostate and circumcision of a 71-year-old man who was a Jehovah's witness. Bleeding became a problem and the patient died three days later.*

> *A urologist in a specialty hospital inserted a urethral stent into an 83-year-old Jehovah's witness with prostatic symptoms. Six weeks later the stent was removed and a transurethral resection of prostate done. Bleeding occurred and the patient died.*

These cases are very distressing for those managing the patients. Perhaps these patients should have been taken back to theatre in a further attempt to arrest the bleeding, but ultimately the responsibility for these deaths must be that of the patients and their relatives.

Prostatectomy
References see page 300

Table S127 (q 49y)
Was DVT prophylaxis used?

	(n=174)
Yes	41
No	133

If yes, which method was used?

	(n=41)
Heparin	8
Stockings	25
Pneumatic boots, cuffs etc	5
Heparin/stockings	1
Stockings/pneumatic boots, cuffs etc	1
Not stated	1

The responses demonstrate that, in practice, urologists do not routinely use thromboembolic prophylaxis. Subcutaneous heparin is not used because of fear of bleeding. These data suggest that the time has come for urologists to question the policy of withholding DVT prophylaxis.

The risk of pulmonary embolism was apparently higher in those having retropubic prostatectomy. It would seem that these high-risk patients should have thromboembolic prophylaxis.

Many urologists fear that the use of heparin or warfarin will increase operative or postoperative bleeding, which is already a major hazard of prostatectomy. Is this really true? Careful studies have shown that prophylaxis may be carried out using either heparin or even warfarin.[37, 38, 39] There could be no risk of increased bleeding if the prophylaxis were graduated compression stockings or pneumatic boots. Clearly there is a problem here which deserves further research. There is no room for complacency.

Pulmonary emboli (see also pages 68 to 70)

That 19 pulmonary emboli were confirmed at postmortem in those patients who died after prostatectomy (see Table S126) is probably an underestimate of the real incidence of this problem and draws attention to a complication, the importance of which appears to be underestimated by surgeons performing prostatectomy.

> An 89-year-old man needed a transurethral resection of the prostate for severe prostatism. He was prepared for surgery with the collaboration of a geriatrician. He suffered from cardiac failure, oesophageal reflux and was almost immobile due to arthritis. No thromboembolic prophylaxis was used. A Registrar operated with a Consultant present. The patient was discharged on the twelfth day but died in the car in which he was being driven home. He had had a pulmonary embolism.

A Consultant Surgeon with an interest in vascular surgery operated on an 83-year-old man who presented with acute retention of urine. No prophylaxis (not even stockings) was given against thromboembolic phenomena. A retropubic prostatectomy was done and the patient died of a pulmonary embolism on the fourth postoperative day.

A general surgeon with an interest in coloproctology admitted a patient (aged 79 years) in acute urinary retention. The patient was demented, had ischaemic heart disease, atrial fibrillation, previous deep venous thromboses and was permanently anti-coagulated (ASA 4). Anticoagulation was withdrawn. A transurethral resection was done by this surgeon, who admitted a low experience of endoscopic procedures, following which the patient had a pulmonary embolism which he survived. The patient died following the onset of venous gangrene in both legs.

A Registrar working with a general surgeon with an interest in urology operated electively on a 79-year-old man. The patient was under the care of a geriatrician and had a past history of hypertension and a cerebrovascular accident. He was not in retention. The operation was a transurethral resection of the prostate and took one and a half hours. The patient died nine days later following a pulmonary embolism.

Fluid overload

One of the recognised hazards of transurethral resection is fluid overload leading to heart failure or the transurethral resection syndrome.

A 79-year-old man with ischaemic heart disease died five days after an uneventful transurethral resection of prostate. The death was unexpected but the fluid charts showed that an excess of dextrose saline had been infused intravenously. A postmortem confirmed severe pulmonary oedema.

Several similar cases were reported. After transurethral resection of the prostate, patients should be given saline, plasma expanders or blood but not 5% dextrose or dextrose saline. Clearly, intravenous fluids should not be given unless clinically indicated, but drips are usually inserted in order to provide venous access and fluids are given to promote a diuresis. Once patients are drinking adequately postoperatively, the drip can be removed. This avoids the temptation to continue intravenous fluids unnecessarily with risk of overloading in the elderly.

Surgical misjudgement

There were a number of cases where the indications for and the objectives of prostatectomy were questionable.

> *A 59-year-old man was terminally ill with carcinomatosis originating from a bronchial carcinoma. He also suffered from epilepsy and thrombocytopaenia. He developed acute retention of urine and a transurethral resection of prostate was done. He died ten days later from carcinomatosis.*

Was this surgeon's judgement good?

> *An 85-year-old man with known carcinoma of the prostate presented in renal failure due to ureteric obstruction. A transurethral resection of prostate and stenting of the ureteric orifices was done. The patient died rapidly in renal failure.*

Was this surgeon's judgement better?

> *An 80-year-old man weighing only 45kg was known to have chronic obstructive airways disease, pulmonary tuberculosis and a peptic ulcer. He was not in retention but an elective transurethral resection of the prostate was done for symptoms. He died with bronchopneumonia.*

The advisers wondered whether a small indwelling catheter or a spiral would not have been more appropriate management.

> *A general surgeon with an interest in urology operated on a 71-year-old asthmatic man with a benign prostatic enlargement and a left hydronephrosis. Following a transurethral resection of prostate, the surgeon proceeded to do a laparotomy with the intention of performing a pyeloplasty. During this procedure the spleen was torn leading to a splenectomy. The pyeloplasty was abandoned. The patient died 24 hours later following a myocardial infarction.*

The advisers found this case astonishing. They could not imagine how a 71-year-old man would need a pyeloplasty, let alone via a laparotomy, at the same time as prostatic resection.

Thirteen days after he had presented with acute urinary retention, an 89-year-old man, who was classed as ASA 3 due to chronic obstructive airways disease and hypertension, underwent a transurethral resection of prostate under spinal anaesthesia. Three days later he developed a strangulated inguinal hernia which was not treated because he was "unfit".

If he was fit enough for the transurethral resection of prostate, why was he declared unfit for surgery of his strangulated hernia?

CRANIOTOMY

SURGICAL PROCEDURE

Deaths - Craniotomy

Index Cases - Surgery for posterior fossa lesions

KEY ISSUES

Nowadays, all patients requiring intracranial surgery should be managed by neurosurgeons in appropriate units.[40, 41]

SAMPLE

Deaths

335 surgical death questionnaires sent out

200 returned (return rate 60%)

198 suitable for analysis

Index Cases

43 index case questionnaires were returned (see page 19).

AUDIT

Table S128 (q 98)
Has this death been considered, (or will it be considered) at a local audit/quality control meeting?

	Deaths (*n*=198)
Yes	128
No	62
Not answered	7
Not known/not recorded	1

At least 31% of deaths were not considered at audit meetings. Fifteen of the patients who were not considered at audit meetings had head injuries.

PATIENT PROFILE

The median age of the patients was 55 years. The male to female ratio was 1.4 :1. Ninety per cent of the admissions were urgent or emergencies and 72% of the patients were in ASA classes 3, 4 and 5; these patients often had multiple injuries associated with head injuries and were seriously ill.

Table S129 (q 4)
Age at final operation

	Deaths (*n*=198)	Index (*n*=43)
<10 years	3	6
10 - 19	6	4
20 - 29	19	1
30 - 39	21	3
40 - 49	28	5
50 - 59	40	14
60 - 69	47	6
70 - 79	29	3
80 - 89	5	1

Table S130
Diagnoses leading to craniotomy (deaths)

	(n=198)
Acute subdural haematoma	46
(mostly traumatic; one spontaneous haematoma in acute myeloid leukaemia)	
Malignant cerebral/cerebellar tumours	31
Subarachnoid haemorrhage	26
Intracerebral/cerebellar haemorrhage	17
Meningioma (all sites)	16
Diffuse brain injury	13
Intracranial aneurysms and A-V malformations	12
Cerebral/cerebellar metastases	11
Extradural haematoma	7
Acoustic neuroma	6
Pituitary adenoma	4
Chronic subdural haematoma	3
Others	6
Cerebral/cerebellar infarcts, craniopharyngioma, rheumatoid arthritis of atlanto-axial joint)	

Figure S2 (qs53 and 81)
Number of days between operation and death

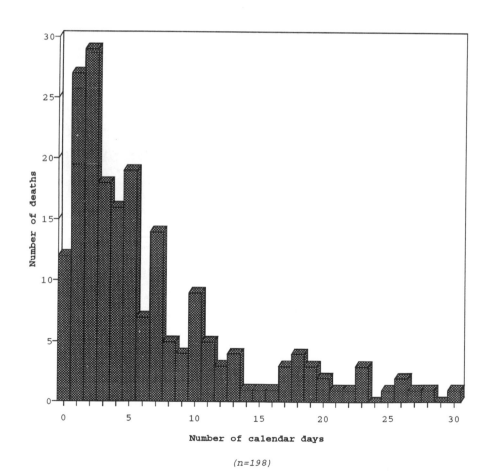

Number of calendar days

(n=198)

Craniotomy

References see page 300

Table S131 (q 47)
ASA Class

	Deaths (*n*=198)		Index (*n*=43)
1	20		13
2	35		19
3	34		6
4	51		3
5	56		-
Not answered	2		2

THE SURGICAL TEAM

Table S132 (q 1)
Specialty of Consultant Surgeon in charge at time of final operation

	Deaths (*n*=198)		Index (*n*=43)
Neurosurgery	193		43
Paediatric neurosurgery	1		-
Orthopaedic	2		-
General surgery	2		-

There were four head injuries operated on by orthopaedic or general surgeons. Once the acute problem has been dealt with and the airway has been assured, the patient should be transferred to a neurosurgical unit, provided that other injuries permit this, as further neurosurgical intervention may be required in the early postoperative period.

> *A 66-year-old man was involved in a road traffic accident and suffered cerebral contusions and a unilateral subdural haematoma. The orthopaedic Consultant in charge discussed the case with the regional neurosurgical unit before proceeding to evacuate the intracranial haematoma. The patient failed to regain consciousness and died.*

Unfortunately the intervention was not successful despite appropriate consultation. *Intradural* haemorrhage is rarely suited to non-specialist intervention but a deteriorating patient with an *extradural* haematoma may be saved by non-specialist intervention. Provided that the dura is not opened serious problems with brain swelling and haemorrhage from the brain are unlikely to occur.

A 19-year-old man suffered a head injury and a computerised tomography scan confirmed an acute extradural haemorrhage. A general surgeon performed emergency burr holes and produced an immediate improvement. Twenty-four hours after the initial burr holes, a further collection of blood was identified in the extradural space. At this point a general surgical Senior Registrar re-explored the extradural space. The patient died five days after the accident.

The initial urgent intervention was undertaken by the receiving general surgeon, but the patient should then have been transferred to a specialist centre as soon as possible after injury. Intracranial complications may develop and require expert management. Patients with intracranial haematoma have repeatedly been shown to do better in specialist units.[42]

Table S133 (q 39)
Which grade of surgeon made the final decision to operate?

	Deaths (n=198)	(Locum)	Index (n=43)
Registrar	13		-
Senior Registrar	12	(1)	2
Consultant	173	(5)	41

In 93% of cases a Consultant or Senior Registrar made the decision to operate. In 7% of cases (all emergency situations) the decision was taken by the Registrar without consultation.

Table S134 (q 54)
What was the grade of the most senior operating surgeon?

	Deaths (n=198)	(Locum)	Index (n=43)	(Locum)
Senior House Officer	-		1	
Registrar	55	(1)	2	(1)
Senior Registrar	40	(1)	7	
Associate Specialist	2	(1)	-	
Consultant	101	(2)	33	

Table S135 (q 57)
Was a more senior surgeon immediately **available, i.e. in the operating room/suite?**

	Deaths (n=198)	Index (n=43)
Yes	32	5
No	64	5
Not applicable (Consultant operating)	100	33
Not answered	2	-

In 67% of cases where a trainee was operating, there was no senior supervision immediately to hand. This is not necessarily inappropriate as many (91%) of the trainees had been in the specialty of neurosurgery for six months or more .

TIME OF SURGERY

Table S136 (q 53)
Day and time of start of operation

	Deaths (n=198)	Index (n=43)
Weekday, 08.00 to 18.00	113	36
Weekday, outside these hours	38	4
Weekday, time not given	4	-
Weekend	43	3

Table S137 (q 2)
In which type of hospital did the last operation take place?

	Deaths (n=198)	Index (n=43)
District General	53	12
University/Teaching	107	2
Surgical Specialty	37	6
Other Acute/Partly Acute	1	2

Table S138 (q 31)
Did the patient's condition deteriorate during transfer?

	Deaths (n=198)	Index (n=18)
Yes	14	-
No	106	18
Not answered	3	-

The initial treatment in the first hour after head injury is vital. Adequate ventilatory support to enable transfer is essential.
Further assessment by means of modern imaging techniques enables a proper surgical plan.

One-hundred-and-twenty-three patients (62%) were transferred from other hospitals; 109 (89%) were transferred from hospitals within the same NHS Region. Lack of resources caused minimal problems with admissions and any reported delays did not affect the outcome of the patients reported to the Enquiry. In general however, the earlier patients are admitted into units familiar with the care of head injury, the lower the morbidity and mortality, and delays are to be avoided.

Table S139 (q 71)
Which of the following are available in the hospital in which the final operation took place?

	Deaths (n=198)	Index (n=43)
Theatre recovery area	121	34
Adult intensive care unit	179	35
Adult high dependency unit	106	26
Paediatric ICU/HDU	57	15
None of the above	2	-
Not answered	1	-

According to the information submitted to the Enquiry on the questionnaires, in 13 adult deaths, the four hospitals in which surgery took place had neither a recovery ward nor an intensive care unit. These hospitals had a high dependency unit only (see Glossary, Appendix B).

Table S140 (q 74)
Were you at any time unable to transfer the patient into an ICU/HDU within the hospital in which the surgery took place?

	Deaths (n=198)	Index (n=43)
Yes	5	1
No	183	27
Not answered	10	15

The main reason for inability to admit to an intensive care unit was a lack of beds and staff. Other reasons for delays in treatment due to circumstances other than clinical were delayed referrals, delay whilst awaiting investigations, lack of operating time and Christmas theatre closures.

Table S141
Complications after craniotomy (deaths)

	(n=198)
Respiratory problems (including 7 pulmonary emboli)	46
Persistent coma	34
Cardiovascular problems	20
Cerebrovascular accidents	16
Intracerebral haemorrhage	14
Subdural haematoma	6
Brain stem failure	3
Meningitis	3
Epilepsy	3
Renal failure	3
Problems with diabetes mellitus	3
Ventricular haemorrhage	2
Recurrent subarachnoid haemorrhage	2
Extradural haemorrhage	2
Hydrocephalus	2
CSF fistula	1
Coagulopathy	1
Diarrhoea	1
Gout	1
Diabetes insipidus	1

NB this can be a multiple entry

SPECIFIC PROBLEMS IN NEUROSURGERY

Essential services

A neurosurgical unit, regardless of whether it is set up in a District General Hospital, a Teaching Hospital or in a specialty unit, must be fully supported 24 hours a day with participation from cooperative neurologists and neuroradiologists, adequate intensive care beds, theatre time and neurosurgically trained nurses including theatre nurses.

There was one instance in the reported cases where the referral of a patient with a subarachnoid haemorrhage was delayed until the *weekly* medical ward round had taken place. Apparently such an occurrence was commonplace on this unit. This delay was an adverse factor in this patient's outcome.

> *A 50-year-old woman suffered a subarachnoid haemorrhage from a left posterior communicating artery aneurysm. There was an initial delay in treatment due to a doctor-imposed delay in referral. This led to the patient arriving at the neurosurgical unit in a dehydrated condition. The neurosurgeon was then faced with the problem that the radiology department would not provide angiography within 24 hours of a request. Thus a further delay occurred before surgery, at which an anterior communicating aneurysm was also clipped, could take place. The patient developed delayed cerebral ischaemia and died.*

Delay in performing angiography can lead to re-bleeding. The benefit of clipping the incidental anterior communicating artery aneurysm in a patient with a poor clinical status is doubtful.

It is particularly important that the neurosurgeons are supported by adequate facilities and both medical and nursing personnel to ventilate patients' lungs on site. Patients are now transferred stabilized and ventilated so there is a need for an increase in the number of beds with adequate ventilators. Time can be lost whilst referrals are made to a unit which can offer to take a ventilated patient.

Acute subdural haematomas in the elderly

It is generally accepted that the mortality and morbidity for severe head injuries increase with advancing age and carry an overall mortality of 61% to 100%.[42]

> *A 74-year-old woman suffered a head injury. There was an acute subdural haematoma and temporal lobe contusions. Her intracranial pressure was monitored and, despite the fact that she was described as moribund, a Consultant made the decision to operate. The surgery was done by a Registrar. The patient died with bronchopneumonia. A postmortem revealed an undiagnosed fracture of the second cervical vertebra but no spinal cord injury.*

Was this intervention appropriate?

Surgery for metastases

Overall palliative benefit of removal of single metastasis in the brain appears to be considerably greater than that which can be achieved using radiotherapy or dexamethasone.[43] The majority of patients with multiple metastases, however, have irresectable disease and should not be considered for surgery.

> *A 68-year-old man presented with multiple cerebellar metastases from a known bronchial carcinoma. Surgery was performed to remove the metastases. Later the same day a further craniotomy was done to relieve intracranial pressure and insert a ventricular drain. The patient died soon after.*

Given the primary diagnosis, the presence of multiple metastases and their site, was this surgery reasonable?

Debulking primary tumours

Debulking primary tumours (such as glioblastoma multiforme, highly malignant oligogliomas, and anaplastic astrocytomas) gives surprisingly good symptomatic control.

> *A locum Consultant working in a Teaching Hospital operated on a 67-year-old man with a glioblastoma involving the internal capsule and lentiform nucleus. A respiratory problem arose and the patient was admitted to the intensive care unit where he stayed for four days until he died.*

Craniotomy
References see page 300

Given the awful prognosis, was a decision to admit the patient to the ICU reasonable, particularly in the light of the general underprovision of intensive care facilities?

Anticoagulants

Anticoagulation can cause neurosurgical problems. There were pulmonary emboli in three per cent of the deaths following craniotomy. There is a need to define the role of anticoagulants in neurosurgery as a means of preventing thromboembolic problems. When should anticoagulation start postoperatively?

> *A 63-year-old woman was known to suffer from deep venous thromboses and was anticoagulated. When surgery was planned for a malignant cerebral glioma the warfarin was withdrawn. A successful operation to decompress the tumour was done. Thirty-six hours later heparin anticoagulation was given and the patient rapidly developed an intracerebral haematoma in the tumour bed. A Senior Registrar then spent five and a half hours attempting to arrest the haemorrhage. The patient died on the operating table.*

This patient was expected to die from her primary pathology. Was it reasonable to re-operate? This case highlights the dilemma concerning the timing of re-introducing anticoagulants.

Postmortem information

There was a marked absence of post mortem information in the group. Many patients underwent Coroners' post mortems and information did not reach the surgeon (see also pages 54 to 60).

Inappropriate operations

> *A 46-year-old alcoholic woman with known carcinomatosis developed a subarachnoid haemorrhage. A Registrar discussed the case with his Consultant and then proceeded to remove the intracranial haematoma and clip a middle cerebral aneurysm. The patient died from carcinomatosis ten days later.*

> *A 77-year-old man, with advanced motor neurone disease, sustained a head injury and developed an acute subdural haematoma. His Glasgow coma score was 5. He was expected to die; a fact of which the family were aware. On a Sunday afternoon a Registrar operated without success.*

The wisdom of these procedures must be questionable.

PRIMARY ELECTIVE TOTAL HIP REPLACEMENT

SURGICAL PROCEDURE

Primary elective total hip replacement

The underlying diseases which necessitate total hip replacement are arthropathies of the hip: two of these, osteoarthropathy and rheumatoid arthritis, are major public health problems. The rate of total hip replacement varies widely between Districts, additionally many of these operations are carried out in the private sector. Total hip replacements were performed 30,000 times as a primary procedure in NHS hospitals in England in 1989-90; in addition, the incomplete data suggest that in excess of 8,000 operations were performed in the private sector.[44]

KEY ISSUES

1   The incidence of pulmonary embolism was high.

2   There was a low return rate of completed questionnaires.

SAMPLE

Deaths

134 surgical death questionnaires sent

   87 returned (return rate 65%)

   85 death questionnaires suitable for analysis

Index Cases

357 index case questionnaires returned (see page 19).

A total of 768 questionnaires were sent out to orthopaedic surgeons asking for an index case. A total of 357 index questionnaires were available for analysis, and if one adds the 18 surgeons who took the trouble to contact the Enquiry and explain why they would not be returning the questionnaire, this makes a return rate of 49%. This is a disappointingly low rate of cooperation by orthopaedic surgeons.

AUDIT

Table S142 (q 98)
Has this death been considered, (or will it be considered) at a local audit/quality control meeting?

	Deaths (n=85)	
Yes	58	68%
No	23	27%
Not answered	4	

Twenty-seven per cent of these cases were not considered at an audit meeting. More could be done.

PATIENT PROFILE

The median age for the patients who died was 75 years and the male to female ratio was 1:1.2. Most patients were in ASA classes 1 and 2 (63, 74%); all cases were under the care of appropriate orthopaedic specialists.

Table S143 (q 4)
Age at final operation

	Deaths (n=85)	Index (n=357)
20 - 29 years	-	2
30 - 39	-	4
40 - 49	-	10
50 - 59	3	58
60 - 69	15	104
70 - 79	36	125
80 - 89	29	52
90 - 99	2	2

Table S144 (q 47)
ASA Class

	Deaths (n=85)	Index (n=357)
1	25	154
2	38	147
3	10	27
4	1	1
Not answered	11	28

Figure S3 (qs 53 and 81)
Number of days between operation and death

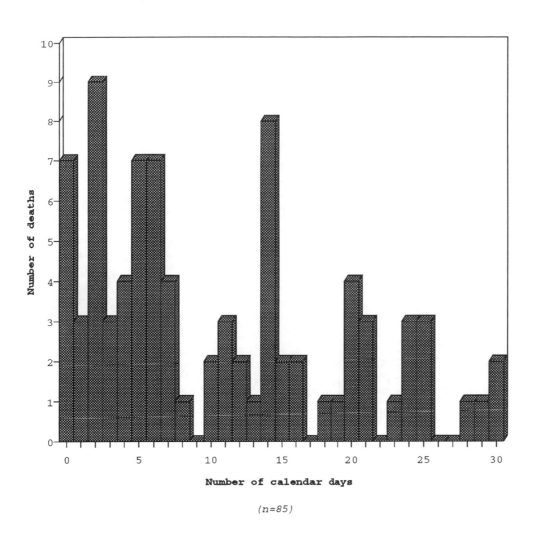

(n=85)

THE SURGICAL TEAM

Decision-making and timing of surgery

Consultants were involved in decision-making in 95% of cases and in the remainder the decisions regarding surgery were not made at a level less than that of Registrar. This is a dramatic improvement on previous NCEPOD Reports.

Primary Elective Total Hip Replacement
References see page 300

Table S145 (q 54)
What was the grade of the most senior operating surgeon?

	Deaths (n=85)	(Locum)	Index (n=357)	(Locum)
Senior House Officer	-		2	
Registrar	12	(1)	26	
Staff Grade	2		8	
Senior Registrar	5		43	(4)
Clinical Assistant	2	(1)	1	
Associate Specialist	3		11	(2)
Consultant	61	(1)	253	(3)
Not answered	-		3	

Table S146 (q 57)
Was a more senior surgeon immediately available, ie in the operating room/suite?

	Deaths (n=85)	Index (n=357)
Yes	15	72
No	9	26
Not applicable (Consultant operating)	61	253
Not answered	-	5
Not known	-	1

There was only one case amongst the deaths when a Registrar was operating alone and unsupervised. Consultants operated on 72% of the patients who died and 71% of the index cases.

TIME OF SURGERY

Table S147 (q 53)
Day and time of start of operation

	Deaths (n=85)	Index (n=357)
Weekday, 08.00 to 18.00	84	352
Weekday, outside these hours	-	1
Weekday, time not given	1	4

RESOURCES
Table S148 (q 62)
Classify the final operation

	Deaths (*n*=85)		Index (*n*=357)
Scheduled	3		18
Elective	80		337
Not answered	2		2

Table S149 (q 63)
In view of your answer to q 62, was there any delay due to factors other than clinical?

	Deaths (*n*=85)		Index (*n*=357)
Yes	8		76
No	71		258
Not answered	6		23

Delays in operation

In the eight deaths, Consultants reported that delays were due to: long waiting lists (5), budget problems (1), medical problems (1) and lack of instruments (1). There were no deaths as a result of these delays. In the 76 index cases where delays were cited, these were: long waiting list (52), budget problems (8), lack of beds (6), patient-imposed delay (6), medical problems (2), Christmas holiday closures (1), and Consultant staff shortages (1).

Table S150 (q 2)
In which type of hospital did the last operation take place?

	Deaths (*n*=85)		Index (*n*=357)
District General	57		231
University/Teaching	9		55
Single Specialty Hospital	8		51
Other Acute/Partly Acute	-		4
Defence Medical Services	-		4
Independent	11		12

Table S151 (q 71)
Which of the following are available in the hospital in which the final operation took place?

	Deaths (n=85)	Index (n=357)
Theatre recovery area	75	345
Adult intensive care unit	48	208
Adult high dependency unit	20	97
Paediatric ICU/HDU	6	45
None of the above	2	2
Not answered	3	2

Table S152 (q 74)
Were you at any time unable to transfer the patient into an ICU/HDU within the hospital in which the surgery took place?

	Deaths (n=85)	Index (n=357)
Yes	6	23
No	73	294
Not answered	6	40

Services such as intensive care and high dependency units which would facilitate the care in the event of complications in these elderly patients were not always available. This can be seen not only in the reports of those patients who died but also from the data relating to index cases. When it was necessary to transfer a patient to an ICU/HDU, specialists reported their inability to transfer patients in six cases of those who died and 23 of the index cases. Reasons given for being unable to transfer a patient into an ICU/HDU were lack of beds, absence of a unit locally and no beds in the adjacent hospital's intensive care unit. Amongst the index cases, the most common reason for inability to admit to a unit was the physical absence of such a unit in the hospital in which the operation took place (17 out of 23 cases, 74%). Orthopaedic surgeons might feel more comfortable and less vulnerable if they were performing total hip surgery in an establishment providing all the facilities which might be found in a well-equipped acute modern hospital.

Table S153
Postoperative complications (deaths)

	(*n*=85)
Pulmonary embolism	36
Cardiac problems	34
Gastrointestinal	13
Respiratory infection	10
Genito-urinary	6
Cerebrovascular accident	6
Primary haemorrhage	2
Fat embolus	2
Miscellaneous	4
(prostatic complications, wound infection, uncontrolled diabetes and septicaemia)	

NB this can be a multiple entry

Pulmonary embolism (see also pages 68 to 70)

Thirty (35.3%) of the 85 patients who died had a pulmonary embolism confirmed by postmortem. The remaining six cases of pulmonary embolism did not have a postmortem and the diagnosis is based on clinical investigations. Pulmonary embolism was the leading cause of death following this procedure.

Table S154
Was DVT prophylaxis used? (deaths)

	(*n*=85)
Yes	52
No	33

If yes, which method was used?

	(*n*=52)
Heparin	23
Heparin/stockings	5
Stockings	6
Dextran	4
Plaquenil	3
Plaquenil/stockings	1
Dextran/stockings	2
Aspirin	1
Warfarin	2
Calf stimulation	1
Not stated	4

Thromboembolic phenomena are a problem in elective hip replacement[45] and there appears to be no easy answer as to the best method of prophylaxis. There is no evidence from the above table that prophylaxis is effective. To provide an answer to which method is most effective in reducing death rates from pulmonary emboli there would need to be a controlled prospective randomised double-blind, multi-centred trial involving large numbers of patients.

Nevertheless, to date it would seem that the most effective prophylactic drug for patients undergoing hip surgery is a low-molecular-weight heparin.[46] The low-molecular-weight heparins prevent thrombosis more effectively than conventional heparins but the risk of major bleeding is the same with both. Also the once-daily regimen for low-molecular-weight heparins is more convenient but it remains to be seen whether the high cost of these newer heparins is offset by savings on the treatment of deep venous thrombosis and pulmonary embolism and a reduction in the number of fatal pulmonary emboli.

It should be pointed out that comments and observations pertaining to patients undergoing primary elective total hip replacement and the incidence of thromboembolic phenomena cannot be extrapolated to elderly patients with proximal femoral fractures (see the 1990 NCEPOD Report[3]) as the populations are different.

General complications

A 62-year-old man who was known to suffer with severe heart failure and ischaemic heart disease was selected to have a total hip replacement. He arrested on the table during the surgery. The surgical note states "surgery was going satisfactorily when there were 'anaesthetic problems'". Hypotension, after the insertion of the cement, but before the end of the procedure, developed. Postmortem showed that the patient died from a fat embolus and the pathologist stated "there is no surgical or orthopaedic cause for the death."

The advisers felt that it is not uncommon for the surgeon to blame the anaesthetist for deterioration of the patient on the table, when in fact it is related to what has just been done. The pathologist's comment does nothing to further the education of surgeons, and could mislead a Coroner.

An 80-year-old man had a right total hip replacement in a District General Hospital. The Registrar operated. The supervising Consultant was apparently in the adjacent theatre. There was a major problem with intraoperative bleeding requiring a 10 unit blood transfusion, and the operation took three hours. Postoperatively no thromboembolic prophylaxis was given. The patient was treated in the intensive care unit but died of "irreversible shock" five days later. No postmortem was done. No anaesthetic questionnaire was returned.

This vignette conveys many messages. Nowhere in the documents returned to the Enquiry was there an explanation for the cause of the intraoperative haemorrhage.

Jehovah's witnesses

> *An orthopaedic surgeon in a District General Hospital needed to perform a total hip replacement on a 73-year-old man. The patient was fit (ASA 2) and was a Jehovah's witness. The surgeon left the operation to the Registrar. There was considerable bleeding during surgery and the patient suffered a myocardial infarction. After 24 days of ill health postoperatively he died in cardiac failure.*

Should the Consultant Orthopaedic Surgeon have undertaken to do this operation personally?

Fluids

Many cases of cardiac failure in all specialties occur because of postoperative fluid mismanagement.

> *An 80-year-old man suffered with impaired pulmonary and renal function. Following a multi-disciplinary collaborative effort he was subjected to surgery which went well. However in the immediate postoperative period he was given massive volumes of intravenous fluid, rapidly developed pulmonary oedema and died despite large doses of diuretics.*

Postmortems (see also pages 54 to 60)

There was a low utilization of postmortems examinations.

> *A 72-year-old woman was treated in a District General Hospital. She was a known high-risk case for a total hip replacement which the surgeons felt to be necessary. Her problems included an active carcinoma of the breast, ischaemic heart disease with atrial fibrillation and chronic active hepatitis. Arrangements were made to give her subcutaneous heparin for prophylaxis against thromboembolic problems and her surgery was done by a Consultant. She developed a stroke two days postoperatively coupled with a gastrointestinal haemorrhage, and died on the 28th postoperative day. No postmortem was done (the reason being that she presented a high risk to medical personnel) and the Coroner was not informed.*

> *A 69-year-old man had a total hip replacement by a Consultant in a District General Hospital. He was known to have a peptic ulcer and therefore heparin was not used as a deep venous thrombosis prophylaxis. Four days after surgery he was found dead in bed. No postmortem was done. The death certificate stated that death was due to "postoperative bleeding and respiratory distress".*

Six days after a total hip replacement a 78-year-old woman died apparently of dehydration. Throughout the postoperative period she had suffered with uncontrolled diarrhoea but no diagnosis had been made although a mention was made of pseudomembranous colitis. There was no postmortem.

There appears to be no proven or satisfactory explanation for this man's death. The lack of postmortems in these cases is a handicap to audit.

SURGICAL MANAGEMENT OF BURNS

SURGICAL PROCEDURE

Surgery for initial or long-term treatment of burns.

KEY ISSUES

1   Death was usually due to the severity of the initial burns surgery or the smoke inhalation suffered.

2   The overall standard of care appeared to be high and was Consultant-led.

SAMPLE

Deaths

25 surgical death questionnaires sent out

18 returned (return rate 72%)

18 questionnaires suitable for analysis

Index Cases

38 index case questionnaires returned (see page 19).

A total of 102 questionnaires were sent out to plastic surgeons for index case information. Thirty-eight questionnaires were returned (a return rate of 37%). This return rate seems very low although 15 surgeons responded stating that they did not treat burns patients. Even allowing for these replies there is still a low return rate of index cases or replies from plastic surgeons.

PATIENT PROFILE

The mean age of the patients was 52 years and there were twice as many men as women. All cases were urgent or emergency admissions and 78% were ASA classes 3 or 4. Eleven patients were transferred to specialised units without mishap or deterioration during the transfer period.

THE SURGICAL TEAM

Table S155 (q 1)
Specialty of Consultant Surgeon in charge at time of final operation

	Deaths (n=18)	Index (n=38)
Plastic	16	38
General surgery with interest in vascular surgery	1	-
Orthopaedic	1	-

> *A 46-year-old man suffered 80% self-inflicted burns. A request for admission to a burns unit was refused on clinical prognostic grounds so he was admitted to a general ward under the care of a general surgeon with an interest in vascular surgery. An escharotomy was done. The patient died 48 hours after admission.*

The advisers considered that it was inappropriate for a general surgeon to care for this man, and he should have been cared for in a specialist unit where there would be a better understanding of terminal care. The man was dying and the escharotomy was pointless. In general, burns patients are better cared for in a burns unit; however circumstances may sometimes dictate that local care is preferred. If this is the case then advice should be sought from a burns specialist.

Decision-making

Consultants and Senior Registrars were involved in the decision-making in 94% of cases.

Table S156 (q 54)
What was the grade of the most senior operating surgeon?

	Deaths (n=18)	(Locum)	Index (n=38)	(Locum)
Senior House Officer	-		3	
Registrar	3		10	
Staff Grade	-		1	
Senior Registrar	2		3	
Consultant	13	(1)	21	(1)

TIME OF SURGERY

Table S157 (q53)
Day and time of start of operation

	Deaths (n=18)		Index (n=38)
Weekday 08.00-18.00	15		34
Weekday, outside these hours	1		3
Weekday, time not given	-		1
Weekend	2		-

RESOURCES

Table S158 (q 2)
In which type of hospital did the last operation take place?

	Deaths (n=18)		Index (n=38)
District General	8		12
University/Teaching	4		14
Single Specialty Hospital	5		9
Defence Medical Services	1		3

Table S159 (q 34)
To what type of area was the patient first admitted?

	Deaths (n=18)		Index (n=38)
Medical ward	1		1
Surgical ward	1		15
Mixed medical/surgical ward	1		1
High dependency unit	1		8
Intensive care unit	6		3
A/E holding area	1		4
Burns unit	7		5
Paediatric ward	-		1

A 45-year-old mentally subnormal woman suffered 45% scalds. She was treated in a general surgical ward by a plastic surgeon. There were no intensive care beds available. She underwent grafting by the Consultant Surgeon but developed wound infections, septicaemia and heart failure. She died 12 days after the accident.

It would appear that the area of care in the form of a general surgical ward was inappropriate for this patient. Why was she not transferred to a specialist unit? Did the fact that she was on a general surgical ward contribute to the occurrence of infection in this case?

An 87-year-old woman suffered 11% sca'ds. She remained in a District General Hospital and had surgery to graft her burns two weeks after the injury. She was only referred to a specialist unit later when problems arose. She died in the high dependency unit of the receiving burns unit. The cause of death was septicaemia.

Was the location appropriate?

Table S160 (q 71)
Which of the following are available in the hospital in which the final operation took place?

	Deaths (n=18)		Index (n=38)
Theatre recovery area	12		35
Adult intensive care unit	16		24
Adult high dependency unit	12		13
None of the above	1		-

Table S161
Complications following burns surgery (deaths)

	(n=18)
Respiratory	14
Cardiovascular	10
Septicaemia	6
Wound infection	3
Renal failure	3
Coagulopathy	2
Cerebrovascular accidents	2
Allergic reactions	1

NB this can be a multiple entry.

Smoke inhalation

The most common problem coexisting at the time of injury was smoke inhalation and subsequent respiratory complications (10 patients, 56%). The pulmonary complications of this injury appeared to be underestimated initially. Inhalational injuries are becoming more of a problem. If patients are not admitted to burns units then advice on the management of pulmonary problems should be sought from someone experienced in managing them.

ORAL/MAXILLOFACIAL SURGERY

SURGICAL PROCEDURE

Deaths - any oral/maxillofacial surgery

Index cases - any oral/maxillofacial surgery lasting more than one hour.

KEY ISSUES

1   Seventeen of the deaths followed surgery for head and neck malignancies. The remainder of the procedures were for dental problems and facial trauma.

2   There is scope for joint audit with anaesthetists when problems with fluid balance and (or) airway management occur.

3   Maxillofacial surgery requires adequate training and competence in the use of appropriate local anaesthetic techniques.

SAMPLE

Deaths

42 surgical death questionnaires sent out.

29 returned (return rate 69%).

29 questionnaires suitable for analysis.

Index Cases

94 index case questionnaires were returned (see page 19).

AUDIT

Table S162 (q 98)
Has this death been considered, (or will it be considered) at a local audit/quality control meeting?

	Deaths (n=29)
Yes	17
No	10
Not answered	2

Thirty-four per cent of deaths were not considered at a surgical audit meeting despite the fact that many surgeons spend time on a monthly basis participating in audit. Audit for this discipline may need to cover a wider geographical area. However, all deaths should be audited even at a local level. There seems to be scope for joint audit with anaesthetists about problems with the airway, and fluid balance.

PATIENT PROFILE

Table S163 (q 4)
Age at final operation

	Deaths (n=29)	Index (n=94)
<10 years	1	2
10 - 19	-	10
20 - 29	2	30
30 - 39	-	12
40 - 49	1	15
50 - 59	2	16
60 - 69	6	5
70 - 79	7	3
80 - 89	7	1
90 - 99	3	-

Table S164 (q 63)
Was there any delay due to factors other than clinical?

	Deaths (n=29)	Index (n=94)
Yes	2	12
No	27	77
Not answered	-	5

In those patients who died, surgery was performed expeditiously where necessary and only one case was delayed due to deficiencies in resources; surgery for a patient with head injuries and facial fractures was delayed because the CT scanner was difficult to reach from the maxillofacial unit which was at the opposite end of the hospital to the scanner suite.

Delays in the index cases were reported to be due to insufficient operating time, waiting list delays, delays in transfer of the patient, lack of experienced operating surgeons, absence of beds in the intensive care unit and Christmas theatre closures. However the most common reason for delay was that the patient chose to delay surgery for various personal reasons.

THE SURGICAL TEAM

Table S165 (q1)
Specialty of Consultant Surgeon in charge at time of final operation

	Deaths (n=29)	Index (n=94)
Oral/Maxillofacial	24	94
Plastic	3	-
Otolaryngology	1	-
General with interest in vascular surgery	1	-

Table S166 (q 54)
What was the grade of the most senior operating surgeon?

	Deaths (n=29)	(Locum)	Index (n=94)	(Locum)
Senior House Officer	3		1	
Registrar	2		4	
Senior Registrar	2		6	
Associate Specialist	-		1	
Consultant	22	(3)	78	(1)
Other	-		2	
Not answered	-		2	

This specialty is Consultant-led with 86% of Consultants making the final decision to operate. In 97% of cases there was consultation prior to surgery.

> *A general surgical Registrar on a firm with a vascular interest excised a Merkel cell tumour from the cheek of a 93-year-old man. The Consultant did not see the patient. The patient developed bronchopneumonia and died.*

In three of the five cases (deaths) when a Senior Officer or Registrar was operating, a more senior surgeon was available. It is noted in the index cases that a Senior House Officer (Consultant available in the rest room) did a case taking more than one hour. The advisers questioned whether this was appropriate.

TIME OF SURGERY

Table S167 (q53)
Day and time of start of operation

	Deaths (n=29)		Index (n=94)
Weekday, 08.00-18.00	26		86
Weekday outside these hours	1		4
Weekday, time not given	2		3
Weekend	-		1

RESOURCES

Table S168 (q 2)
In which type of hospital did the last operation take place?

	Deaths (n=29)		Index (n=94)
District General	18		61
University/Teaching	11		20
Single Specialty Hospital	-		3
Other Acute/Partly Acute	-		2
Defence Medical Services	-		5
Independent	-		3

Table S169 (q 76)
What were the indications for the admission to ICU/HDU?

	Deaths (n=11)		Index (n=30)
Specialist nursing	8		22
Presence of experienced intensivists	8		9
General monitoring	9		24
Metabolic monitoring	3		-
Ventilation	8		4
Anaesthetic complications	-		1
Co-incident medical diseases	3		-
Inadequate nursing on general wards	1		7
Other	-		6
Not answered	-		4

Eleven cases were admitted to an intensive care unit. Traditionally maxillofacial units have often used high dependency unit type facilities on wards, as the main postoperative care is aimed at airway management. There are divided responsibilities over airway management, fluid balance and monitoring. It must be agreed who leads and where responsibilities begin and end. Responsibility for the postoperative care of these patients must be shared but close collaborative care is essential. Clearly during anaesthesia and surgery the anaesthetist has the primary role; this is often continued or transferred to an intensivist if the patient is admitted to the intensive care unit. The dangerous time occurs when patients are either admitted directly to the ward from theatre or are discharged from the ICU. Patients undergoing maxillofacial procedures have special problems regarding airway management. Specialist ward nurses are ideal but, with the contraction of services, there is often a wide case-mix in a ward and specialist nursing may no longer be available.

An 81-year-old woman had surgery for a retromolar squamous cell carcinoma. She also suffered from respiratory disease, hypertension and cardiac failure. After appropriate preparation, a full collaborative team performed radical surgery with primary reconstruction. She was nursed on the intensive care unit overnight and then electively discharged to the ward. Whilst on the ward, three days after surgery, she developed respiratory distress and become comatose. A tracheostomy was done and she was re-admitted to ICU but she died ten days after surgery. There was no postmortem.

Why was she discharged from the intensive care unit?

Table S170
Complications after maxillofacial surgery (deaths)

	(n=29)
Respiratory problems	15
Cardiovascular	15
Wound complications	4
Cerebrovascular accident	3
Bleeding directly related to surgery	3
Coagulopathy	2
Renal failure	2
Gastrointestinal problems	2
Septicaemia	1
Carcinomatosis	1

NB this can be a multiple entry

A five-year-old boy with multiple medical problems (supravalvular aortic stenosis, Williams' syndrome, hypercalcaemia, nephrocalcinosis and mental subnormality) required the removal of eight carious deciduous teeth. A locum Consultant Surgeon and a Consultant Anaesthetist treated the child. A period of bradycardia occurred during the anaesthetic, which was treated with atropine, and the operation was completed in six minutes. The child suffered a cardiac arrest in the recovery period and could not be resuscitated.

The operation was justified in view of the risk of infection from carious teeth in the presence of congenital heart disease. It is possible that this child would not have died if he had not had an operation. The pathologist commented on the preventable nature of dental caries in a child of this age. It was noted that he lived in an area without fluoride supplementation and a high incidence of dental decay. Williams' syndrome is rare, but it is known to be associated with the occurence of bradycardia and sudden death during anaesthesia.

Inappropriate general anaesthesia

There were several instances where inappropriate general anaesthetics were given to elderly and infirm patients in order to perform relatively simple procedures such as dental extraction. This led to deaths from chest infection and other respiratory complications. Outpatient care in ambulant patients is to be preferred, and, in any case, proper consultation with specialist anaesthetists should occur.

OTOLARYNGOLOGICAL SURGERY

SURGICAL PROCEDURE

Deaths - any otolaryngological surgery

Index cases - any otolaryngological surgery lasting one hour or more

KEY ISSUES

1   The overall delivery of care was good with procedures carried out by appropriately skilled staff.

2   Many of the operation notes were brief and illegible.

3   Intensive care facilities should be available where needed.

4   Immediate operation is essential in the event of an oesophageal perforation.

SAMPLE

Deaths

97 death questionnaires were sent out

63 returned (return rate 65%)

63 questionnaires suitable for analysis

Index Cases

190 index case questionnaires returned (see page 19).

AUDIT

Table S171 (q 98)

Has this death been considered, (or will it be considered) at a local audit/quality control meeting?

	Deaths (n=63)
Yes	32
No	22
Not answered	9

PATIENT PROFILE

The median age of the patients was 71 years and 30 (48%) patients were in ASA classes 3, 4, or 5. The male to female ratio was 2.3:1. Operations for malignancies accounted for 35% of the deaths. Many patients were poor risks and often tracheostomy was the final operation done by an ENT surgeon as part of a much longer and devastating illness or following a major accident.

Table S172 (q 4)
Age at final operation

	Deaths (n=63)	Index (n=190)
<10 years	1	8
10 - 19	1	23
20 - 29	-	36
30 - 39	1	29
40 - 49	4	29
50 - 59	4	18
60 - 69	15	24
70 - 79	21	20
80 - 89	13	3
90 - 99	3	-

Table S173 (q 12 Deaths and q 11 Index)
Initial admission intention for the last operation performed

	Deaths (n=63)	Index (n=190)
Elective	27	178
Urgent	16	5
Emergency	20	7

Table S174 (q 16)
Admission

	Deaths (n=63)		Index (n=190)
Weekday	56		162
Weekend	6		28
Public Holiday	1		-

Although delays in admission and operation caused no problems, delays in diagnosis and referral did occur.

> *A woman with dyspnoea was admitted under the care of a medical team as she was known to have chronic respiratory disease. Two weeks were spent investigating her before a diagnosis of carcinoma of the larynx was made; she was then appropriately referred to an ENT surgeon. At operation a diagnostic endoscopy was done, followed by a tracheostomy. The patient died six days later and a postmortem confirmed pulmonary metastases.*

The advisers considered that the surgical management of this case was appropriate given the late presentation and referral. However the operative note in this case was inadequate and omitted the fact that a tracheostomy had been done.

Table S175 (q 47)
ASA Class

	Deaths (n=63)		Index (n=190)
1	9		141
2	22		30
3	17		9
4	11		2
5	2		-
Not answered	2		8

The difference in the ASA classes between those who died and the index group is a reflection of the increased age and incidence of malignancy in the former group.

THE SURGICAL TEAM

Table S176 (q 1)
Specialty of Consultant Surgeon in charge at time of final operation

	Deaths (n=63)		Index (n=190)
Otolaryngology	58		190
General	3		-
Cardiothoracic/Thoracic	2		-

Decision-making

Consultants made the decision to operate or were informed of the case in 92% of those cases who subsequently died and 92% of the index cases.

Table S177 (q 54)
What was the grade of the most senior operating surgeon?

	Deaths (n=63)	(Locum)	Index (n=190)	(Locum)
Senior House Officer	4		-	
Registrar	7	(1)	14	
Staff Grade	-		1	
Senior Registrar	6		12	(1)
Clinical Assistant	-		1	
Associate Specialist	1		2	
Consultant	44	(2)	160	(1)
Not answered	1		-	

Table S178 (q 57)
Was a more senior surgeon immediately available i.e. in the operating room/suite?

	Deaths (n=63)	Index (n=190)
Yes	6	25
No	12	4
Not applicable (Consultant operating)	44	160
Not answered	1	1

Consultants operated on 70% of those who died and provided appropriate cover for trainees operating alone.

TIME OF SURGERY

Table S179 (q 53C)
Day and time of operation

	Deaths (n=63)	Index (n=190)
Weekday, between 8.00 to 18.00	54	184
Weekday, outside these hours	1	3
Weekday, time not given	7	3
Weekend	1	-

RESOURCES

Table S180 (q 2)
In which type of hospital did the last operation take place?

	Deaths (n=63)	Index (n=190)
District General	51	127
University/Teaching	11	42
Single Specialty Hospital	-	10
Other Acute/Partly Acute	-	4
Defence Medical Services	-	5
Independent	1	2

Amongst those who died, there were four delays due to lack of theatre space and intensive care beds, and two due to patient reluctance to undergo surgery. Delays in the index group were due to long waiting lists (10), a medical complication which caused surgery to be oeferred (1), and theatre closures (1).

Table S181 (q 71)
Which of the following are available in the hospital in which the final operation took place?

	Deaths (n=63)	Index (n=190)
Theatre recovery area	56	186
Adult intensive care unit	55	134
Adult high dependency unit	13	51
Paediatric ICU/HDU	11	50
None of the above	1	3
Not answered	2	1

Eight cases (deaths) were operated on in units without an intensive care unit. In the index group 56 patients were in a similar position. In one case where the patient subsequently died the surgeon could not admit the patient to an ICU when it was needed, as the unit was on another site and had no beds. A similar problem occurred in nine index cases.

Table S182
Complications in ENT surgery (deaths)

	(*n*=63)
Respiratory infection	30
Cardiac problems	17
Carcinomatosis	8
Septicaemia	7
Oesophageal perforation	3
Cerebrovascular accident	3
Pulmonary embolism	2
Meningitis	2
Urinary retention	1

NB this can be a multiple entry

Topical cocaine

A 75-year-old man with severe cardiovascular disease (ischaemic heart disease and left bundle branch block) also had "mild to moderate" sleep apnoea. A Registrar did a septoplasty and turbinectomy and used topical cocaine during the procedure. The patient died following an acute myocardial infarct.

A 77-year-old man had a debulking procedure for a recurrent malignant melanoma in the nose to improve his airway. He died two days later from meningitis.

Topical cocaine was used in both cases. In the first case it is questionable whether a patient with advanced cardiac disease should have surgery for a mild condition. Is it advisable to use topical cocaine in the elderly?

Rigid oesophagoscopy and perforation of the oesophagus

> *A 62-year-old woman, under the care of a psychiatrist, had weight loss and dysphagia. It was realised that these were due to an organic problem and she was referred to an ENT surgeon for endoscopy. Rigid oesophagoscopy was carried out by a junior Registrar in the presence of a Consultant. The oesophagus was perforated. Mediastinitis occurred and the patient died of septicaemic shock.*

Why was this patient not referred to a thoracic surgeon when the oesophagus was perforated?

> *A 65-year-old woman suffered with dysphagia and underwent a rigid oesophagoscopy done by a Consultant. The oesophagus was perforated and the patient was transferred to an intensive care unit where she stayed for ten days. A cardiothoracic opinion was sought but no operative intervention was advised.*

Fibreoptic oesophagoscopy may be a preferable technique.

Staffing problems

> *A lone ENT Consultant with no junior staff support, operated on a 78-year-old man with a pharyngeal pouch. No DVT prophylaxis was used, as is this surgeon's usual practice. The operation was appropriately carried out, but the patient died of a pulmonary embolism on the eleventh day.*

The advisers commented that it was impossible for the Consultant to deliver a good standard of care without supporting staff. Having said this, they were also critical of the lack of DVT prophylaxis in a elderly patient undergoing a prolonged procedure.

198

OPHTHALMIC SURGERY

SURGICAL PROCEDURE

Deaths - any ophthalmic surgery

Index cases - any ophthalmic surgery lasting one hour or more

A principal operation in this section is cataract surgery. In 1989/90 75,400 cataract operations were performed in the NHS in England; 53% of these operations were on patients aged over 75 years of age (13% in adults of 85 years or over).[47]

KEY ISSUES

1   The quality of care in this group was high and Consultant-led. All surgery was performed by surgeons specialising in ophthalmology.

2   Deaths are uncommon in ophthalmic surgery and were unrelated to the type of procedure.

3   There is scope for the greater use of local anaesthetic techniques.

SAMPLE

Deaths

44 surgical death questionnaires sent out

33 returned (75% return rate)

Index Cases

138 index case questionnaires returned (see page 19).

AUDIT

Table S183 (q 98)
Has this death been considered (or will it be considered) at a local audit/quality control meeting?

	Deaths (n=33)
Yes	8
No	21
Not answered	1
Not known/not answered	3

Audit in ophthalmology is usually designed to look at outcomes, topics or specific procedures. The College of Ophthalmologists recommends meetings on a two-monthly basis. Deaths are unusual, so it is surprising that 21 deaths were not discussed. The advisers suggested that deaths or mishaps should be discussed in a multi-disciplinary meeting with anaesthetists.

PATIENT PROFILE

The median age was 79 years and only eight patients were in ASA classes 3, 4, or 5 (24%). Eighty-eight per cent of the surgery was elective with most of the patients undergoing surgery for cataracts. Despite the high age of the group, surgery was necessary to improve the poor quality of life imposed by the incapacity of impaired vision.

Table S184 (q 4)
Age at final operation

	Deaths (n=33)	Index (n=138)
< 10 years	-	6
10 - 19	-	5
20 - 29	-	18
30 - 39	-	15
40 - 49	-	8
50 - 59	-	13
60 - 69	3	25
70 - 79	14	36
80 - 89	15	9
90 - 99	1	3

Table S185 (q 47)
ASA Class

	Deaths (n=33)	Index (n=138)
1	5	88
2	17	33
3	6	3
4	2	-
5	-	-
Not answered	3	14

Decision-making

Consultants were involved in 30 cases (91%) prior to surgery, reflecting the extent of Consultant leadership in the specialty.

Table S186 (q 54)
What was the grade of the most senior operating surgeon?

	Deaths (Locum) (n=33)		Index (Locum) (n=138)	
Senior House Officer	1		1	
Registrar	2		5	
Staff Grade	2	(1)	-	
Senior Registrar	4		10	(1)
Clinical Assistant	-		1	
Associate Specialist	1		-	
Consultant	23	(2)	121	

Table S187 (q 57)
Was a more senior surgeon immediately available, i.e. in the operating room/suite?

	Deaths (n=33)	Index (n=138)
Yes	5	9
No	5	7
Not applicable (Consultant operating)	23	121
Not answered	-	1

TIME OF SURGERY

Table S188 (q53c)

Day and time of operation

	Deaths (n=33)	Index (n=138)
Weekday, between 08.00 and 18.00	26	120
Weekday, outside these hours	-	10
Weekday, time not given	6	2
Weekend	1	6

RESOURCES

Table S189 (q 62)
Classify the final operation

	Deaths (n=33)	Index (n=138)
Emergency	-	2
Urgent	1	31
Scheduled	2	29
Elective	29	74
Not answered	1	2

Table S190 (q 63)
In view of your answer to q 62, was there any delay due to factors other than clinical?

	Deaths (n=33)	Index (n=138)
Yes	5	18
No	25	113
Not answered	3	5
Not known/not recorded	-	2

Of those who died the delays were due to; patient imposed-delays (3), bed shortage (1) and long waiting lists where the wait was deleterious to the patient's condition (1). Of the index cases delays were due to; patient-imposed delay (5), long waiting lists (5), lack of theatre space or staff (3), lack of beds (3), lack of a suitable corneal graft (1) and a doctor-related delay (1).

Table S191 (q 2)
In which type of hospital did the last operation take place?

	Deaths (n=33)	Index (n=138)
District General	22	76
University/Teaching	4	30
Single Specialty Hospital	4	25
Other Acute/Partly Acute	2	1
Defence Medical Services	-	2
Independent	1	3
Not answered	-	1

Table S192 (q 71)
Which of the following are available in the hospital in which the final operation took place?

	Deaths (n=33)	Index (n=138)
Theatre recovery area	32	134
Adult intensive care unit	21	83
Adult high dependency unit	10	33
Paediatric ICU/HDU	5	29
None of the above	-	1
Not answered	1	1

The advisers stated that full intensive care services were not essential as a support for ophthalmic surgery. Normal recovery room facilities were important, together with access to anaesthetic skills if needed. There should be protocols for a selection of patients who might need onward transfer to a high dependency unit after surgery. It was recommended that there should be greater use of local anaesthetic techniques to avoid the complications of general anaesthesia.

Table S193
Complications of ophthalmic surgery (deaths)

	(n=33)
Cardiac problems	18
Respiratory infections	13
Cerebrovascular accident	4
Miscellaneous (pulmonary embolism, stress ulcer and renal failure)	3

NB this can be a multiple entry

Inappropriate surgery

An 81-year-old patient was in hospital because of gastrointestinal haemorrhage. He was known to have a cataract, and his vision was 6/12. A cataract extraction and intraocular lens insertion were carried out. Gastrointestinal bleeding recurred and the patient died six days after surgery.

The advisers considered that this was an inappropriate operation for a patient with a high-risk gastrointestinal problem and reasonable vision.

Blank page
References see page 300

ANAESTHESIA

Blank page
References see page 300

INTRODUCTION

This part of the Report is based solely on the information contained in questionnaires received from anaesthetists about 1616 patients who died and 1689 index cases (see Glossary, Appendix B). Each death questionnaire, on receipt in the office, was stripped of all identifying features and the data were entered on the database. Each was then scanned by the anaesthetist coordinator who selected those for the attention of a panel of Consultant Anaesthetists. The criteria for this subsequent scrutiny were *inter alia* age, early death, level of monitoring, solo anaesthetist, occurrence of critical events, deaths of ASA 1 patients, deaths after elective operations or other events which were apparent on individual inspection; the visual inspection was supplemented by a computer search for these and a few other items. A random selection of other questionnaires not so selected was also seen by the panel.

A total of 858 anaesthetic questionnaires were thus read. The panel wrote brief accounts of each case and, after discussion, some of these accounts form the basis of the vignettes in this Report. All of these are directly based on the information which was contained in the questionnaires. There is no other source of data and no modification is introduced. The advisers were derived from nominations from the Association of Anaesthetists of Great Britain and Ireland and The Royal College of Anaesthetists and relevant specialist societies. The group was:

D J Dye	(Chepstow)
J C Edwards	(Southampton)
G S Ingram	(London)
M J Lindop	(Cambridge)
S M Lyons	(Belfast)
R A Mason	(Swansea)
J M Millar	(Oxford)
F J M Walters	(Bristol)

They met on eight occasions. This represents a considerable and sustained effort on the part of these Consultants and it is a pleasure to record and acknowledge the substantial contribution which they make to this process. They have also contributed to the text of this report, have seen various drafts and have agreed the general messages contained therein.

The answers to each question are presented in turn in tabular form. Some of these prompt comment but others are merely matters of record. Some answers are analysed in more detail with reference to other answers where this seems helpful. Illustrative vignettes are provided to amplify the message of the tables and these inevitably include details from other parts of the questionnaire.

HOSPITALS

Table A1 (q 1)
In what type of hospital did the anaesthetic take place?

	Deaths (*n*=1616)		Index (*n*=1689)
District General	1093		1095
University/Teaching	373		376
Surgical specialty	103		106
Other acute/partly acute	4		26
Community	1		2
Defence Medical Services	5		30
Independent	37		54

Table A2 (q 2)
Is this hospital part of, or wholly, an NHS Trust?

	Deaths (*n*=1616)		Index (*n*=1689)
Yes	375		446
No	1239		1239
Not answered	2		4

ANAESTHETISTS

Table A3 (q 3)

If you were not involved in any way with this anaesthetic and have filled out this questionnaire on behalf of someone else, please indicate your position

	Deaths (n=297)		Index (n=188)
Chairman of Division	41		41
College Tutor	36		16
Duty Consultant	84		41
Other Consultant	82		71
Other	54		19
Other anaesthetists	(n=54)		(n=19)
Senior House Officer	21		6
Registrar	13		9
Senior Registrar	11		1
Residual other	5		2
Not stated	4		1

We are particularly grateful to those Consultants who were not involved in the administration of a particular anaesthetic but who nevertheless completed the questionnaire. It could be argued that the "duty Consultant" was involved by virtue of being "on call" and that this should have been less arduous than completion by those who were much more distantly involved, namely those who were Chairmen of Divisions or Clinical Directors, or merely "other Consultants".

NCEPOD is largely intended as a Consultant-based Enquiry although it is recommended that, as a training exercise, completion of questionnaires may be by trainees. We are also grateful to those who were not involved with the anaesthetic but did it for their peers who may have moved to another hospital.

Anaesthesia
References see page 300

Table A4 (q 4)
Grade(s) of anaesthetist(s) present

	Deaths (n=1616)	(Locums)	Index (n=1689)	(Locums)
Senior House Officer	582	(21)	387	(11)
Registrar	401	(45)	290	(28)
Senior Registrar	258	(19)	135	(16)
Consultant	973	(35)	1263	(51)
Staff Grade	25		46	(2)
Associate Specialist	55	(8)	58	(6)
Clinical Assistant	43	(6)	52	(3)
General Practitioner	2		-	
Hospital Practitioner	3		7	
Other	1		6	
Not answered	6		2	

NB this can be a multiple entry

It is important to recognise the various categories of locum appointments. These are different and distinct. The category and its significance varies with the grade. A locum *Consultant* may be: an accredited Senior Registrar who is "acting up", a visitor of equivalent experience from abroad, a Consultant who has retired (early or late) and is filling the vacant post, or a peripatetic individual who is not accreditable. Locum *Senior Registrars* are usually appropriately qualified doctors who seek substantive employment but accept a temporary post until they are successful. There are also Registrars and Senior House Officers with similar, but earlier, difficulty with their career progression. Finally there are those in these grades who apparently travel from District to District taking positions for brief periods.

There is no official recognition of these categories (and there may be more) so NCEPOD amalgamates them all in the knowledge that this is imprecise.

Table A5 (q 4)
Grades of anaesthetists working alone

	Deaths (n=917)	(Locums)		Index (n=1141)	(Locums)
Senior House Officer	168	(14)		72	(5)
Registrar	120	(30)		103	(20)
Senior Registrar	89	(7)		63	(9)
Consultant	462	(25)		770	(49)
Staff Grade	15			32	(1)
Associate Specialist	34	(4)		52	(4)
Clinical Assistant	27	(4)		40	(2)
Hospital Practitioner	2			6	
Other	-			3*	

* Two "Clinical Medical Officers" and one not stated.

Forty-three per cent of patients who died were anaesthetized by a team of anaesthetists. This is a very similar proportion to that published on 1990 data.[3] Surgeons seldom, if ever, work unassisted by doctors, but anaesthetists of all grades frequently work by themselves. The contrast between anaesthesia and surgery in this aspect remains stark; invariably surgeons have medically qualified assistants or colleagues, anaesthetists usually do not.

Registrars worked alone in 7% of all patients who died, but a quarter of these anaesthetists were locums. It is not acceptable that a substantial proportion (15%) of the solo anaesthetists who were junior trainees were also locums.

When departments or directorates are compelled to employ locum anaesthetists it might help the locums if clear local protocols existed about their responsibilities and the sources of advice and assistance irrespective of their grade.

Table A6 (qs 4 and 30)

Anaesthetist working alone/classification of operation (deaths)

(*n*=917)

	Emergency (*n*=90) %		Urgent (*n*=269) %		Scheduled (*n*=390) %		Elective (*n*=163) %		Not answered (*n*=5) %	
Senior House Officer *n*=168	17	*10.1*	100	*59.5*	47	*28.0*	4	*2.4*	-	
Registrar *n*=120	18	*15.0*	46	*38.4*	45	*37.5*	10	*8.3*	1	*0.8*
Senior Registrar *n*=89	21	*23.6*	24	*27.0*	36	*40.4*	7	*7.9*	1	*1.1*
Consultant *n*=462	32	*6.9*	78	*16.9*	227	*49.1*	122	*26.4*	3	*0.7*
Staff Grade *n*=15	-		7	*46.7*	4	*26.7*	4	*26.6*	-	
Associate Specialist *n*=34	1	*2.9*	9	*26.5*	16	*47.1*	8	*23.5*	-	
Clinical Assistant *n*=27	1	*3.7*	4	*14.8*	15	*55.6*	7	*25.9*	-	
Hospital Practitioner *n*=2	-		1	*50.0*	-		1	*50.0*	-	

The fact that solo trainee (Senior House Officer/Registrar) anaesthetists might have to anaesthetize patients for emergency life-saving operations is not satisfactory. However, these emergency procedures were not, in the main, operations which come strictly into the NCEPOD classification of emergency (viz. life-saving operations simultaneous with resuscitation, see Glossary, Appendix B). Most were urgent, i.e. a category (life-saving operation preceded by resuscitation) which allows some delay while extra staff can be obtained.

Twenty-one per cent (100/480 - see Table A21, page 224) urgent patients were anaesthetized by solo Senior House Officers. These, by definition, were operations which, although life-saving, could be delayed in order for resuscitation to take place. Thus there was time for the mobilization of extra staff. The solo Senior House Officers sought advice from other staff on 49 occasions and mostly this was from more senior anaesthetists; Consultants and Senior Registrars were involved on 28 of these occasions.

Recognition of basic specialist training programmes by the Royal College of Anaesthetists may involve inspection of trainee logbooks. The absence of evidence of Consultant supervision for ASA 3, 4 or 5 patients in these logbooks does not support a case for accreditation by the Royal College.

Senior House Officers should never anaesthetize patients without direction by a Senior Registrar or Consultant. This recommendation particularly applies to isolated anaesthetizing locations and very sick patients.

Table A7 (qs 4 and 30)

Anaesthetist working alone/classification of operation (index cases)

(*n*=1141)

	Emergency (*n*=4) %		Urgent (*n*=51) %		Scheduled (*n*=355) %		Elective (*n*=712) %		Not answered (*n*=19) %	
Senior House Officer *n*=72	1	*1.4*	9	*12.5*	19	*26.4*	40	*55.5*	3	*4.2*
Registrar *n*=103	-		4	*3.9*	37	*35.9*	59	*57.3*	3	*2.9*
Senior Registrar *n*=63	1	*1.6*	6	*9.5*	26	*41.3*	29	*46.0*	1	*1.6*
Consultant *n*=770	1	*0.1*	29	*3.8*	236	*30.6*	495	*64.3*	9	*1.2*
Staff Grade *n*=32	-		2	*6.2*	10	*31.3*	20	*62.5*	-	
Associate Specialist *n*=52	1	*1.9*	-		15	*28.8*	33	*63.5*	3	*5.8*
Clinical Assistant *n*=40	-		-		8	*20.0*	32	*80.0*	-	
Hospital Practitioner *n*=6	-		-		2	*33.3*	4	*66.7*	-	
Other *n*=3	-		1	*33.3*	2	*66.7*	-		-	

Anaesthesia

References see page 300

Table A8 (q 6)

Did the anaesthetist (of whatever grade) seek advice from another anaesthetist at any time?

	Deaths (n=1616)		Index (n=1689)
Yes	248		39
No	1334		1637
Not answered	18		7
Not known	16		6

If yes, grade of most senior anaesthetist from whom advice sought

	Deaths (n=248)		Index (n=39)
Senior House Officer	5		-
Registrar	33		1
Senior Registrar	28		1
Consultant	176		36
Staff Grade	2		-
Associate Specialist	1		-
Clinical Assistant	1		-
Not answered	2		1

There was evidence of some peer consultation but mostly advice seemed to be sought from more senior colleagues. There were several Consultants who asked their colleagues for assistance or advice. This should be encouraged.

Table A9 (qs 4 and 6)
Grade of most senior anaesthetist and whether advice was sought (deaths)

(*n*=1616)

	All	Advice sought	Advice not sought	Not known/ not answered
Senior House Officer	172	83	79	10
Registrar	205	67	132	6
Senior Registrar	155	29	122	4
Consultant	973	49	917	7
Staff Grade	20	4	16	-
Associate Specialist	45	11	33	1
Clinical Assistant	37	5	31	1
General Practitioner	1	-	1	-
Hospital Practitioner	2	-	2	-
Not answered	6	-	1	5

Forty-six per cent of Senior House Officers (79/171), when they were the most senior, did not seek advice about patients who subsequently died (77% for index cases), see also Table A8. It must be assumed that Senior House Officers who seek advice from Consultants are then in a position to provide better care to patients.

Table A10 (qs 4, and 6)
Grade of most senior anaesthetist and whether advice was sought (index)

(*n*=1689)

	All	Advice sought	Advice not sought	Not known/ not answered
Senior House Officer	73	15	56	2
Registrar	124	8	113	3
Senior Registrar	81	6	74	1
Consultant	1263	6	1250	7
Staff Grade	38	1	37	-
Associate Specialist	57	1	56	-
Clinical Assistant	42	2	40	-
General Practitioner	-	-	-	-
Hospital Practitioner	6	-	6	-
Other	3	-	3	-
Not answered	2	-	2	-

Table A11 (q 7)

Did any colleague(s) come to help at any time?

	Deaths (n=1616)		Index (n=1689)
Yes	109		20
No	1455		1635
Not answered	41		30
Not known	11		4

If yes, grade(s) of anaesthetist(s) who came to help

	(n=109)		(n=20)
Senior House Officer	18		6
Registrar	26		2
Senior Registrar	14		-
Consultant	60		12
Staff Grade	2		-
Associate Specialist	1		-
Clinical Assistant	1		-
Other	3		-
Not answered	1		1

NB this can be a multiple entry

Qualifications of the anaesthetist (q 9)

The answers to this question cannot be related to others and publication would serve merely to confuse.

Non-trainees' current practice (q 10)

Cardiac Surgery	93%
Neurosurgery	85%
Plastic Surgery	85%

Regular NHS commitments to specialist surgical disciplines by non-trainees is recorded here for the three operations studied.

All the cardiac patients were anaesthetized by Consultants and 93% had *regular* sessions in the subspecialty.

THE PATIENT AND OPERATION

Table A12 (qs 15 and 16)
Days from operation to death or discharge

	Deaths (n=1616)		Index (n=1689)
Same day	129		10
Next day	167		86
2 days	156		104
3 days	106		117
4 days	96		122
5 days	81		153
6 to 10 days	305		611
11 to 15 days	237		293
More than 15 days	339		174
Discharge date not stated	n/a		19

Figure A2 (see Table A12)
Number of days between operation and death

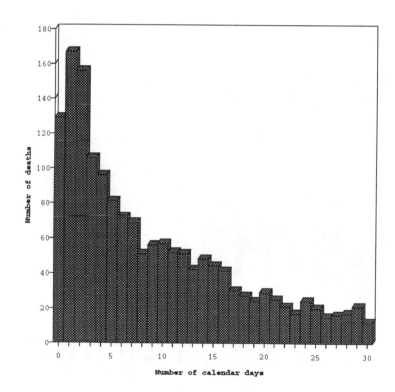

It is commonly believed that early, as opposed to late, deaths may be related to the anaesthetic. Certainly more patients died in the first few days. This is particularly noticeable in Figure A3 (overleaf) where it is clear that there are more ASA 3, 4 and 5 patients than ASA 1 and 2 who die in the first three days.

Table A13 (qs 15, 16, and 39)
Interval between operation and death by ASA grade

	All deaths	%	1		2		3		4		5		Not answered	
							ASA Grade (n=1616)							
All deaths	1616	*100.0*	42	*2.6%*	340	*21.0%*	623	*38.5%*	461	*28.5%*	143	*8.9%*	7	*0.4%*
Same day	129	*8.0*	1		24		42		37		24		1	
Next day	167	*10.3*	4		19		52		57		35		-	
2 days	156	*9.6*	3		32		62		42		15		2	
3 days	106	*6.6*	7		12		40		29		18		-	
4 days	96	*5.9*	4		22		36		25		9		-	
5 days	81	*5.0*	2		18		25		28		7		1	
6 to 10 days	305	*18.9*	6		72		117		90		19		1	
11 to 15 days	237	*14.7*	7		57		99		68		6		-	
More than 15 days	339	*21.0*	8		84		150		85		10		2	

Forty-one per cent ASA 5 and 15% ASA 3 patients died on the same day or the next after operation.

Figure A3 (qs 15, 16 and 39)
Early deaths by ASA grade

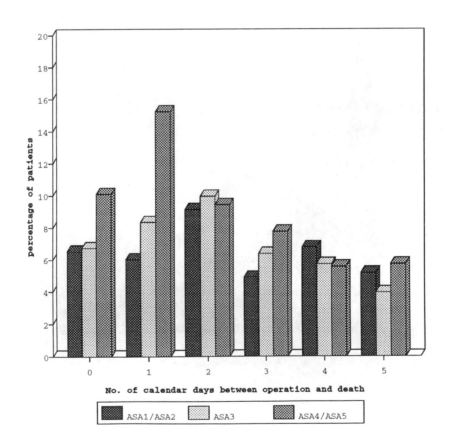

Age

The two samples are not similar in terms of their ages. Twice as many index patients (see page 19 and Glossary, Appendix B) were less than 70 years of age than those who died.

Figure A4 (q 12)
Age at operation

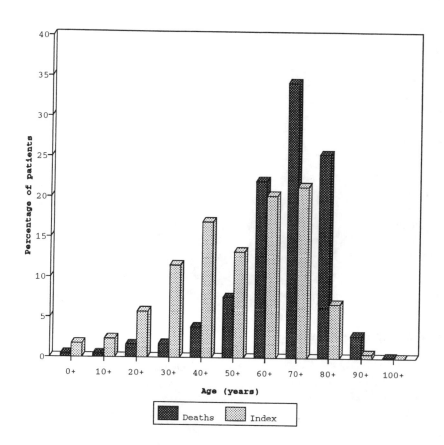

TRANSFERRED PATIENTS

Table A14 (q 17)
Was the patient transferred from another hospital?

	Deaths (n=1616)		Index (n=1689)
Yes	246*		43
No	1367		1642
Not answered	3		4

* Operations

	Deaths
Craniotomy	115
Amputations of the lower limb	44
Colorectal resection	27
Coronary artery bypass graft	24
Burns surgery	11
Prostatectomy	5
Oral/Maxillofacial surgery	4
Otolaryngological surgery	4
Strangulated hernia	3
Hysterectomy	3
Total hip replacement	2
Pulmonary resection	2
Oesophagectomy	1
Breast surgery	1

Table A15 (q 18)
From which type of hospital was the patient transferred?

	Deaths (n=246)	Index (n=43)
District General Hospital	168	30
University/Teaching Hospital	19	9
Surgical Specialty Hospital	3	-
Other Acute/Partly Acute Hospital	13	-
Community Hospital	23	2
Independent Hospital	4	-
Other	15*	1*
Not answered	1	1

* Most of these were psychiatric hospitals or homes for the elderly. One patient who died came from abroad.

Table A16 (q 19)
Who accompanied the patient during transit?

	Deaths (*n*=246)	Index (*n*=43)
Ambulance crew	141	23
Relatives	22	12
Nurse	84	5
Anaesthetist	40	2
Other doctor	5	1
Not known/not recorded	64	12
Not answered	14	1

NB this can be a multiple entry

	Deaths	
	Craniotomy (*n*=115)	All other operations (*n*=131)
Ambulance crew	64	77
Relatives	11	11
Nurse	43	41
Anaesthetist	35	5
Other doctor	3	2
Not known/not recorded	26	38
Not answered	7	7

NB this can be a multiple entry

Table A17 (q 20)
Was there any special care of the airway during transfer?

	Deaths (n=246)	Index (n=43)
Yes	71	3
No	141	35
Not known/not recorded	27	5
Not answered	7	-
If yes,		
Added oxygen	49	2
Pharyngeal airway	6	-
Tracheal tube	46	1
Controlled ventilation	44	1

NB this can be a multiple entry

This is an important matter for those who care for patients with head injuries and particularly for neurosurgeons.

One-hundred-and-fifteen transferred patients, out of the 246 who subsequently died, had a craniotomy.

	Deaths	
	Craniotomy (n=115)	Other (n=131)
Yes	49	22
No	51	90
Not known/not recorded	13	14
Not answered	2	5
If yes,		
Added oxygen	33	16
Pharyngeal airway	5	1
Tracheal tube	40	6
Controlled ventilation	36	8

NB this can be a multiple entry

Four patients whose tracheas were intubated and who subsequently died were transferred in an ambulance **without** medical attendants. (Three had craniotomies and one a coronary artery bypass graft.)

Table A18 (q 21)
Did the patient's condition deteriorate during transfer?

	Deaths (n=246)		Index (n=43)
Yes	7*		-
No	148		36
Not answered	86		7
Not known	5		-

* Five of these were neurosurgical patients; in two of these there were changes in size of the pupil, one patient had a grand mal fit, one bled, and in one the level of consciousness deteriorated.

Table A19 (q 24)
Was cardiorespiratory resuscitation required immediately on arrival?

	Deaths (n=246)		Index (n=43)
Yes	16*		-
No	221		41
Not known	6		1
Not answered	3		1

* All these patients received intravenous fluids with various appropriate additives (vasopressors, inotropes or antibiotics). Two were resuscitated with the aid of counter-pulsation.

Written protocols about the transfer of patients are useful since there seems to be no recognised practice about this increasingly common part of hospital work. Attention should be paid to the desirability of medical supervision for the most seriously ill.[42]

Table A20 (q25)
What was the patient's neurological status at the time of arrival?

	Deaths (n=246)		Index (n=43)
Glasgow Coma Scale less than 7*	66		2
Glasgow Coma Scale 7 or more	156		35
Not known/not recorded	11		2
Not answered	13		4

* see Glossary, Appendix B

CLASSIFICATION OF THE OPERATION

Table A21 (q 30)
Classification of the operation

	Deaths (n=1616)	%		Index (n=1689)	%
Emergency	192	11.9		7	0.4
Urgent	480	29.7		72	4.3
Scheduled	664	41.1		555	32.8
Elective	272	16.8		1030	61.0
Not answered	8	0.5		25	1.5

Direct inspection of the questionnaires about the 192 surgical procedures labelled as emergencies suggests that, with the exception of many neurosurgical procedures, the label "emergency" may be applied inappropriately. Five operations out of the seven so labelled amongst the index cases are not usually regarded as life-saving procedures (see also Tables A6 and A7).

THE PATIENT'S CONDITION BEFORE OPERATION

Table A22 (q 31)
Was a record of the patient's weight available?

	Deaths (n=1616)	Index (n=1689)
Yes	832	1313
No	772	368
Not answered	12	8

Fluid administration, drug dosage and (for children at least) tracheal tube size and length can be predicted on the basis of weight, height and (or) surface area. If patients are weighed there should be a record in the notes. If they are not weighed this is an indicator of the quality of care. Sometimes it is not practical for them to be weighed. Doubtless most anaesthetists do make a reasonable guess at induction of anaesthesia and make suitable adjustments to the doses of drugs, but the absence of a record of this simple variable may reflect poor quality of care.

Table A23 (q 32)
Was a record of the patient's height available?

	Deaths (n=1616)	Index (n=1689)
Yes	215	196
No	1379	1472
Not answered	22	21

Patients tend to know their own height quite accurately and it is surprising that this knowledge is not transferred to their records. Anaesthetists learn about complex algebraic manipulations in pharmacokinetics but do not use this elementary information; if they did use it, height would be recorded as a standard in the notes.

Table A24 (q 33)
Was an anaesthetist *consulted* by the surgeon (as distinct from informed) before the operation?

	Deaths (n=1616)		Index (n=1689)
Yes	726		304
No	844		1364
Not known/not recorded	29		8
Not answered	17		13

Any professional communication between the disciplines about patients is to be encouraged but there is no sign that change has happened since our last Report.[3] More consultation took place in the case of patients who subsequently died than did amongst the index cases. There may be little point in formal consultation on every occasion unless there is a specific problem or a high-risk procedure is proposed.

Table A25 (q 34)
Did an anaesthetist visit the patient before operation?

	Deaths (n=1616)		Index (n=1689)
Yes	1539		1632
No	63		49
Not known/not recorded	9		5
Not answered	5		3

If yes, was this anaesthetist present at the start of the operation?

	Deaths		Index
Yes	1447		1508
No	88		116
Not known/not recorded	2		-
Not answered	2		8

This table demonstrates an improvement in professional practice: that 95% of patients are seen by an anaesthetist before operation and that 90% are seen by their "own" anaesthetist is very satisfactory.

The advisers were unanimous that anaesthetists should always visit their patients in the ward before operation. Organizational arrangements must allow for proper assessment of patients before operation if the quality of care is to be maintained in the face of pressure to admit patients to hospital on the day of operation.

Table A26 (q 35)
Were any investigations done before the operation?

	Deaths (n=1616)		Index (n=1689)	
Yes	1604		1587	
No	11		94	
Not answered	1		8	

Investigations before operation

		%		%
Haemoglobin	1585	98.0	1556	92.1
Packed cell volume (haematocrit)	1266	78.3	1320	78.2
White cell count	1519	94.0	1457	86.3
Sickle cell test (eg Sickledex)	31	1.9	29	1.7
Coagulation screen	422	26.1	168	9.9
Plasma electrolytes - Na	1542	95.4	1188	70.3
- K	1532	95.8	1177	69.7
- Cl	563	34.8	430	25.5
- HCO_3	782	48.4	584	34.6
Blood urea	1485	91.9	1125	66.6
Creatinine	1310	81.2	974	57.7
Serum albumin	842	52.1	545	32.3
Bilirubin	746	46.2	487	28.8
Glucose	833	51.5	468	27.7
Urinalysis (ward or lab)	712	44.1	803	47.5
Blood gas analysis	244	15.1	39	2.3
Chest X-ray	1256	77.7	764	45.2*
Electrocardiography	1366	84.5	989	58.6*
Respiratory function tests	130	8.0	81	4.8
Echocardiography	98	6.1	50	3.0
Special cardiac investigation	131	8.1	33	2.0
Special neurological investigation	150	9.3	40	2.4
Other	54	3.3	63	3.7
Not answered	4	0.2	0	0.0
(though answered "yes" to 35a)				

NB this can be a multiple entry

* These figures are surprisingly high in view of the nature of the index cases and the guidelines of the Royal College of Radiologists[48] and the remainder of the evidence that many of the index patients were young and free from intercurrent disease. Is it possible that some of these patients were over-investigated?

Anaesthesia
References see page 300

Table A27 (q 36)
Coexisting medical diagnoses

	Deaths (n=1616)	Index (n=1689)
None	203	716
Respiratory	483	229
Cardiac	941	431
Neurological	289	118
Endocrine	304	140
Alimentary	254	118
Renal	213	53
Musculoskeletal	180	134
Haematological	130	45
Genetic abnormality	7	5
Other	36*	50
Not known	5	-
Not answered	46	101

NB this can be a multiple entry

* These patients included 17 with sepsis.

Risk factors

NCEPOD has previously suggested[3] that discussion between surgeons and anaesthetists before a decision to proceed in particular patients might be helpful.

> *A Consultant Anaesthetist (FFARCS, 1977), was not so consulted in this case. The patient was a 78-year-old man with urinary retention and he was to have a transurethral resection of prostate. Two operations for carcinoma of the parotid gland had already been performed. He was hypertensive, had suffered a cerebrovascular accident, had angina, was in atrial fibrillation and had had a previous myocardial infarct. He was receiving beta-blocking drugs and diuretics. An appropriate general anaesthetic was given, with suitable instrumental monitoring, but there was an episode of hypertension at the end of the procedure accompanied by ECG changes of ischaemia (raised ST segments). Two litres of intravenous crystalloid solution and two units of blood were transfused during and immediately after the operation. He died the next day from what may have been pulmonary oedema.*

Overt or silent myocardial ischaemia is a well recognized risk factor and yet this patient had an operation which lasted one hour and was done by a Registrar who had done four of these procedures before. Would the decision to operate have been the same if discussion about the risks had taken place?

Table A28 (q 37)

What drug or other therapy was the patient receiving at the time of operation (but excluding premedication or drugs for anaesthesia)?

	Deaths (n=1616)	Index (n=1689)
None	175	627
Analgesic - aspirin	205	71
Analgesic - other non-narcotic	397	304
Analgesic - narcotic	333	59
Anti-angina	270	100
Antiarrhythmic	252	60
Anticoagulant	220	60
Anticonvulsant	68	20
Antidepressant	61	34
Antidiabetic	193	54
Antihypertensive	315	226
Anti-infective	366	90
Anti-Parkinson's	19	5
Anxiolytic	48	15
Benzodiazepines	150	74
Bronchodilator	205	104
Cardio- or vaso-active drug	198	35
Contraceptive	12	43
Corticosteroid	187	91
Cytotoxic	29	44
Diuretic	520	144
H_2 blockers	186	94
Psychotropic	63	20
Other*	305	257
Not answered	14	-
Not known	28	42

NB this can be a multiple entry

* This includes, in both groups, a random selection of laxatives, eye drops, antidiarrhoeal agents, thyroxine and other drugs not previously specified.

Table A29 (q 38)
Was there any history of a drug (including anaesthetic) reaction (excluding minor reactions to penicillin)?

	Deaths (n=1616)	Index (n=1689)
Yes	87	166
No	1473	1482
Not known/not recorded	6	-
Not answered	50	41

Most of the cases in both series were reactions to antibiotics including penicillin or sulphonamides despite the request to exclude these. The other commonly reported group of drugs were mild analgesics; there were a few patients who had reacted adversely to opioids.

One patient in each series was known to have had suxamethonium apnoea previously. Several patients had a history of more than one drug sensitivity. One patient amongst the index cases had had angioneurotic oedema after penicillin. The remainder in the "other" category included iodine, hormone replacement therapy, lipstick and elastoplast.

Figure A5 (q 39)
ASA grade

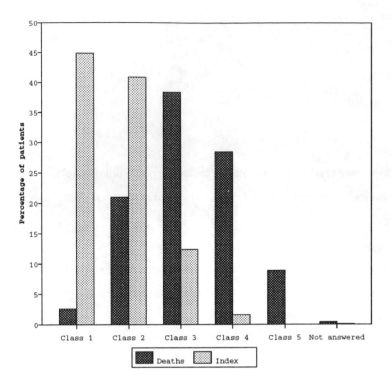

The difference between patients who died and the index cases as indicated by the ASA grade allocated by the anaesthetist is quite obvious: the patients who died were much the sicker group despite the well-recognised tendency for anaesthetists to allocate patients to a higher ASA grade in response to their knowledge that the patient subsequently died! Thirty-seven per cent of the patients who died were ASA 4 or 5.

Table A30 (qs A39/S42)
ASA grade (deaths) - comparison of anaesthetic and surgical questionnaires

ASA grade (Surgical questionnaire)	ASA grade (Anaesthetic questionnaire) (n=1616)					Not answered
	1	2	3	4	5	
1	20	47	29	4	3	-
2	11	168	158	58	7	-
3	1	49	246	134	10	1
4	2	14	94	183	55	2
5	-	1	3	18	51	-
Not answered	1	14	23	14	3	2
SQ not received	7	47	70	50	14	2

Figure A6 (qs A39/S42)
Comparison of anaesthetists' grading with surgeons' grading of ASA class

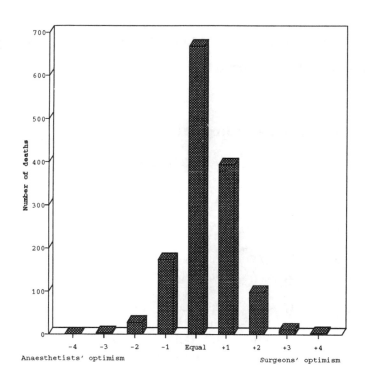

This graph is almost identical to the one which appears in the NCEPOD 1990 Report.[3] Anaesthetists remain less optimistic in terms of ASA grading than surgeons, and therefore tend to grade patients in worse ASA grades than do surgeons, assuming that these are independent assessments. This difference is not absolute but it may reflect different perceptions. A patient with ischaemic gangrene of a leg appears curable to the surgeon because if the leg is removed the patient may recover. The anaesthetist is more likely to note the presence of a mortal pathological process in the whole patient.

Table A31
Grade of the most senior anaesthetist by the patient's ASA grade (deaths)

(*n*=1616)

ASA grade

	All	1	%	2	%	3	%	4	%	5	%	Not answered
Senior House Officer	172	1	0.6	29	16.9	91	52.9	48	27.9	3	1.7	-
Registrar	205	2	1.0	20	9.8	76	37.1	77	37.6	30	14.6	-
Senior Registrar	155	1	0.6	22	14.2	44	28.4	57	36.8	30	19.4	1
Consultant	973	37	3.8	243	30.0	359	36.9	257	26.4	71	7.3	6
Staff Grade	20	-		6	30.0	7	35.0	5	25.0	2	10.0	-
Associate Specialist	45	1	2.2	8	17.8	21	46.7	12	26.7	3	6.7	-
Clinical Assistant	37	-		11	29.7	19	51.4	4	10.8	3	8.1	-
General Practitioner	1	-		-		1	100.0	-		-		-
Hospital Practitioner	2	-		-		2	100.0	-		-		-
Not answered	6	-		1	16.7	3	50.0	1	16.7	1	16.7	-

Sixty-nine per cent of patients who died and were graded as ASA 4 or 5 were anaesthetized by Senior Registrars or Consultants but 26% were anaesthetized by Senior House Officers or Registrars. This is unacceptable.

Table A32
Grade of the most senior anaesthetist by the patient's ASA grade (index)

(*n*=1689)

ASA grade

	All	1	%	2	%	3	%	4	%	5	Not answered
Senior House Officer	73	35	47.9	28	38.4	10	13.7	-		-	-
Registrar	124	64	51.6	48	38.7	10	8.1	2	1.6	-	-
Senior Registrar	81	34	42.0	34	42.0	10	12.3	3	3.7	-	-
Consultant	1263	547	43.3	526	41.6	167	13.2	21	1.7	-	2
Staff Grade	38	22	57.9	11	28.9	5	13.2	-		-	-
Associate Specialist	57	34	59.6	18	31.6	4	70.0	1	1.8	-	-
Clinical Assistant	42	18	42.9	22	52.4	2	4.8	-		-	-
General Practitioner	6	3	50.0	3	50.0	-		-		-	-
Hospital Practitioner	3	1	33.3	2	66.7	-		-		-	-
Not answered	2	1	50.0	1	50.0	-		-		-	-

Tables A31 and A32 confirm the fact that the two samples of patients came from different populations. However the tables show that the majority of the index patients were anaesthetised by Consultants.

PREPARATION OF PATIENT BEFORE OPERATION

Table A33 (q 40)
When was the last fluid/food given by mouth?

	Deaths (n=1616)		Index (n=1689)
More than 6 hours before	1376		1478
Between 4 - 6 hours before	89		140
Less than 4 hours before	14		21
Not known/not recorded	127		40
Not answered	10		10

Table A34 (q 41)
Indicate measures taken to reduce gastric acidity and volume, as prophylaxis against acid aspiration.

	Deaths (n=1616)		Index (n=1689)
None	1173		1343
Antacids	60		26
H_2 antagonists*	147		121
Metoclopramide**	133		230
Nasogastric/stomach tube	159		13
Other***	13		3
Not known/not recorded	3		1
Not answered	33		19

NB this can be a multiple entry

*   Includes those who received omeprazole.

**   Includes patients who received other antiemetics.

***   Includes eight patients amongst those who died whose tracheas were already intubated. One patient rejected the nasogastric tube.

Table A35 (q 42)
Did the patient receive intravenous fluid therapy in the 12 hours before induction?

	Deaths (n=1616)		Index (n=1689)
Yes	678		78
No	921		1610
Not known/not recorded	10		-
Not answered	7		1
Nature of fluid(s)			
Crystalloid or dextrose	583		64
Colloid	149		4
Whole blood	64		4
Red cell component	36		7
Other components, e.g. platelets	33		1
Mannitol	37		1
Not answered	31		7

NB this can be a multiple entry

Table A36 (q 43)
Was anything added to the IV solution(s)?

	Deaths (n=678)		Index (n=78)
Yes	224		24
No	381		37
Not known/not recorded	11		1
Not answered	62		16

(See also Table A43, page 239)

Table A37 (q 44)

Were measures taken to improve the respiratory system *before* **induction of anaesthesia?**

	Deaths (n=1616)	Index (n=1689)
Yes	313	132
No	1237	1489
Not known/not recorded	2	-
Not answered	64	68
Treatments		
Antibiotic therapy	110	19
Bronchodilators	111	61
Chest physiotherapy	202	70
Airway management	30	5
Other	14*	10**
Not answered	-	2

* Three patients needed to have a pleural effusion drained; two each required urgent administration of diuretics, treatment of cardiac failure and intermittent positive pressure ventilation of their lungs.

** Six patients received steroids for bronchospasm by inhalation or injection.

Table A38 (q 45)
Were premedicant drugs prescribed?

	Deaths (n=1616)	Index (n=1689)
Yes	792	1412
No	812	275
Not answered	12	2

Premedicant drugs prescribed

	Deaths	Index
Atropine	39	108
Chloral hydrate	-	2
Diazepam	108	200
Droperidol	49	54
Fentanyl	16	5
Glycopyrronium	19	17
Hyoscine	104	147
Lorazepam	91	114
Ketamine	1	1
Metoclopramide	127	305
Midazolam	4	4
Morphine	51	85
Papaveretum	125	152
Pethidine	97	134
Prochlorperazine	31	40
Temazepam	276	672
Promethazine	69	113
Trimeprazine	3	13
Other	121*	143
Not answered	5	6

* This group included - glyceryl trinitrate patch (26), diamorphine (5), H_2 antagonists (17), and steroids (18), and an assortment of other analgesics, sedatives, antiemetics, antibiotics and antacids.

The popularity of the benzodiazepine drugs as premedicant drugs in both groups of patients is now very clear.

Table A39 (qs 39 and 45)
Premedication by ASA grade (deaths)

(*n*=1616)

	All	%	ASA 1 and 2	%	ASA 3	%	ASA 4 and 5	%	Not answered
Yes	792	*100*	273	*34.5*	338	*42.7*	178	*22.4*	3
No	812	*100*	108	*13.3*	279	*34.3*	422	*52.0*	3
Not answered	12		1		6		4		1

It is interesting to note that about half of the patients received premedication and 77% of these were ASA grades 1 to 3. More than half of those who did not receive premedicant drugs were ASA 4 or 5.

Table A40 (qs 39 and 45)
Premedication by ASA grade (index)

(*n*=1689)

	All	%	ASA 1 and 2	%	ASA 3	%	ASA 4 and 5	%	Not answered
Yes	1412	*100*	1230	*87.1*	167	*11.8*	13	*0.9*	2
No	275	*100*	220	*80.0*	41	*14.9*	14	*5.1*	-
Not answered	2		2		-		-		-

Most index cases (84%) received drugs before operation and, of these, 99% were ASA grades 1 to 3.

Table A41 (q 46)
Was *non-invasive* **monitoring established just** *before* **the induction of anaesthesia?**

	Deaths (n=1616)		Index (n=1689)
Yes	1406		1317
No	175		353
Not known/not recorded	24		18
Not answered	11		1
Monitors			
ECG	1176		975
BP	1042		902
Pulse oximetry	1107		991
Other*	36		23
Not answered	8		6

NB this can be a multiple entry

* Includes measurements of expired carbon dioxide and inspired oxygen.

The use of oximetry before induction has increased marginally (from 63% to 69% of patients who died) from the previous NCEPOD Report.[3] The total absence of instrumental monitoring at this stage in 11% of deaths is noteworthy, has not changed much and is a cause for continued concern.

Table A42 (q 47)
Was *invasive* **monitoring established** *before* **induction of anaesthesia (e.g. central venous pressure, arterial line)?**

	Deaths (n=1616)		Index (n=1689)
Yes	283*		43**
No	1289		1597
Not known/not recorded	5		2
Not answered	39		47

* Most of these patients had arterial lines (203); usually radial where specified (one dorsal pedis) and 125 had central venous lines. The incidence of pulmonary arterial catheters was quite low.

** All refer to the use of arterial lines and 10 included central venous pressure in addition.

Table A43 (q 48)

Was it necessary to take measures additional to those specified in questions 24 and 43 to improve the patient's cardiovascular function just before and at the induction of anaesthesia?

	Deaths (n=1616)	Index (n=1689)
Yes	212	61
No	1367	1599
Not known/not recorded	5	2
Not answered	32	27
Measures		
Crystalloid IV fluids	103	33
Colloid IV fluids	69	9
Whole blood transfusion	21	3
Blood components	20	1
Antiarrhythmic drugs	7	1
Cardiac glycoside	18	2
Diuretics	7	1
Vasopressors	27	7
Inotropic drugs	26	2
Other*	34	6

* Includes a miscellany of glyceryl trinitrate patches, therapeutic additions to intravenous fluids, antibiotics and even anaesthetic drugs.

Table A44 (q 49)

Was there an inappropriate delay before the start of the operation?

	Deaths (n=1616)		Index (n=1689)
Yes	35		20
No	1553		1649
Not known/not recorded	7		8
Not answered	21		12

Due to non-availability of;

	Deaths		Index
Radiology	1		-
Haematology	-		2
Operating theatre	21		6
Anaesthetist	2		-
Anaesthetist's assistant	1		-
Surgeon	5		2
Theatre staff	1		-
Portering staff	-		1
Other	8		6
Not answered	-		3

NB this can be a multiple entry

The non-availability of an *operating room* was the most frequent cause of inappropriate delay. Nineteen of these were designated emergency cases but were unlikely to have been emergency, life-saving procedures with resuscitation simultaneous with surgery (the CEPOD definition - see Glossary, Appendix B). Amongst the patients who died, these operations were:

	Deaths (n=21)
Amputations of the lower limb	9
Colorectal resection	7
Oesophagectomy	2
Otoloryngology	1
Craniotomy	1
Coronary artery bypass graft(s)	1

Table A45 (q 50)

Were any measures taken (before, during or after operation) to prevent venous thrombosis?

	Deaths (n=1616)	Index (n=1689)
Yes	737	840
No	841	814
Not known/not recorded	10	18
Not answered	28	17

Measures	Deaths (n=737)		Index (n=840)	
	Before/during	After	Before/during	After
Aspirin	74	36	24	29
Heparin	331	310	324	333
Dextran infusion	19	17	59	38
Leg stockings	182	157	311	253
Calf compression/ stimulation	130	13	167	37
Warfarin	26	14	9	34
Other	23*	17	26**	18
Not answered	1	2	-	-

NB this can be a multiple entry

* Includes 13 patients who had spinal or epidural anaesthetics, five who had some form of ankle, heel or calf support and one who had antiplatelet drugs.

** Eight patients were receiving a variety of antiplatelet drugs and peripheral vasodilators. On six occasions antimalarial drugs were mentioned in this section.

Leg stockings, calf compression or stimulation are relatively cheap and risk-free methods and their increased use may be indicated. The usage reported here may be much lower than is actually the case because the use of some of these methods is not always recorded formally in the notes.

There are still surgeons who are fearful of prophylaxis for deep vein thrombosis and pulmonary embolism, particularly urologists, orthopaedic and neurosurgeons. However it is particularly alarming to note that fatal pulmonary embolism occurs in the absence of prophylaxis in patients who had two or more risk factors for this complication.

An otherwise fit 51-year-old obese (93kg) woman was to have a total abdominal hysterectomy for a benign condition. She had varicose veins. She died four days after surgery from a pulmonary embolism. No prophylaxis of any type was used.

Another obese woman was to have a similar operation but for malignant disease. She was 77 years old and had previously had a myocardial infarction. There was no prophylaxis. She died two days later after pulmonary embolism from pelvic vein thrombosis demonstrated at postmortem.

Both these women were anaesthetized by Consultant Anaesthetists in District General Hospitals. Pelvic surgery is a risk factor, so is obesity, so is malignant disease and so are varicose veins.

A 72-year-old man was admitted to a District General Hospital for a transurethral resection of his prostate. The presence of hyponatraemia, ketones in the urine (on ward testing) and leucocytosis seem to have been ignored. No prophylaxis for deep vein thrombosis was used. An operation was done and he died 18 days later of pulmonary thromboembolism, having been readmitted to hospital eight days after operation with diabetic ketoacidosis. The surgeon (urologist) considered that "death had nothing to do with surgery" and he did not attend the autopsy.

Many patients died of pulmonary embolism notwithstanding prophylactic efforts, and NCEPOD does not have sufficient information about those who survive to settle this matter, but there is sufficient evidence (see Venous Thromboembolism section pages 68 to 70) to justify much more research. Each hospital should have a protocol for the prevention and management of deep venous thrombosis and pulmonary embolism. There is a need for consultation between surgeons and anaesthetists about the use of spinal and epidural anaesthesia when anticoagulation of any type is proposed.

These are further examples in which cross-consultation between anaesthetists and surgeons might change practice and influence outcomes.

Some of the less aggressive prophylactic treatments may be attractive and even effective in some circumstances. However, desperate conditions may require that the risk of surgical haemorrhage be accepted.

An obese (119kg) 62-year-old was to have a total hip replacement in a District General Hospital. He was hypertensive and had ischaemic heart disease. The Consultant Anaesthetist (FFARCS, 1973) did a femoral nerve block and administered a continuous infusion of propofol and allowed him to breathe isoflurane through a laryngeal mask airway. Leg stockings were used during the operation. No other prophylactic measures were reported. Pulmonary embolism was proven at autopsy after he died on the fourteenth day.

THE ANAESTHETIC

Table A46 (qs 51 and 53)
Duration of procedure (from time of start of anaesthetic to transfer out of operating room)

	Deaths (*n*=1616)	Index (*n*=1689)
<30 minutes	59	28
>30 minutes	395	367
>1 hour	543	777
>2 hours	373	399
>4 hours	190	88
Not answered	56	30

There were 96 (6%) operations on patients who subsequently died which were conducted between 22.00 and 07.00 hours. (This period was chosen to span midnight since this is recognised to be a period of low alertness in the circadian rhythm).

244

Table A47
Most senior member of staff present when the time of start of anaesthetic was recorded as being after 22.00 and before 07.00 hours

	Deaths (n=97)	
	Anaesthetist	Surgeon
Senior House Officer	23	2
Registrar	31	52
Senior Registrar	21	27
Staff Grade	-	2
Associate Specialist	1	-
Clinical Assistant	1	-
Consultant	20	14

These data ignore the type of surgery and seem to indicate that marginally more senior surgeons are involved with operations out of hours, except for Consultants. It must also be recalled in this context that anaesthetists are usually working alone.

Operations should not often need to be performed at night unless that operation is life-saving.[49] The distribution of grades of staff was similar in both disciplines: about half the operations were managed by Senior House Officer and Registrar surgeons and anaesthetists. It is to be hoped that these staff were not expected to take serious responsibility before adequate rest was possible.[50] This is a difficult problem for the organization of Consultants whose hours of work are not controlled and for whom substitutes are less frequently available.

Table A48
Did the anaesthetist seek advice at any time from another anaesthetist (when the time of the start of the anaesthetic was recorded as being after 22.00 and before 07.00 and the most senior anaesthetist present at the start of the anaesthetic was a Senior House Officer or Registrar) ?

	Deaths (n=54)	Index (n=2)
Yes	26	1
No	25	1
Not known/not recorded	2	-
Not answered	1	-

If yes, what was the grade of the most senior anaesthetist from whom advice was sought?

	Deaths	Index
Senior House Officer	1	-
Registrar	4	-
Senior Registrar	7	-
Consultant	14	1

Table A49

Did any colleagues come to help at any time (when the time of the start of anaesthetic was recorded as being after 22.00 and before 07.00 and the most senior anaesthetist present at the start of the anaesthetic was a Senior House Officer or Registrar) ?

	Deaths (n=54)	Index (n=2)
Yes	6	-
No	46	2
Not answered	1	-
Not known/not recorded	1	-

If yes, what was the grade of the most senior anaesthetist who came to help?

Registrar	2
Senior Registrar	3
Consultant	1

Table A50

What was the grade of the most senior operating surgeon (when the time of the start of the anaesthetic was recorded as being after 22.00 and before 07.00, and the most senior anaesthetist present at the start of the anaesthetic was a Senior House Officer or Registrar) ?

	Deaths (n=54)	Index (n=2)
Senior House Officer	2	-
Registrar	33	-
Senior Registrar	14	2
Consultant	3	-
Staff Grade	2	-

Successive reports have indicated the desirability of the availability of emergency operating rooms during the day. The previous tables show what happens when operations do take place out of hours, who is available to help and who actually comes in.

Table A51 (q 54)

What was the grade of the most senior surgeon in the operating room?

	Deaths (*n*=1616)	%	Index (*n*=1689)	%
Senior House Officer	32	2.0	13	0.8
Registrar	395	24.4	168	9.9
Senior Registrar	182	11.3	134	7.9
Associate Specialist	17	1.1	18	1.1
Clinical Assistant	8	0.5	7	0.4
Staff Grade	11	0.7	11	0.7
Consultant	961	59.5	1328	78.6
Other	-		1*	0.1
Not known/not recorded	4	0.2	4	0.2
Not answered	6	0.4	5	0.3

* Clinical Medical Officer

An 87-year-old patient with serious cardiovascular disease (receiving betablockers, nitrates, nifedipine and frusemide) was described as ASA 4. An elective total hip replacement was done in a District General Hospital by a Registrar who took 2.5 hours during the day to do the operation. The Registrar anaesthetist, with two years' experience but no qualifications in anaesthesia, spoke to a Consultant Anaesthetist. A combined general/epidural anaesthetic was done and the blood pressure was maintained at 70-80 mmHg throughout with intermittent ephedrine. The patient died two hours after arrival in the recovery room.

Consultation between surgeons and anaesthetists beforehand might have ensured both a more expeditious operation and perhaps more appropriate anaesthesia. Consultant Surgeons may need to choose patients for operation with as much attention to their *general* state of health as to the suitability of the surgical procedure for their Registrars (see also Table A24). This selection could be incorporated into the information recorded on the waiting list, which should perhaps even include the ASA grade.

Table A52 (q 55)
Did you have non-medical help with anaesthesia?

	Deaths (n=1616)		Index (n=1689)
Yes	1602		1662
No	11		21
Not answered	3		6
Non-medical help			
Trained anaesthetic nurse	299		331
Trainee anaesthetic nurse	14		27
Theatre nurse	124		124
Trained operating department assistant	1173		1161
Trainee operating department assistant	79		92
Operating department orderly	51		54
Ward nurse	38		43
Physiological measurement technician	44		20
Other*	29		25
Not answered	10		15

NB this can be a multiple entry

* This group includes a variety of staff in both series. Perfusionists often helped anaesthetists and student nurses were mentioned twice. An escort nurse, an "untrained" nurse, a student nurse and a medical student were mentioned once each amongst the index cases.

This represents an improvement over the figure in our previous Report.[3]

The Basic Specialist Training guide of the Royal College of Anaesthetists states unequivocally that "no anaesthetist should be expected to work without properly trained assistants".

> *A Consultant and Registrar without non-medical assistance anaesthetized a patient (ASA 2, 77 years old) in a general hospital for an abdominoperineal excision of rectum. Critical events were reported in the questionnaire as bradycardia and hypotension. There was no anaesthetic record sent to us and no report of what instrumental monitoring was used. Atrial fibrillation and an assumed myocardial infarction developed seven days later; the patient died on the eleventh day but no autopsy was performed.*

A Senior Registrar anaesthetized an 86-year-old patient for a laparotomy for perforated bowel. The procedure started at 20.45 hours and lasted over two hours. The patient was ASA 5 and was comprehensively monitored, but hypotension was persistent until, after 2.5 litres of crystalloid and 800 ml of colloid, inotropes were used. The Senior Registrar was advised by a Consultant but otherwise worked solo in a District General Hospital. Furthermore, there was no non-medical assistance for the anaesthetist for this very poor risk patient who died two days later.

This patient was 78 years old (70kg, ASA 4, hypertensive) and was anaesthetized for a laparotomy by a Registrar, who had the DA. Help was sought and obtained from both a Senior Registrar and Consultant. There was no non-medical help provided. The four-hour operation (hemicolectomy) for carcinoma of the colon was performed by a Registrar after consultation with his Consultant. The ileum was torn during the operation. Arrhythmias developed in the recovery period, after an episode of possible aspiration, and the patient died 18 hours later. Bilateral adrenal haemorrhages were found at autopsy.

All these patients were probably doomed to die. Is it appropriate to expect medical staff to do all the unskilled tasks associated with anaesthesia and surgery **and** to attend to the acute changes in their patient's condition?

Table A53 (q 56)
Is there an anaesthetic record for this operation in the notes?

	Deaths (n=1616)		Index (n=1689)
Yes	1573		1654
No	40		21
Not answered	3		14

Most anaesthetic records are satisfactory but some are not. There were many instances when copies of anaesthetic records were not returned despite positive answers to this question. NCEPOD received a very few single sheets with unstructured writing without a grid for physiological variables. Most were not so unsatisfactory as this and there were many which were completed in an exemplary fashion. The grid is particularly useful because conscientious completion enables slow changes and trends to be noticed promptly.

> One Consultant Anaesthetist (FFARCS, 1964) gave an anaesthetic in a University Hospital for a prolonged and major procedure. He did not visit the patient beforehand but graded the 62-year-old patient as ASA 2. The patient had chronic rheumatoid arthritis and was described as "Cushingoid". No invasive arterial blood pressure monitoring was used for a transoral operation to remove the odontoid peg which lasted four and a half hours. There were nine recordings of non-invasive blood pressure and pulse during the operation. The patient died of a pulmonary embolism, despite prophylaxis with intermittent calf compression.

The inadequacy of the recordings is obvious but relatively unimportant in the light of the many other short-comings in the management by the anaesthetist of this patient. These may or may not have affected the outcome.

Table A54 (q 57a)
Did the patient receive intravenous fluids *during* the operation?

	Deaths (*n*=1616)	Index (*n*=1689)
Yes	1523	1474
No	83	206
Not known/not recorded	4	4
Not answered	6	5

Intravenous fluids during operation

Crystalloid

Dextrose 5%	79	58
Dextrose 4% saline 0.18%	178	185
Dextrose 10%	26	12
Saline 0.9%	383	243
Hartmann's (compound sodium lactate)	1022	1154
Other crystalloid	57	32

Colloid

Modified gelatin	668	424
Human albumin solution	65	22
Starch (HES)	101	65
Dextran	33	59
Mannitol	65	14
Other colloid	24	-

Blood

Whole blood	257	126
Red cell component	257	143
Other blood component	91*	16

* This figure included 21 patients who received pump blood in the process of cardiopulmonary bypass and 48 who received fresh frozen plasma.

Anaesthesia
References see page 300

The natures and volumes of intravenous fluids are often grossly inappropriate. The group of anaesthetists was forced to observe that many patients were over-transfused with fluids during and immediately after the operation. The two examples below suffice.

An 82-year-old patient who weighed 56kg (ASA 2) was anaesthetized in a District General Hospital for anterior resection of colon by a Consultant (FFARCS, 1982) and Registrar anaesthetist. He was given a general anaesthetic combined with an epidural. There was no blood loss. Five litres of fluid were given during the procedure and 2.5 litres afterwards. The central venous pressure was reported to have been measured but no record of its values appear on the anaesthetic record. Oxygen saturation figures were consistently recorded at 90-94% and the inspired oxygen concentration was 27% throughout. He was grossly hypertensive and had a tachycardia immediately after admission to the recovery room. He died the next day; autopsy showed pulmonary oedema, venous congestion and pleural effusions. The pathologist states the cause of death as acute heart failure "occasioned by the stress of surgery".

A Consultant Anaesthetist (FFARCS, 1983) anaesthetized an 84-year-old woman in an Independent Hospital for a scheduled total hip replacement. There was clinical and laboratory evidence of ischaemic heart disease, cardiac failure and renal impairment. Bradycardia and hypotension occurred during the operation. She remained drowsy afterwards and was given naloxone (although narcotic drugs were not used). Subsequently 7.5 litres of fluid were given in 24 hours despite the absence of urine output. She died the next day.

Table A55 (q 59a)
Were monitoring devices used during the management of this patient?

	Deaths (n=1616)	Index (n=1689)
Yes	1609	1687
No	-	-
Not answered	7	2

Table A56 (q 59bf)
Monitoring devices used (deaths)

(n=1616)

	Anaesthetic room*	Operating room
ECG	1058	1575
Pulse oximeter	994	1534
Indirect BP	901	1331
Pulse meter	137	252
Oesophageal or precordial (chest wall) stethoscope	37	42
Fresh gas O_2 analyser	147	581
Inspired gas O_2 analyser	139	823
Inspired anaesthetic vapour analyser	40	264
Expired CO_2 analyser	166	1112
Airway pressure gauge	246	1008
Ventilation volume	134	723
Ventilator disconnect device	196	1024
Peripheral nerve stimulator	28	325
Temperature	46	224
Urine output	130	568
Central venous pressure	109	399
Direct arterial BP (invasive)	151	371
Pulmonary arterial pressure	24	52
Intracranial pressure	1	7
Other	6	41

* The apparent discrepancy between the use of the anaesthetic room and the operating room is exaggerated by the fact that in 346 cases the section in the questionnaire for the anaesthetic room was blank. This may mean either that the room or the instruments were not used there.

Table A57 (q 59b to f)
Monitoring devices used (index)

	(n=1689)	
	Anaesthetic room*	Operating room
ECG	980	1654
Pulse oximeter	977	1648
Indirect BP	841	1583
Pulse meter	119	298
Oesophageal or precordial (chest wall) stethoscope	24	32
Fresh gas O_2 analyser	127	699
Inspired gas O_2 analyser	94	1011
Inspired anaesthetic vapour analyser	34	359
Expired CO_2 analyser	114	1312
Airway pressure gauge	130	1139
Ventilation volume	72	786
Ventilator disconnect device	109	1144
Peripheral nerve stimulator	24	364
Temperature	6	102
Urine output	25	237
Central venous presure	16	94
Direct arterial BP (invasive)	31	120
Pulmonary arterial pressure	4	8
Intracranial pressure	-	1
Other	1	15

NB this can be a multiple entry

* See note to Table A56.

It is quite clear that the clinical practice of anaesthesia has changed over the last ten years. More instrumental monitors are not only available but now they are used. Ninety-nine per cent of the deaths and 98% of the index cases were monitored with an electrocardiograph. Oximetry was used in 95% of patients who died and 98% index cases. This is one indicator of the high standards of anaesthesia revealed in this Enquiry and is a vivid illustration of improvement. The use of invasive vascular monitoring seems notably to have increased.

Expired carbon dioxide monitoring is still not so common as oximetry. Sixty-nine per cent and 78% of patients in the two groups were monitored in this way (see also Table A64).

Expired carbon dioxide analysis is one, although not the only, means whereby satisfactory airway management can be assured and its use may save lives. However the answers to question 68 indicate that many anaesthetists do not use capnography for this purpose. In 58% of deaths (53% of index cases) capnography was used to confirm accurate placement of the tracheal tube, perhaps after the tracheal tube was seen going through the cords, (see page 259). The other life-saving device is a ventilator disconnect device and 85% of patients who died and 83% index patients who received controlled ventilation of the lungs (q 67) were monitored with its aid. Some capnographs have apnoea alarms incorporated and these function as disconnect alarms.

The difference of usage of many instruments for monitoring according to the location (anaesthetic or operating room) persists. The NCEPOD 1990 Report[3] suggested that more departments should reconsider the use of anaesthetic rooms and perhaps certain patients should be anaesthetized in the operating room.

There were 125 coronary artery bypass grafts. Pulmonary artery pressure monitoring was used in 41 of these patients in the operating room.

Table A58 (q 60)
Was there any malfunction of monitoring equipment?

	Deaths (n=1616)	Index (n=1689)
Yes	17	23*
No	1571	1630
Not known/not recorded	6	10
Not answered	22	26

* Two reports concerned ventilator alarms which failed to function in a consistent manner, once because the inflation pressure in use was too low. A variety of gas analysers and automatic blood machines were reported to have broken down but none were related to a life-threatening event.

Total failure of electricity supplies just after induction of anaesthesia limits the usefulness of mains-powered monitors if there is no *back-up supply*.

> *An Associate Specialist (with the part 1 FRCA and 20 years' experience) anaesthetized a 75-year-old patient with diabetes and arteriosclerosis for a below knee amputation. There was a history of angina and antihypertensive therapy was already prescribed. Pethidine (75mg) was given in the premedication. Nitrous oxide, oxygen and halothane were breathed spontaneously through a laryngeal mask airway, after induction with propofol. Intramuscular pethidine (4 hourly prn) was prescribed for pain after operation. It is apparent from the record that the cessation of the electrical supply immediately after induction did not affect the management of the anaesthetic. The patient had a fatal pulmonary embolism seven days later: no prophylaxis had been given.*

Should surgery be postponed in these circumstances? There should always be a back-up electrical supply.

Table A59 (q 61)
Did anything hinder full monitoring?

	Deaths (n=1616)	Index (n=1689)
Yes	81	68
No	1506	1597
Not known/not recorded	3	7
Not answered	26	17

In 36 of the patients who died the non-availability of monitors particularly in the anaesthetic room was the given reason for the hindrance. The presence of extensive burns, gross obesity, or the absence of limbs was the source of physical limitation to full monitoring on 12 occasions.

All except three out of 68 answers amongst index cases were as a result of the non-availability of a variety of fundamental monitoring devices, often in the anaesthetic room.

Table A60 (q 62)
What was the position of the patient during surgery?

	Deaths (n=1616)	Index (n=1689)
Supine	1286	1097
Lateral	87	185
Prone	13	10
Sitting	7	8
Lithotomy	207	307
Other	7	72*
Not known/not recorded	1	4
Not answered	8	6

* Includes 26 in the head-up position, 18 head-down, 5 in the park bench (partly lateral position) and several in various combinations of position.

Table A61 (q 64)
What type of anaesthetic was used?

	Deaths (n=1616)	Index (n=1689)
General alone	1159	1291
Local infiltration alone	-	1
Regional alone	123	50
General and regional	162	205
General and local infiltration	69	72
Sedation alone	1	-
Sedation and local infiltration	4	1
Sedation and regional	96	69
Not answered	2*	-

* Refer to one lost anaesthetic record and one record which was not sent to us.

The use of regional anaesthesia in any combination (381 occasions amongst the deaths, 324 in the index cases) seems to be increasing slowly.

Table A62 (q 64)
What type of anaesthetic was used in solo practice (deaths)?

	All (n=1616)	%	Solo SHO (n=168)	%	Solo Consultant (n=462)	%
General alone	1159	71.7	136	80.9	313	67.8
Regional alone	123	7.6	14	8.3	43	9.3
General and regional	162	10.0	9	5.4	57	12.3
General and local infiltration	69	4.3	-		17	3.7
Sedation alone	1	0.1	-		-	
Sedation and local infiltration	4	0.2	1	0.6	2	0.4
Sedation and regional	96	5.9	8	4.8	30	6.5
Not answered	2	0.1	-		-	

We analysed the practice of solo Senior House Officers and that of solo Consultants amongst the deaths in the hope that some differences might be apparent. There were no obvious differences in the types of hospital involved, the nature of operation (emergency, urgent, scheduled, or elective), the interval between operation and death, the use of a recovery area, the use of monitoring devices, the incidence of early postoperative complications, or the place of death.

Senior House Officers were more likely than Consultants to use general anaesthesia alone, although the use of regional anaesthesia alone was similar. The combination was more favoured by the Consultants.

GENERAL ANAESTHESIA

Table A63 (q 65)

Did you take precautions *at induction* **to minimise pulmonary aspiration?**

	Deaths (*n*=1390)*	Index (*n*=1568)*
Yes	459	201
No	907	1352
Not known/not recorded	12	7
Not answered	12	8

Precautions

Cricoid pressure	357	81
Postural changes - head up	18	18
Postural changes - head down	2	5
Postural changes - lateral	2	1
Preoxygenation without inflation of the lungs	392	152
Aspiration of nasogastric tube	131	16
Other	6	1
Not answered	3	9

NB this can be a multiple entry

* This total refers to all those (Table A62) who received *general* anaesthesia.

Seventy-eight per cent of the 459 patients known to have had precautions taken, had cricoid pressure applied and 85% received oxygen beforehand without inflation of the lungs.

Table A64 (q 66)
How was the airway established during anaesthesia?

	Deaths (n=1390)	Index (n=1568)
Face mask (with or without oral airway)	63	67
Laryngeal mask	147	209
Orotracheal intubation	1140	1245
Nasotracheal intubation	25	69
Tracheostomy	28	15
Other*	30	19
Not answered	11	5

NB this can be a multiple entry

* Refers to patients in whom double lumen and (or) bronchial tubes were inserted.

Analysis of the answers to question 59 (for deaths) with the data of this table shows that 77% of patients whose tracheas were intubated (tube or tracheostomy) had expired carbon dioxide monitoring during the operation. The figure is 82% for index patients.

Table A65 (q 67)
What was the mode of ventilation during the operation?

	Deaths (n=1390)	Index (n=1568)
Spontaneous	196	220
Controlled	1176	1341
Both	10	3
Not answered	8	4

Table A66 (q 68)

If the trachea was intubated, how was the position of the tube confirmed?

	Deaths (n=1390)	Index (n=1568)
Tube seen passing through cords	1020	1241
Chest movement with inflation	967	1140
Auscultation	783	775
Expired CO_2 monitoring	801	833
Oesophageal detector device	7	4
Other*	32	31
Not known/not recorded	18	13
Not answered	220	246

NB this can be a multiple entry

* It is disappointing to have to comment that there are still anaesthetists (responding in both series of questionnaires) who consider that arterial blood gas analysis (five questionnaires) or oximetry (15 questionnaires) are appropriate methods whereby the position of a **tracheal** tube may be confirmed.

The differentiation between oesophageal and tracheal intubation should not be made on the basis of decreased oxygen saturation because this would only take place after an interval and valuable time be lost.

Oximetry is of course valuable in the event of accidental **bronchial** intubation[51] and it is possible that some of the these 15 refer to this application. Other appropriate confirmatory techniques included fibreoptic bronchoscopy and the use of chest x-ray when the tube was already in place beforehand.

Table A67 (q 69)
Were muscle relaxants used during the anaesthetic?

	Deaths (*n*=1390)		Index (*n*=1568)
Yes	1182		1363
No	201		201
Not known/not recorded	2		-
Not answered	5		4
Relaxants			
Depolarising	445		257
Non-depolarising	1100		1282
Not answered	6		7

NB this can be a multiple entry

The fact that 29% of patients who subsequently died and who received non-depolarising muscle relaxant drugs were monitored with a peripheral nerve stimulator may not be surprising but it does seem to indicate that this device is not regarded highly by anaesthetists. Many anaesthetists do not use a neuromuscular monitor. These are relatively inexpensive items, could be more widely available and are useful aids when modern neuromuscular blocking agents are given.

Table A68 (q 70)
How was general anaesthesia maintained?

	Deaths (*n*=1390)		Index (*n*=1568)
Nitrous oxide	1262		1512
Volatile agent	1274		1501
Narcotic agent	1001		1160
Intravenous	154		88
Not answered	8		5

NB this can be a multiple entry

Table A69 (q 71)
Were there any problems with airway maintenance or ventilation?

	Deaths (n=1390)		Index (n=1568)
Yes	62		32
No	1316		1521
Not known/not recorded	5		7
Not answered	7		8

These cases illustrate vividly the value of oximetry. Many questionnaires state that the problem was detected because the oxygen saturation was noted to be declining. Pulmonary oedema, pulmonary haemorrhage, excessive secretions, pneumothorax and accidental bronchial intubation were all diagnosed after desaturation was noted.

Difficulty with the airway was also noted at laryngoscopy.

Table A70 (q 72)
Was the method of airway management changed during the operation?

	Deaths (n=1390)		Index (n=1568)
Yes	61		30
No	1324		1530
Not answered	5		8

There was no instance when the change of airway management was the result of a serious event and most may be regarded as routine.

REGIONAL ANAESTHESIA

Table A71 (q 74)

If the anaesthetic included a regional technique, which method was used?

	Deaths (n=381)		Index (n=324)
Epidural - caudal	17		45
- lumbar	67		86
- thoracic	36		24
Interpleural	-		1
Intravenous regional	-		-
Peripheral nerve block	32		18
Plexus block	6		10
Subarachnoid (spinal)	225		145
Surface	4		3
Not answered	-		1

NB this can be a multiple entry

Table A72 (q 75)

Which agent was used?

	Deaths (n=381)		Index (n=324)
Local	377		315
Narcotic	42		61
Other	1*		-
Not answered	2		5

NB this can be a multiple entry

* This patient was reported to have received clonidine into the epidural space.

SEDATION (as opposed to General Anaesthesia)

Table A73 (q 76)
Which sedative drugs were given for this procedure (excluding premedication)?

	Deaths (n=101)	Index (n=70)
Inhalant	7	5
Narcotic analgesic	7	6
Benzodiazepine	86	50
Sub-anaesthetic doses of IV anaesthetic drugs	15	25
Other	1	3*
Not answered	-	1

NB this can be a multiple entry

* Droperidol was given on these three occasions.

Table A74 (q 77)
Was oxygen given?

	Deaths (n=224)	Index (n=120)
Yes	188	99
No	17	16
Not known/not recorded	2	2
Not answered	17	3
Indication		
Routine	162	93
Otherwise indicated*	35	6
Not answered	2	3

NB this can be a multiple entry

* These all appeared to be soundly based clinical indications (e.g. low oxygen saturation, pulmonary oedema, restlessness).

The anaesthetic questionnaire suggested that this question should be answered if sedation and (or) regional anaesthesia were performed. Oxygen administration (84%) is commendable. Some anaesthetists might think that this percentage should be higher in this group of patients.

SPECIAL CARE AREAS
Table A75 (q 78)
Which special care areas are available in the hospital in which the operation took place?

	Deaths (n=1616)		Index (n=1689)
Recovery area or room*	1446		1626
High dependency unit (HDU)*	284		313
Intensive care unit (ICU)*	1180		959
Other	51		32
Not answered	29		14

NB this can be a multiple entry

* see Glossary, Appendix B for definitions

The descriptive term "special care area" is naturally not interpreted identically by all respondents. The "other" group amongst the deaths contained: 22 reports which referred to cardiac surgical, coronary care, cardiac intensive care, postoperative cardiac intensive care, cardiac recovery unit or cardiothoracic units; 15 reports to neurosurgical units; 4 to renal units, 1 to "special nose care" and the remainder to a mixture of other locations. There were similar descriptions amongst the index cases.

The answers to 170 questionnaires (deaths) and 63 index cases indicate that no recovery room was available in the hospital. This figure must not be extrapolated to numbers of hospitals, but it does suggest that there are still at least several which do not provide this basic service for safe surgery.

Comparison with the previous NCEPOD 1990 Report[3] shows that there is little change in the provision of HDUs amongst both series of patients.

It is important in this context to emphasise that the mere existence of an area or room labelled 'recovery' does not satisfy the clinical need for this essential service. Recovery rooms must be suitably equipped and staffed with trained personnel 24 hours a day.

Table A76 (q 79)
After leaving the operating room, did the patient go to a specific recovery area or room?

	Deaths (n=1616)		Index (n=1689)
Yes	1142		1551
No	422		134
Died in theatre*	47		N/A
Not known/not recorded	2		1
Not answered	3		3

* The difference between this table and table A96 (q 96) is accounted for by the fact that three patients returned to theatre for further operations and died there.

Anaesthesia
References see page 300

Table A77 (q 80)

Were you unable at any time to transfer the patient into an ICU, HDU etc?

	Deaths (*n*=1616)		Index (*n*=1689)
Yes	51		39
No	1408		1514
Not known/not recorded	6		8
Not answered	151		128
If yes, why?			
Closed at night	2		1
Closed at weekend	-		1
Understaffing	5		4
No HDU in hospital	4		11
No ICU	1		9
Lack of beds	32		14
Other	3		5
Not answered	7		4

NB this can be a multiple entry

One patient amongst the deaths had to be denied admission because of an outbreak of a drug-resistant infection in the unit.

Difficult decisions

> *A Consultant anaesthetized an 89-year-old patient in a District General Hospital. The patient was mentally retarded and in congestive cardiac failure (described as ASA 4) but a total hip replacement (for painful osteoarthritis) was undertaken. He died the next day in left ventricular failure possibly after a myocardial infarction. "A decision had been taken between the surgeons, anaesthetist and relatives that we would do the operation even though he was a high risk. He was not to be admitted to ICU in view of his ill-health and age".*

This may be the appropriate management of scarce resources (ICU), but what about the resources for anaesthesia, orthopaedic surgery and the prosthesis? The prognosis was appalling; should any operation at all have been undertaken having decided not to treat its probable complications?

The matter of rational use of resources is always difficult particularly when they are scarce. One particularly tragic case is an example of the problem.

> A Consultant Anaesthetist (FFARCS, 1985), assisted by a Senior House Officer in a District General Hospital, anaesthetized a 52-year-old woman who had no living relatives, was partially sighted, severely physically handicapped from cerebral palsy and had faecal peritonitis from perforated diverticulitis. Aspiration of stomach contents into the lungs happened before induction of anaesthesia at which time she was already severely hypotensive. A Registrar surgeon performed the operation after consultation with his Consultant Surgeon. The anaesthetist states "aggressive medical therapy and intensive care facilities were not appropriate".

Who can disagree, but why then was the operation done?

Table A78 (q 81a)
Were monitoring devices used during the management of this patient in the recovery room?

	Deaths (n=1142)	Index (n=1551)
Yes	1083	1470
No	33	58
Not known/not recorded	12	14
Not answered	14	9

Fifteen patients died in the recovery room (Table A96, page 285) but all these were monitored at least with pulse oximetry. Thirty-three patients did not receive standard monitoring in the recovery room: NCEPOD does not know about the *availability* of instruments for monitoring either in the recovery or operating room.

Table A79 (q 81b to f)
Monitoring devices used in recovery

	Deaths (n=1142)	Index (n=1551)
ECG	538	566
Pulse oximeter	834	1114
Indirect BP	1026	1378
Pulse meter	115	144
Oesophageal or precordial (chest wall)	5	8
Stethoscope		
Inspired gas O_2 analyser	14	8
Expired CO_2 analyser	11	3
Airway pressure gauge	21	3
Ventilation volume	20	3
Ventilator disconnect device	18	3
Peripheral nerve stimulator	8	4
Temperature	85	92
Urine output	194	162
CVP	69	23
Direct arterial BP (invasive)	35	16
Pulmonary arterial pressure	2	-
Intracranial pressure	-	-
Other*	13	4

NB this can be a multiple entry

* Most of these patients were diabetics who had blood glucose estimations performed.

One can anticipate that the use of oximetry in the recovery room will soon match its use in theatre. The NCEPOD 1990 Report[3] showed that 52% of those patients who died were monitored in the recovery room with oximetry. The figure here is 73%.

Table A80 (q 82)
Who decided that the patient should be discharged from the recovery room?

	Deaths (*n*=1142)	Index (*n*=1551)
The most senior anaesthetist	653	782
Another anaesthetist	92	72
Surgeon	12	16
Nurse	318	654
Other	7	1
Not applicable (i.e. died in recovery room)	15	-
Not known/not recorded	21	14
Not answered	24	12

The respective roles of nurses and anaesthetists in the decision about individual patients is usually determined by customary local practice but this might be improved were there to be written protocols about criteria to be met by every patient before their discharge to wards. The routine use of oximetry before induction and during recovery would enable clinicians to state that all patients should have a saturation equivalent to, or better than, that before operation before they were returned to the ward. If this figure were not to be achieved medical review would follow. Furthermore, a local protocol would aid the prescription of supplementary oxygen on the wards. This might prevent premature discharge of patients after major operations particularly when this is done merely to make room for the next patient.

Table A81 (q 84)
Had this patient recovered protective reflexes before discharge from the recovery area?

	Deaths (*n*=1142)	Index (*n*=1551)
Yes	999	1486
No	45	11
Not known	57	39
Not applicable (died in recovery area)	15	-
Not answered	26	15

Table A82 (q 85)
Where did this patient go next (after the recovery area)?

	Deaths (n=1142)		Index (n=1551)
Ward	989		1445
High dependency unit	43		64
Intensive care unit	55		20
Specialised ICU	27		5
Home	-		3
Another hospital	2		-
Other	3*		8**
Not applicable (death in recovery area)	15		-
Not answered	8		6

* Back to theatre

** Five patients were in private (individual) rooms and three were in intensive nursing areas on wards.

Table A83 (q 86)
Where did the patient go on leaving the operating room?

	Deaths (n=422)*		Index (n=134)*
Ward	12**		16
High dependency unit	17		11
Intensive care unit	278		59
Specialised ICU	101		20
Another hospital	1		-
Other	-		6
Not answered	13		22

* patients who did not go to a specific recovery area

** Five of the 12 patients who died had craniotomies and went directly to the ward and in three of these patients it was obvious that a decision was taken that treatment should be abandoned. There was no explanation offered in three questionnaires. Three other questionnaires stated that the recovery room was not staffed at night. One patient was discharged to an ENT ward to be "specialled" after a tracheostomy; "a recovery room was not necessary". The tube blocked and she died.

Recovery room

Recovery from anaesthesia can be hazardous. There were four questionnaires for index cases which stated that recovery took place in a corridor. One patient was a child in a University Hospital. One patient had a total hip replacement in a District General Hospital, one had an operation for detached retina and one had induced hypotension for a middle ear operation. NCEPOD was not told why this happened, although in three instances it was clear that there was no recovery room in the hospital, and no harm occurred.

These hospitals may not of course be recognised for training by The Royal College of Anaesthetists (although trainees were involved in two of the anaesthetics) but most questionnaires (89% deaths, 96% index cases) affirm the availability of recovery rooms for patients. This indicates that this provision is so widespread that it could now be regarded as obligatory.

There are three case reports in which the use of a recovery room may have been appropriate. There are several points in addition, which need consideration.

A Registrar (who started training in 1986 but did not state the date of his FFARCS diploma) performed a continuous epidural anaesthetic in the early evening in a District General Hospital for a 71-year-old, ASA 4 man (untreated atrial fibrillation, pleural effusion, renal failure, jaundice) who had a leg amputated by a Registrar surgeon. The Registrar anaesthetist did not consult with anyone. There was no surgical form returned to NCEPOD. He was discharged to the ward with an epidural infusion of bupivacaine. The patient died three days later of respiratory failure. There was no explanation why the available essential services were not used.

A Consultant (FFARCS, 1981) anaesthetized an 80-year-old patient in a District General Hospital. A laparotomy and colostomy were done by a Registrar Surgeon but the patient died one hour later at 02.30hours. The recovery room was closed at night. No surgical form was returned to NCEPOD.

A Senior House Officer anaesthetist (qualified 1987, no qualifications in anaesthesia) consulted a Senior Registrar about an 81-year-old patient who needed to have a laparotomy for intestinal obstruction caused by carcinoma of the colon. There is an impeccable anaesthetic record. A Hartmann's procedure was done by a Registrar at midnight. No Consultant Surgeon was involved at all. The recovery room was not open at night so the patient was discharged to the ward at 04.00hours. Papaveretum 10mg 1M was prescribed on demand and the patient died 13 hours later. An autopsy was done, the report was available to the Registrar Surgeon who stated "we knew why he died; he was old, infirm, and with a life-threatening condition". The postmortem report was not sent to NCEPOD.

The common feature of these three reports is that no recovery room was available when trainee staff were operating on sick patients. Should patients with continuous regional anaesthesia be sent back to a ward? Should patients be sent back to the ward to die so soon after operation? Should such patients be sent back to the ward at night when it is known that nursing staff may be at a premium? How is the Registrar surgeon to learn if the Consultant Surgeon is not involved?

Table A84 (q 87)
Was controlled ventilation used postoperatively?

	Deaths (n=1616)		Index (n=1689)
Yes	386		59
No	1059		1507
Not answered	109		123
Not applicable	62		-
(patient died in theatre or recovery area)			
If yes, why?			
Respiratory inadequacy	170		9
Control of intracranial pressure or other neurosurgical indications	83		4
Part of the management of pain	60		17
Other reasons	190*		41
Not answered	15		3

NB this can be a multiple entry

* Most in this category were patients after cardiopulmonary bypass surgery and ventilation of the lungs was part of routine practice. A substantial number of cases were elderly, septic, cold or those whose lungs were ventilated until cardiovascular stability was achieved.

CRITICAL INCIDENTS DURING ANAESTHESIA AND RECOVERY

Table A85 (q 88a)
Did any events, which required specific treatment, occur during anaesthesia or recovery?

	Deaths (n=1616)	Index (n=1689)
Yes	415	142
No	1141	1490
Not known/not recorded	4	3
Not answered	56	54

Table A86 (q88)
Did any events which required specific treatment, occur during anaesthesia or recovery when the anaesthetist was working alone?

	Deaths			
	Solo Senior House Officer		Solo Consultant	
	(n=168)	%	(n=462)	%
Yes	30	17.8	109	23.6
No	135	80.4	340	73.6
Not answered	2	1.2	12	2.6
Not known/not recorded	1	0.6	1	0.2

Events which needed special treatment during operation or recovery were slightly more frequent in the Consultants' practice.

Table A87 (q 88b)
Critical incidents

	Deaths (n=1616)	Index (n=1689)
Air embolus	1	1
Airway obstruction	18	2
Anaphylaxis	1	-
Arrhythmia	106	39
Bronchospasm	15	9
Cardiac arrest (unintended)	73	1
Convulsions	5	1
Cyanosis	34	4
Disconnection of breathing system	1	2
Hyperpyrexia	1	-
Hypertension	21	12
Hypotension	215	55
Hypoxia	53	6
Misplaced tracheal tube	4	3
Pneumothorax	6	-
Pulmonary aspiration	4	-
Pulmonary oedema	30	-
Respiratory arrest (unintended)	17	3
Wrong dose or overdose of drug	4	-
Other	54*	14

NB this can be a multiple entry

* These include 13 cases of haemorrhage, eight cases of respiratory inadequacy, five ischaemic records on ECG, and two surgical mishaps.

Many of these *are* multiple entries; nevertheless the rate of occurrence of these events is 4.5 times greater amongst the deaths than amongst the index cases.

CRITICAL INCIDENTS (DEATHS)

Airway obstruction

There was one death, amongst 18 reports, which may have important lessons.

> *A 64-year-old patient had carcinoma of the floor of the mouth which was treated in a District General Hospital by a 12-hour freeflap reconstruction. A series of operations had been done previously including hemimandibulectomy seven years earlier. The nasotracheal tube was removed at the end of the operation. Airway obstruction developed while he was in the recovery room. A Senior Registrar anaesthetist had apparently managed this solo (with the non-medical assistance of an ODA). There were no beds in the ICU and so the patient was kept in the recovery room. He became restless. Junior oral surgical staff managed him initially with two doses of intramuscular papaveretum (20mg and 10mg) at 2.75 hours intervals. One hour after the second dose the duty Consultant and Senior House Officer were called from another emergency case to assist with resuscitation which failed. Autopsy showed widespread oedema in the neck and larynx. Death was as a result of cerebral hypoxia.*

Should the non-urgent operation have been carried out when it was known that there were no beds available in the ICU? Should the anaesthetist have removed the nasotracheal tube so soon, should a tracheostomy have been done and should junior oral surgical staff (who may not have medical qualifications) be left to be responsible for such a compromised airway?

Anaphylaxis (or possible)

There was one report amongst the deaths.

> *A 26-year-old woman was to have a total dental clearance in a District General Hospital. Premedication was with 5mg morphine and 0.3mg atropine. She was anaesthetized by a Consultant (FFARCS, 1976) with propofol and suxamethonium given through a 23-gauge cannula and the mouth was infiltrated with prilocaine and octapressin (presumably by the oral surgeon but no surgical questionnaire was received by NCEPOD). The patient became cyanosed after induction and bronchospasm developed. There was no hypotension at this stage. The nasotracheal tube was changed for an orotracheal one and two doses of hydrocortisone and chlorpheniramine were given and 0.1mg naloxone. No operation was done and she was moved to the ICU where alcuronium was given presumably to facilitate IPPV. The reaction continued (or another developed) and was managed with fluids and "vasopressors". The diagnosis was confirmed by laboratory tests. She died on the third day.*

The word *adrenaline* occurs neither on the questionnaire nor on the anaesthetic record.

Bronchospasm and hypotension were reported on a questionnaire completed by a Registrar (qualified 1972, no other qualifications admitted). A Consultant's advice was sought. The patient was 64 years old and had a hiatus hernia which prevented her from lying flat. A laparotomy followed by a Hartmann's operation was done between 23.00 hours and 01.15 hours by a Registrar surgeon; the delay was because of over-running of elective lists. The systolic blood pressure became unrecordable at induction of anaesthesia (thiopentone and suxamethonium with cricoid pressure) but after 15 minutes reached 80 mmHg. The CVP was then 22 cm H_2O after 2.5 litres of intravenous fluid. A nasogastric tube was inserted at this time. Ventilation of the lungs was with 100% oxygen. The bowel was found to be perforated and the patient become septicaemic. She died 11 days later on the ward after a period of IPPV in the ICU.

Was this also anaphylaxis (not so diagnosed)?

A 90-kg man was admitted for a dacrocystorhinostomy by ophthalmic surgeons. The anaesthetist noted a large pharyngeal swelling after induction of anaesthesia and the dacrocystorhinostomy operation was abandoned. He was 51 years of age and was described as ASA 2 by a Clinical Assistant (qualified 1961, 18 years in anaesthesia but no qualifications) who was to anaesthetize him for his radical pharyngeal operation in a District General Hospital, three weeks later. No anaesthetic record was received by NCEPOD but the almost indecipherable surgical note indicates that his chest stopped moving early in the procedure. Cardiorespiratory resuscitation including treatment with bronchodilators and steroids was unavailing and autopsy revealed widespread severe coronary artery disease but no evidence of a recent infarct. No more details are available.

Was this the result of a tracheal tube misplacement/dislodgement, disconnexion, anaphylaxis or a severe arrhythmia? The absence of the anaesthetic record precludes further comment.

Pulmonary aspiration

> *A Consultant (FFARCS, 1978) and a Senior House Officer anaesthetized this 84-year-old man (ASA 4) for an urgent laparotomy for perforated diverticulitis. Oximetry was not used in the anaesthetic room during induction of anaesthesia. A nasogastric tube was in place before the operation. Local anaesthetic was injected through the cricothyroid membrane into the trachea and directly sprayed onto the vocal cords before awake tracheal intubation. The patient was lying in the head up position. He vomited during the tracheal intubation, aspirated stomach contents, suffered unremitting bronchospasm during the procedure and died nine days later of persistent respiratory failure.*

An attempt to empty the stomach should always be made before operation although it should be well known that this does not guarantee that the stomach will be empty.

Should the anaesthetic technique be modified when there is an obvious risk of regurgitation?

Regurgitation

> *A Senior House Officer, advised by a Clinical Assistant, anaesthetized an 82-year-old patient, who was found to have ischaemic bowel, in a District General Hospital. The most senior anaesthetist in the operating room had no qualifications in anaesthesia. The patient was described as ASA 4 although there was not much evidence for this classification in the questionnaire. The anaesthetic record was not sent to NCEPOD. The operating surgeon was a Consultant. The surgical questionnaire states that the stomach was emptied before operation but there is no indication of this in the anaesthetic questionnaire. No narcotics were prescribed. Four hours after the operation (on a Sunday) for an internal hernia with bowel strangulation the patient was discovered to have aspirated stomach contents and died on the ward after numerous attempts at resuscitation. The decision to abandon resuscitation was, it is reported by the Consultant Surgeon, taken by "the anaesthetist."*

Were the supervison of this anaesthetist, and the patient's discharge to the ward, appropriate?

Anaesthesia
References see page 300

Respiratory arrest

A Senior House Officer (without qualifications in anaesthesia) in a University Hospital was to manage a 78-year-old woman (ASA 4) for a sigmoid colectomy without any advice or help from a Consultant Anaesthetist. A Senior Surgical Registrar infiltrated local anaesthetic for the bowel resection and colostomy. The patient was sedated with intermittent midazolam to a total of 7.5mg given before and during the hour-long procedure. Respiratory arrest occurred in the immediate recovery period (treated with flumenazil) and the patient died of respiratory failure nine days later.

Would a more senior anaesthetist have chosen a different technique?

A solo Consultant (FFARCS, 1971) anaesthetized an 80-year-old patient in a District General Hospital, for a sigmoid colectomy. There was an adenocarcinoma of the colon but the surgical questionnaire was not received by NCEPOD. The surgeon was a Consultant. Chronic obstructive airways disease, ischaemic heart disease (previous infarction 18 years ago, angina) and intermittent claudication were being treated. A thoracic epidural with local anaesthetic was combined with general anaesthesia. Systolic hypotension was managed solely with fluids (2 litres Ringer lactate, 1 litre polygeline and 500ml Dextran 70). There was an estimated 300-ml blood loss and 30ml of urine collected over the two-hour operation. The fluid balance charts for the 48-hour period before death showed a positive balance of 7 litres. No central venous pressure measurements were made. During the immediate recovery the patient complained of angina which was unresponsive to nitrates. Agitation was managed with midazolam which provoked apnoea. Intravenous fentanyl had been used and diamorphine was being given into the epidural space; naloxone reversed the apnoea. Later recovery was complicated also by frequent anginal episodes, oliguria, hypotension, congestive cardiac failure refractory to inotropes and death occurred in the ICU to which he could not be admitted immediately after operation because of lack of beds.

It seems doubtful that the outcome would have been different whatever else were done (medical assistance, central venous pressure measurements and early admission to ICU).

Anaesthesia
References see page 300

Unintended cardiac arrest

> *A Consultant Anaesthetist (FFARCS, 1977) assisted by a Senior House Officer managed this 81-year-old patient in a District General Hospital. He was to have an operation for a strangulated hernia but he also had chronic obstructive airways disease and a hiatus hernia. The non-invasive automatic blood pressure monitor did not function "due to excessive patient movement" (was he already hypoxic?). A spinal injection of 3ml 0.5% bupivacaine was given; this was accompanied by oxygen administration but sedative drugs were not given. The patient regurgitated on the table, minor aspiration occurred, and cardiac arrest followed. Full resuscitation failed. The autopsy showed the presence of 80% coronary obstruction and the pathologist opined that the presence of a hiatus hernia had not contributed to the death!*

Pathologists should not make statements which, while laudably supportive of their clinical colleagues, are contrary to the available evidence. The presence of such a coronary disability ensures that these patients are at extreme risk. *Any* threat to the integrity of the airway or even a minor cardiovascular incident in these circumstances may prove lethal.

It is also important that clinicians should be encouraged to attend autopsies so that erroneous comments do not appear on what are public records.

> *A Consultant Anaesthetist (FFARCS, 1989) and a Registrar were responsible for the anaesthetic for this 82-year-old patient in a University Hospital, who was to have a transurethral resection of prostate. He had paroxysmal atrial tachycardia, treated with disopyramide, and was graded as ASA 2. He had a spinal (3.5ml, 2% lignocaine) supplemented with midazolam 2mg intravenously and oxygen was administered as a routine. Nausea, bradycardia and hypotension developed (from 180 to 90 mmHg systolic in 10 minutes) and did not respond to ephedrine, atropine or adrenaline. An anti-emetic was given. Hypoxaemia and loss of consciousness developed and despite paralysis, tracheal intubation IPPV with oxygen, and transvenous pacing, resuscitation had to be abandoned. Autopsy showed 50% reduction in lumen of coronary vessels.*

Spinal or epidural anaesthesia, while excellent for the young and healthy, may not be any safer than general anaesthesia in the elderly or infirm, particularly in the presence of ischaemic heart disease; both are relatively contraindicated in patients with intestinal obstruction. Surgeons need to be informed that spinal or epidural anaesthesia may be no less hazardous than general anaesthesia.

Critical incidents - others

Some of these were supplementary to other events mentioned or similar to these above and many were records of surgical mishaps, commonly surgical damage to adjacent organs or haemorrhage.

Table A88 (q 15/16/88)

Analysis of number of days between operation and death by whether or not a critical incident occurred

(*n*=1616)

	Death same day (*n*=130)		Death next day (n=167)		Death second day (*n*=156)		All deaths (*n*=1616)	
Critical incident	84	65%	66	40%	43	28%	415	26%
No critical incident	39		95		106		1141	
Not known/not recorded	-		2		-		4	
Not answered	7		4		7		56	

Many of the critical events listed are potentially lethal. Nevertheless it is obvious from the table above that more tend to occur when the patient dies on the same day than when death is later. Thus the occurrence of one or more of these events (not strictly critical incidents) may indicate that the patient may die.

Figure A7 (q 15/16/88)
Incidence of critical events according to the day of death

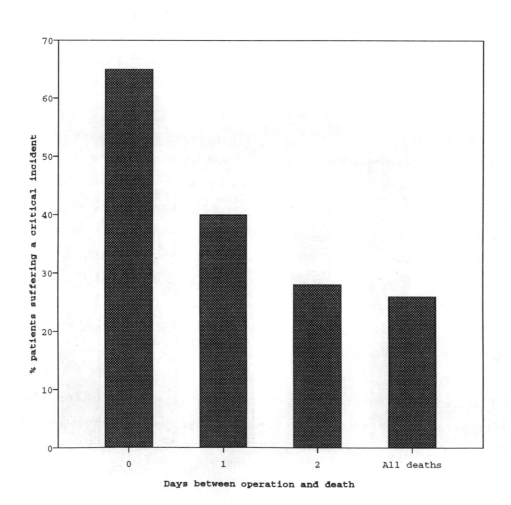

Table A89 (qs 39 and 88)
Occurrence of critical incidents by ASA grade (deaths)

				(n=1616) ASA grade			
	All	1	2	3	4	5	Not answered
All deaths	1616	42	340	623	461	143	7
Critical incident	415	12 *29%*	83 *24%*	149 *24%*	117 *25%*	54 *38%*	-
No critical incident	1141	30	251	449	321	84	6
Not stated/not known	60	-	6	25	23	5	1

The rate of occurrence of critical incidents is not correlated with the ASA grade. There is a suggestion that the occurrence of such an incident in a patient who is ASA 5 may be associated with subsequent death.

Figure A8 (see Table A89)
Occurrence of critical incidents by ASA grade

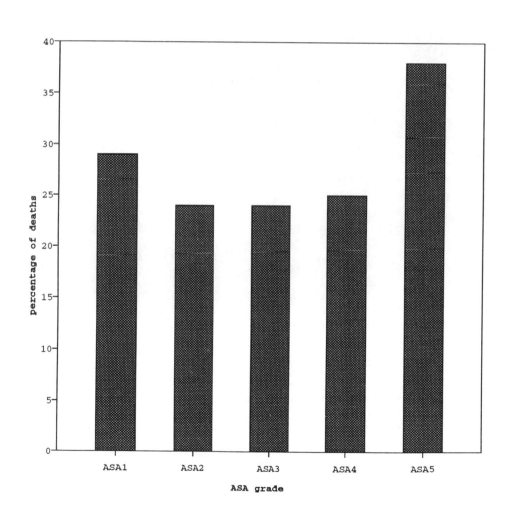

Table A90 (qs 39 and 88)
Occurrence of critical incidents by ASA grade (index)

	All	1		2		3		4		5	Not answered
				(n=1689) ASA grade							
All index cases	1689	759		693		208		27		-	2
Critical incident	142	55	7%	56	8%	28	13%	3	11%	-	-
No critical incident	1490	686		607		172		23		-	2
Not stated/not known	57	18		30		8		1		-	-

The relative rarity of critical events amongst the index cases is obvious.

Table A91 (q 89)

Was there any mechanical failure of equipment (excluding that for monitoring)?

	Deaths (*n*=1616)		Index (*n*=1689)
Yes	1		2
No	1534		1634
Not known/not recorded	6		5
Not answered	75		48

Mechanical failure

	Deaths		Index
Diathermy	-		1
Not specified	1		1

Table A92 (q 90)

Were there early (i.e. up to 7 days) complications or events after this operation?

	Deaths (*n*=1616)		Index (*n*=1689)
Yes	1154		230
No	342		1418
Not known/not recorded	2		2
Not answered	56		39
Not applicable (i.e. death in theatre or recovery area)	62		-

Complications or events

	Deaths		Index
Ventilatory problems	504		52
Cardiac problems	556		34
Hepatic failure	25		-
Septicaemia	179		7
Renal failure	233		4
Central nervous system failure	250		8
Other	215*		152**

NB this can be a multiple entry

* Fifty-three cases of overt haemorrhage or severe coagulation problems.

** Twenty-seven cases of haemorrhage which ranged in severity from a haematoma to occasional gross anaemia (Hb 5gm.dl^{-1}) which required transfusion. Wound and urinary tract infections or pyrexia of unknown source accounted for another 44 cases. There were two reports of postoperative dislocation of hip.

ANALGESIA

Table A93 (q 91)
Were narcotic analgesic drugs given in the first 48 hours after operation?

	Deaths (*n*=1616)	Index (*n*=1689)
Yes	1204	1259
No	315	405
Not known/not recorded	8	6
Not answered	27	19
Not applicable (i.e. death in theatre or recovery area)	62	-

This vignette tells a tragic story of a failure of medical care, not to keep a patient alive, but to ease his passing.

He was 84 years old. He was admitted to a District General Hospital from a residential home. He had ischaemic heart disease and had a pacemaker in place. He was kyphotic, hypothyroid, had glaucoma and a pleural effusion. He was described as ASA 4 and required bilateral amputations because of iliac occlusion. The surgeon was a Senior Registrar. No premedication was given. Seventy milligrams of thiopentone, atropine, atracurium and nitrous oxide (delivered by IPPV) were the sole drugs during the operation given by a Consultant Anaesthetist (FFARCS, 1968). Hypotension was treated with polygeline and by the time he reached the recovery room the blood pressure was normal. He progressively deteriorated and died the next day. No analgesics were given to him at any time.

Even the sickest patients require analgesia, perhaps without operation.

Table A94 (q 92)
Did complications occur as a result of these analgesic methods?

	Deaths (*n*=1204)	Index (*n*=1259)
Yes	48	36*
No	1141	1210
Not known/not recorded	4	1
Not answered	11	12

* Includes 16 cases of nausea and/or vomiting, seven cases of reduced rate of breathing and two cases of hypotension.

Table A95 (q 93)

Were other sedative/hypnotic or other analgesic (non-narcotic) drugs given?

	Deaths (n=1616)	Index (n=1689)
Yes	557	891
No	897	725
Not known/not recorded	8	7
Not answered	92	66
Not applicable (death in theatre or recovery area)	62	-

DEATH

Table A96 (q 96)
Place of death

	(n=1616)
Theatre	50
Recovery area	15
Intensive care unit	414
High dependency unit	44
Ward	985
Home	28
Another hospital	37
Other	28
Not known/not recorded	5
Not answered	10

Comments about appropriate locations for patients after operation have already been made. There are still too many who are discharged from the operating and recovery suite direct to the ward. One patient (see below) could reasonably be considered to have recovered from his operation and therefore to be safe.

> *A 49-year-old patient underwent uneventful surgery and anaesthesia for a single internal mammary artery coronary graft in an Independent Hospital. He was found dead in bed on the fourth day after operation. Death was timed at between 02.10 and 04.30 hours, and presumably was not discovered because he was in a single room.*

There are thus some advantages to open-plan wards for observation of patients but there is no indication why he died.

Table A97 (q 97, death questionnaires)
Do you have morbidity/mortality review meetings in your department?

	(*n*=1616)
Yes	1523
No	81
Not answered	12

It is encouraging that 94% of the respondents could go to mortality review meetings.

If yes, was this case discussed at departmental meeting?

	(*n*=1523)
Yes	480
No	1013
Not known	6
Not answered	24

Hospital type in which deaths occurred but which did not hold morbidity/mortality meetings

	(*n*=81)
District General Hospital	55
University/Teaching Hospital	9
Single Surgical Specialty	9
Other Acute/Partly Acute Hospital	1
Community Hospital	1
Independent Hospital	6

DISCHARGE (index cases)

Table A98 (q 95 index)
Was the date of discharge later than anticipated?

	(*n*=1689)
Yes	118
No	1464
Not yet discharged	1
Not known/not recorded	31
Not answered	75

None of the reasons given appear to be related to the anaesthetic at all. Most of the delays were for minor surgical complications or for social reasons.

Table A99 (q 96 index)
To which destination was the patient discharged?

	(*n*=1689)
Home	1601
Another hospital	41
Convalescent home	23
Rehabilitation	4
Other	13*
Not yet discharged	1
Not known/not recorded	2
Not answered	4

* Most of these were discharged to nursing homes or sheltered accommodation.

AUDIT MEETINGS (index cases)

Table A100 (q 97 index)
Do you have audit meetings in your department?

	(*n*=1689)
Yes	1631
No	39
Not answered	19

It is encouraging that audit meetings are held in connexion with 97% index cases.

Type of hospital in which audit meetings are not held:

	(*n*=39)
District General	19
University/Teaching	5
Surgical Specialty	4
Other Acute/Partly acute	1
Defence Medical Services	2
Independent	8

Table A101 (q 98 index)
Do you have meetings combined with other disciplines?

	(*n*=1689)
Yes	1255
No	402
Not answered	32

SPECIFIC SURGICAL PROCEDURES

Table A102
Anaesthetic questionnaires received and requested

| | Deaths | | Index | |
	received	requested	received	requested
Amputation of part or whole of lower limb	417	696	38	+
Management of strangulated hernia	54	100	6	+
Colorectal resection	314	467	175	+
Any breast surgery	21	36	103	+
Oesophagectomy	60	103	28	+
Pulmonary resection	25	42	19	++
Coronary artery bypass	125	297	32	++
Hysterectomy	65	83	413	783
Prostatectomy	167	238	171	328
Any craniotomy	173	335	37**	103
Total hip replacement	83	134	289	725
Management of burns	16	25	27	98
Any oral/maxillofacial	24	42	79*	198
Any ENT surgery	56	97	158*	408
Any ophthalmic surgery	16	44	114*	379

* Operation time greater than one hour
** Posterior fossa exploration

+   942 combined   (see pages 19 and 39 for full explanation)

++ 132 combined   (see pages 19 and 39 for full explanation)

The numbers in the two series are very different and this, apart from any other differences, makes comparisons between deaths and index cases for specific operations difficult if not impossible. The poor response rates are understandable but very low. Those whose specialty had many deaths were naturally less enthusiastic about the return of index questionnaires.

The table shows the number of questionnaires which were received by NCEPOD for the individual operations. The analysis of the deaths is confined to pooled data because disparate *numbers* of deaths and index cases were received for most of the selected operations. There were also quite gross differences in *medical state* (as indicated by the ASA grades, and ages of patients and by the numbers of their pre-existing medical conditions) between the series of patients.

There was thus no justification for detailed comparisons by the specific operations for deaths and index cases and even when the numbers were sufficient in each group no obvious differences were apparent on a limited analysis (types of hospital, staff, types of anaesthesia, monitoring or types of complications). There are a few isolated comments in the main analysis about specific aspects in relation to specific operations.

ASA Deaths and index
Figures A6 a to c (q 39)
ASA grade
Colorectal resection

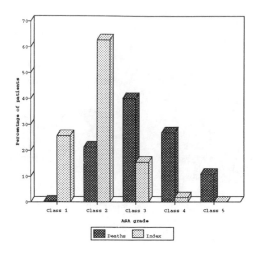

Total hip replacement

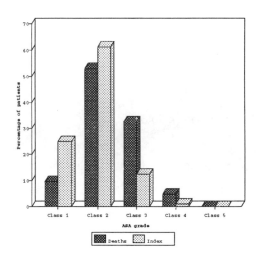

Prostatectomy

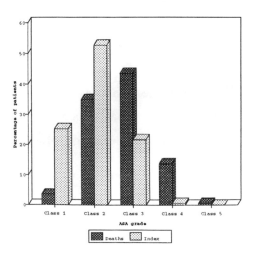

Anaesthesia
References see page 300

The forty-two deaths in ASA 1 patients were examined in conjunction with data from the surgical questionnaires in the attempt to identify why these otherwise fit patients died.

Table A103
Cause of death in ASA1 patients

Operation	All	Acute* heart failure	Pulmonary** embolus	Surgical***	Acute renal failure	Respiratory failure	Multi-organ failure	Unspecified
	(n=42)	(n=9)	(n=10)	(n=9)	(n=2)	(n=2)	(n=2)	(n=8)
Oesophagectomy	12	3	1	3	-	1	-	4
Total hip replacement	8	2	4	1	-	-	-	1
Prostatectomy	6	2	4	-	-	-	-	-
Hysterectomy	6	1	1	-	2	-	1	1
Craniotomy	6	-	-	5	-	1	-	-
Colorectal resection	1	1	-	-	-	-	-	-
Breast surgery	1	-	-	-	-	-	1	-
ENT surgery	1	-	-	-	-	-	-	1
Oral/maxillofacial surgery	1	-	-	-	-	-	-	1

*   Acute heart failure includes left ventricular failure and myocardial infarctions.

**   Pulmonary emboli were proven at autopsy.

***   Surgical denotes local complications e.g. haemorrhage, brain swelling or breakdown of anastomoses.

Table A104
Critical events by operation

	Deaths	%	Index	%
Colorectal resection	314	26	175	10
Total hip replacement	83	30	287	14
Transurethral resection of prostate	167	14	171	4

The substantially higher rate of occurrence of these events amongst the deaths compared with the index cases is confirmatory of the importance of these critical events and follows the same pattern as that for the pooled data from all (selected) operations.

Coronary artery bypass grafts

Repeat operations for coronary artery disease feature fairly frequently in this series. They are not undertaken lightly by experienced specialist surgeons and anaesthetists but sometimes the serious nature of the enterprise is not perceived by others.

> *A Consultant Anaesthetist (FFARCS, 1988) with seven years' experience together with a Senior Registrar, anaesthetized a patient in a University Hospital for a repeat coronary artery bypass graft. They were assisted by a trainee ODA. The patient was 66 years old and was graded, for unrevealed reasons, ASA 4. The Consultant Surgeon had two years' experience, and claimed to have done 50 of these procedures in the past year. The five-hour procedure was expeditiously performed and was apparently successful. The operation involved substantial blood and fluid transfusion and the patient's temperature was 32°C at the end. The trachea was extubated when the patient was awake in the operating room. The anaesthetic record is uninformative and does not reveal, for instance, whether reversal agents were used. There was no left atrial or pulmonary arterial pressure monitoring. Cardiorespiratory arrest occurred for no apparent reason while he was still in the operating room. Cardiopulmonary bypass was established again as soon as possible but despite the fact that all the grafted vessels were functional, independent cardiac function was not achieved and he died.*

Maximal effort has to be employed (delayed tracheal extubation to allow proper rewarming) if the challenges that these seriously ill patients present are to be overcome and many consider that pulmonary artery pressures should be measured in these circumstances.

The "fast-tracking" method of management after operation must be closely monitored by all those involved lest standards slip.

Anaesthesia
References see page 300

Oesophagectomy

An experienced Consultant Anaesthetist (FFARCS, 1965) managed this patient without other medical help in a District General Hospital. The patient was 67 years old (ASA 3, because of angina and chronic obstructive airways disease). No surgical form was received from the locum Consultant Surgeon. Instrumental monitoring of the patient was limited, it is claimed, by inaccessibility. Direct arterial blood pressure was not monitored but non-invasive monitoring was used. The systolic pressure was recorded between 50 and 80 mmHg throughout. Oxygen saturation varied between 97 and 99%. Central venous pressure was not recorded. There was some problem (undefined) with the endobronchial tube during the procedure but it became necessary to intubate the trachea again when the patient was in the recovery room. (Sinus bradycardia followed by ventricular fibrillation had developed.) Two (25mg) doses of pethidine were given at this time. Resuscitation was abandoned after thirty minutes. The hospital had an ICU but the sequence of events described above makes it clear that neither elective ventilation of the lungs, nor admission there, was planned for this patient.

Is it possible that the presence of an additional anaesthetist would have influenced the outcome for this patient? The case seems strong for the use of anaesthesia teams.

Strangulated hernia

A Consultant Anaesthetist (FFARCS, 1985), with a Senior House Officer anaesthetized this 81-year-old patient in a District General Hospital. A repair of a strangulated femoral hernia and bowel resection had been carried out nine days earlier. Large bowel obstruction was now present and a Registrar was deputed to perform the complex operation at 21.00 hours which took 2 hours 35 minutes. The ICU was full. Had it not been, the management at the end of the operation would presumably have been different. Muscle relaxation was reversed but ventilation was inadequate. Doxapram was given without noticeable effect and it is not clear if the tracheal tube was removed. Paralysis was reinstituted, artificial ventilation of the lungs was applied for 20 minutes, reversal repeated but cardiac arrest followed and resuscitation failed.

Did the attempt to manage the problem in an out-of-date manner to avoid intensive therapy hasten this patient's demise?

Colorectal resection

Five out of the 314 patients who had colorectal procedures died in the operating room. The death of one particular patient would not have been averted even if all the factors of management were ideal but they may be contributory in other cases.

> *A Senior House Officer Anaesthetist (DA 1990) in a District General Hospital consulted a Registrar who came to help during the operation. The patient was 91 years old. Carcinoma of the caecum and peritonitis had resulted in the need for laparotomy which was done by a locum Registrar Surgeon. A cerebrovascular accident had occurred six years earlier and the patient was graded ASA 5. The patient had to wait 4-6 hours before an operating room was available and, during this time, deteriorated. The surgeon reported that CT scanning facilities were not available for emergencies. Cardiac arrest occurred during the operation and the patient died.*

Hysterectomy

Five patients died on the day of operation. Two died as a result of severe haemorrhage. One was apparently dying from widespread metastatic disease and was hypoxic, hypocarbic and hypotensive when she was brought to theatre, one 84-year-old had a myocardial infarction on induction of anaesthesia and one 69-year-old died unexpectedly nine hours after operation. Information about the latter patient is limited because the Consultant Anaesthetist, who gave the anaesthetic, completed the questionnaire in a peculiarly unhelpful way so it is not clear what happened.

Total hip replacement

Two patients died in theatre. One was a very poor risk, but active, 91- year-old who had painful osteoarthritis and the other patient died suddenly after a proven fat embolus which happened after the insertion of the cement.

DISCUSSION

Sample

The answers to most of the questionnaires (deaths and index cases) show that the standard of the delivery of anaesthesia in England, Wales and Northern Ireland is good. Comparisons with previous years are not fully valid, because the current sample is very different from those previously used, but the overall picture is one of a very high standard of care. Indeed, there are few demonstrable differences between the management of comparable patients who die and those who survive (index cases).

There are some factors which are noted in the preceding pages which, if corrected or not present, might have made a death less likely. It is inevitable in a report such as this that some emphasis is laid on deficiencies, but this should not be allowed to obscure the reality of widespread good practice.

Readers should remember, that whilst only a few vignettes are published here, the views are formulated after reading 1616 questionnaires which relate to patients who died.

The selection of 15 operations for the Enquiry was for surgical reasons. All deaths after these operations were studied in detail with the exception of colorectal ones. There was a large number of these deaths (1727) and so a random 25% sample was selected and this yielded 314 completed questionnaires from anaesthetists.

Local protocols

Disposition of staff resources on the basis of perceived risk seems a rational approach to clinical practice and perusal of many of the answers to the questions has suggested that some scheme such as is outlined below might be acceptable and even useful. The anaesthetist group is convinced that departments or directorates should consider the production of written protocols for use in their own hospital. Protocols could be written about ASA grades, anaesthesia teams and essential services. A few directorates have already written protocols after the publication of our previous reports.

ASA grade of patient

The ASA system of grading patients is designed not for risk assessment purposes but to enable clinicians to communicate with each other about a patient's overall condition. The group of anaesthetists, on the basis of the questionnaires which they have seen, suggest the following thoughts for consideration.

Some matching between ASA status and the skill (qualifications and(or) experience) of the anaesthetist deployed should be attempted by departments in the design of their local guidelines.

(i)   Good risk 80-year-olds for major surgery should be treated as if they were ASA 4.

(ii)   No ASA 4 or 5 patient should be anaesthetized without detailed discussion with a Consultant (Senior Registrar) anaesthetist.

Anaesthesia
References see page 300

Anaesthesia teams

It is common practice for anaesthetists of all grades to work by themselves (solo) in contrast to the usual practice of surgeons.

There are certain operations which are, and always should be, serviced by a team of anaesthetists. There are several different aspects to this matter;

(i)   This team should normally be led by a Consultant (or experienced Senior Registrar). Careful planning for appropriate staff-patient deployment by departments is required.

(ii)   Anaesthesia for emergency or urgent lifesaving operations should ideally be managed by a team of anaesthetists; two-anaesthetist-teams would usually be the minimum requirement. Many operations, particularly those of long duration will require two anaesthetists (e.g. craniotomy, oesophagectomy, coronary bypass grafts) at least for part of the time e.g. during periods of physiological instability.

(iii)   Trainees need to appreciate that they are part of a team of anaesthetists even if they are working by themselves and should feel able to call for support.

(iv)   Flexibility of staff allocation, so that appropriately experienced anaesthetists are available at critical moments during anaesthesia and operations needs to be encouraged. One Consultant should not be solely responsible for the welfare of a patient or patients for twelve hours. Trainee doctors need instant support in the event of unanticipated crises.

Essential services

NCEPOD and its predecessors have repeatedly made suggestions about the provision of essential services.

It should be possible for **all** patients who have surgical operations to be admitted to a properly staffed and equipped recovery room which is available 24 hours a day.

A fully equipped and staffed high dependency unit (as defined in the Glossary, Appendix B), with provision for safe transport elsewhere to a ward when stable or to an intensive care unit, should be available for all patients wherever major surgery is undertaken.

Operations should not be undertaken in the absence of these services. Admission policies for HDU or ICU should not be affected by the patient's age. Decisions about elderly patients should be made before operation, jointly by surgeons and anaesthetists, and the decision not to operate should not be fudged.

Other topics for protocols for anaesthetic services.

These might include arrangements for the *transfer* of patients, explanations of current local practices for *locums* of any grade, *discharge criteria* for patients who are to return to the ward, *admission criteria* for HDU or ICU, and indications for *oxygen therapy.*

Fluid overload

The administration of intravenous fluids to elderly patients needs to be carefully supervised. Systemic hypotension (in the absence of blood loss) should not be treated solely with large volumes of intravenous fluids but, perhaps in addition, vasopressors should be used more readily. The practice of "fluid loading," so widespread in obstetrics (in association with epidural or spinal anaesthesia) may not be appropriate in the elderly patient who also has ischaemic heart disease. When the vasodilatation caused by these techniques wears off and normal vascular tone returns, all the extra fluid overwhelms the capacity of the diseased circulation and left ventricular failure is almost inevitable.

Non-medical assistants

The provision of competent non-medical assistants is now widespread but must now be invariable. This is a matter for management action.

Pain relief

The provision of pain relief needs attention by anaesthetists since current arrangements are not yet satisfactory everywhere. The Royal College of Anaesthetists is considering a guideline concerned with intramuscular analgesia, but more advanced methods must be dependent upon appropriate nursing and medical support. There were a number of reports of patients who were deemed to have received less than adequate treatment in relation to pain after operation, particularly those whose care after operation was conducted on a general ward, rather that on a high dependency unit.

Anaesthetic records

The standards of these have improved but the variation in design across the countries is very wide. There may be an argument for a standard anaesthetic record. The Royal College of Anaesthetists has now agreed a basic minimum of information which should be included on such a record. There are still a few hospitals which do not appear to provide anaesthetists with a chart on which changes in physiological variables could be plotted against time. Standardization of the record would in addition facilitate external review of the record. Whatever the design of a record the clarity of completion also varies widely. Standardization of charts for automatic blood pressure measurements would also be beneficial.

Instrumental monitoring

The publication[52] of standards (for administration of anaesthesia, monitoring of and support for the patient), which are approved by the World Federation of Societies of Anaesthesiology, makes further comment or suggestions about guidelines on this topic superfluous. The Association of Anaesthetists of Great Britain and Ireland has also published its recommendations.[53] The advisory group of anaesthetists unanimously endorses both the aims and recommendations of these publications and another variant would be undesirable. Thus directorates are advised to introduce their own protocols based on the published efforts of others and NCEPOD does not offer any more confusion on this topic.

Participation in NCEPOD by anaesthetists

Sixty-one per cent of questionnaires about deaths were returned by anaesthetists (see Table M26, page 47). This is too low. Part of the explanation for the low figures is undoubtedly the method whereby NCEPOD arranged for Consultants to receive their questionnaires (See Table M27, page 48). We knew that this was likely to prove unsatisfactory and changes in arrangements have already been made. The failure by surgeons in some particular disciplines is also too high: in the current method their failure probably has a consequent effect on anaesthetists' returns.

Part of the explanation is the recurrent difficulty of discovery of an individual patient's notes. Information retrieval in some institutions has improved over the last two to three years and the problem may soon be solved everywhere. The loss of the notes of dead patients does still happen and some are inevitably secreted in departments of surgery and pathology. Others are destroyed prematurely.

Each Consultant whose name we know who returned at least one questionnaire has been sent a copy of this current Report. The names of all those from whom NCEPOD received at least one completed death or index case questionnaire for 1991/92 and whose names we know are listed in Appendix E.

The information collected by this Enquiry is unique and useful. Its value would be much enhanced if the return rate were substantially increased.

REFERENCES

REFERENCES

1   Buck N, Devlin HB, Lunn JN. *The Report of a Confidential Enquiry into Perioperative Deaths.* Nuffield Provincial Hospitals Trust and The King Edward's Hospitals Fund for London. London, 1987.

2   Campling EA, Devlin HB, Lunn JN. *The Report of the National Confidential Enquiry into Perioperative Deaths 1989.* London, 1990.

3   Campling EA, Devlin HB, Hoile RW, Lunn JN. *The Report of the National Confidential Enquiry into Perioperative Deaths 1990.* London, 1992.

4   *Health Trends* 1986;**18**.

5   *Health Trends* 1990;**22**.

6   *Health Trends* 1991;**23**.

7   Personal communication 17 December 1992 to Ms E A Campling from Mr F Oliphant, Statistics Division 2G, Department of Health.

8   Information Management Group of the NHS Management Executive. *A new format NHS number.* Department of Health. HMSO December 1992.

9   Information Management Group of the NHS Management Executive. *IM & T Strategy Overview.* HMSO December 1992.

10   Personal communication (July 1993) to Mr H B Devlin from tutors of The Royal College of Surgeons of England.

11   Start RD, Delargy-Aziz Y, Dorries CP, Silcocks PB, Cotton BWK. Clinicians and the coronial system: ability of clinicians to recognise reportable deaths. *BMJ* 1993;**306**:1038-41.

12   The Royal College of Pathologists. *Guidelines for Post Mortem Reports.* 1993.

13   Jennett B. Variations in surgical practice: welcome diversity or disturbing differences? *Br J Surg* 1988;**75**:630-631.

14   Office of Population Censuses and Surveys. *Mortality Statistics 1991 - cause.* England and Wales. HMSO 1993.

15   Hull RD, Kakkar VV, Raskoh GE. Prevention of venous thrombosis and pulmonary embolism. In: Fuster V, Verstraete M, eds. *Thrombosis in cardiovascular disorders.* Philadelphia. W B Saunders, 1992:451-64.

16   Parker-Williams J, Vickers R. Major orthopaedic surgery on the leg and thromboembolism. *BMJ* 1991;**303**:531-532.

17   Thromboembolic Risk Factors (THRIFT) Consensus Group. Risk of and prophylaxis for venous thromboembolism in hospital patients. *BMJ* 1992;**305**:567-574.

18   *Prevention of venous thromboembolism - European Consensus Statement 1992.* Med-Orion Publishing Company. London,1992.

19   *Venous Thromboembolism. A continuing challenge.* A symposium organized by the Association of Surgeons of Great Britain and Ireland and The Thrombosis Research Institute. St Helier, Jersey. 3 April 1992. Assoc Surg G.B.I. & The Medicine Group, 1992.

20   Lowe G. *Thromboembolism. Assessing the risk in hospital patients.* Prevention of Venous Thromboembolism. London: Advisa Medica, 1993.

21   Clason AE *et al.* Acute ischaemia of the lower limb; the effect of centralizing vascular surgical services on comorbidity and mortality. *Br J Surg* 1989;**76**:592-3.

22   Bunt TJ, Manship LL, Bynoe RP, Hayes JL. Lower extremity amputation for peripheral vascular disease. A low risk operation. *Am Surg* 1984;**50**:581-4.

23   Malone J M, Moore W, Leal J M, Childers S J. Rehabilitation for lower extremity amputation. *Arch Surg* 1981;**116**:93-8.

24   Williams MH, *et al. An epidemiologically based needs assessement. Hernia repair.* NHS Management Executive, 1993.

25   Stocking B, Jennett B, Spiby J. *Criteria for change. The history and impact of consensus development conferences in the United Kingdom.* The King Edward's Hospital Fund for London, 1991.

26   Matthews HR *et al. Cancer of the Oesophagus.* London:Macmillan Press, 1987.

27   United Kingdom Thoracic Surgical Register of the Society of Cardiothoracic Surgeons of Great Britain and Ireland, 1991.

28   Cashman JN. Non-steroidal anti-inflammatory drugs versus postoperative pain. *J R Soc Med* 1993;**86**:464-7.

29   Nashef SAM. Kakadellis JG, Hasleton PS, Whittaker JS, Gregory CM. Histological examination of peroperative frozen sections in suspected lung cancer. *Thorax* 1993;**48**:388-9.

30   O'Connor GT *et al.* Multivariate prediction of in-hospital mortality associated with coronary artery bypass graft surgery. *Circulation* 1992;**85**:2110-8.

31   Khan SS, *et al.* Increased mortality of women in coronary artery bypass surgery - evidence for referral bias. *Ann Intern Med* 199;**112**:561-7.

32   Steingart RM, *et al.* Sex differences in the management of coronary artery disease. *N Engl J Med* 1991;**325**:226-30.

33   Loft A, *et al.* Early postoperative mortality following hysterectomy; a Danish population based study, 1977-1981. *Br J Obstet Gynaecol* 1991;**98**:147-154.

34   Greer IA, De Swiet M. Thrombosis prophylaxis in obstetrics and gynaecology. *Br J Obstet Gynaecol* 1993;**100**:37-40.

35   Donavan J, *et al. Prostatectomy for benign prostatic hyperplasia. DHA Needs assessment.* NHS Management Executive, 1992.

36   Wenneberg JE *et al.* Use of claims data to evaluate health case outcomes: mortality and re-operation following prostatectomy. *JAMA* 1987;**257**:933-6.

37   Masters RH, *et al.* Incidence of vascular accidents following transurethral prostatectomy. J Urol 1968;100:544-5.

38   Wilson RG, et al. Prophylactic subcutaneous heparin does not increase operative blood loss in transurethral resection of the prostate. *Br J Urol* 1988;**62**:246-8.

39   Parr N J, Loh C S, Desmond A D. Transurethral resection of the prostate and bladder tumour without withdrawal of warfarin therapy. *Br J Urol* 1989;64:623-5.

40   Jamjoom A, *et al.* Outcome following the surgical evacuation of traumatic intracranial haematomas in the elderly. *Br J Neurosurg* 1992;**6**:27-32.

41   *Safe Neurosurgery.* A report from the Society of British Neurological Surgeons, 1993.

42   Teasdale G, *et al.* Management of traumatic intracranial haematoma. *BMJ* 1982;**285**:1695-7.

43   Patchell RA, *et al.* Single brain metastasis : surgery plus radiation or radiation alone. *Neurology* 1986;**36**:447-53.

44   Williams M, *et al. Total hip replacement. DHA Epidemiologically Based Needs Assessment.* NHS Management Executive, 1992.

References

45   Seagroatt V, *et al.* Elective total hip replacement; incidence, emergency readmission rate, and postoperative mortality. *BMJ* 1991;**303**:1431-5.

46   Low-molecular-weight heparins in orthopaedic surgery. *DTB* 1993;**31**:37-8.

47   Frankel S, *et al. Cataract surgery. A DHA Project.* NHS Management Executive, 1992.

48   *Making the best use of a department of clinical radiology: guidelines for doctors. 2nd edition.* Royal College of Radiologists, London, 1993.

49   Surana R, Quinn F, Puri P. Is it necessary to perform appendicectomy in the middle of the night in children? *BMJ* 1993;**306**:1168-9.

50   Wyatt MG, Haighton PWJ, Brodribb AJM. Theatre delay for emergency general surgical patients: a cause for concern? *Ann R Coll Surg Engl* 1990;**72**:236-8.

51   Runciman WB, Webb RK, Barker L, Currie M. The pulse oximeter: application and limitation in an analysis of 2000 incident reports. *Anaesthesia and Intensive care* 1993 (in press).

52   The international task force on safety in anaesthesia. *Eur J Anaesthesiol* 1993;**10**:Supplement 7.

53   *Recommendations on standards of monitoring.* Association of Anaesthetists of Great Britain and Ireland, 1988.

SELECTIVE INDEX OF TABLES

APPENDICES

National Confidential Enquiry Into Perioperative Deaths

35-43 LINCOLN'S INN FIELDS, LONDON WC2A 3PN : Tel: 01-831 6430

ASSOCIATION OF ANAESTHETISTS OF GREAT BRITAIN AND IRELAND   COLLEGE OF ANAESTHETISTS AT THE ROYAL COLLEGE OF SURGEONS OF ENGLAND
ASSOCIATION OF SURGEONS OF GREAT BRITAIN AND IRELAND   FACULTY OF COMMUNITY MEDICINE OF THE ROYAL COLLEGES OF PHYSICIANS OF THE UK
ROYAL COLLEGE OF SURGEONS OF ENGLAND   ROYAL COLLEGE OF PATHOLOGISTS   ROYAL COLLEGE OF OBSTETRICIANS AND GYNÆCOLOGISTS

December 1988

PROTOCOL

This protocol is derived from the CEPOD report* published in December 1987.

1 AIMS

The National Confidential Enquiry into Perioperative Deaths (NCEPOD) is to enquire into clinical practice and to identify remediable factors in the practice of anaesthesia and surgery.

The NCEPOD will investigate deaths which occur in hospital within 30 days of any surgical or gynaecological operation. This will include all procedures carried out by surgeons, whether in the presence or absence of an anaesthetist. Procedures involving local anaesthetics, as well as day cases, are included.

All NHS hospitals within the Regional or Special Health Authorities of England, Wales, Northern Ireland, Guernsey, Jersey and the Isle of Man are to be included in the Enquiry, as well as hospitals managed by the Ministry of Defence, and by the British United Provident Association.

All Consultants (surgeons, gynaecologists and anaesthetists) will be involved in the assessment programme.

2 STEERING GROUP

The Enquiry is overseen by a steering group consisting of the following members:

Chairman	Professor D Campbell	CBE FFARCS FRCS
Vice Chairman	Mr J A P Marston	FRCS
Secretary	Mr H B Devlin	FRCS
Treasurer	Dr M M Burrows	FFARCS
	Professor J P Blandy	FRCS
	Dr N P Halliday	MB BS
	Dr A C Hunt	FRCPath
	Professor A G Johnson	FRCS
	Dr J N Lunn	FFARCS
	Professor R Owen	FRCS
	Professor M Rosen	FFARCS
	Mr S C Simmons	FRCOG
	Professor E D Alberman	FFCM

3 ANNUAL SAMPLE

A sample of all deaths reported will be investigated each year. The **dead cases** sampled will each be compared with similar patients, matched for sex, age, and mode of admission, who underwent similar operations and survived (**survivor cases**). Details of these patients will be obtained from consultants in another NHS Region.

Additionally, details of a large sample of patients undergoing surgery will be sought from all consultants (surgeons, gynaecologists and anaesthetists) each year. These **index cases** will provide a background against which the sample of dead cases and survivor cases will be compared.

Normally, consultants will be asked for details of **one** index case per year. This will depend, however, on the sample of dead cases being studied each year and the discipline of the consultant concerned.

Data will be collected by means of structured **questionnaires,** designed by the specialist groups and approved by the Steering Group.

It is anticipated that all consultants will provide information regarding all **dead** cases in the year's sample, any **survivor** case requested and one **index** case relevant to the sample.

The dead cases will be compared with the survivor cases and both samples with the index case sample. The specialist groups will advise on the sampling and conclusions to be drawn.

4 ANNUAL PROGRAMME

Groups of specialist doctors, formed as a result of nominations from specialist societies and associations and approved by the Steering Group will advise the clinical coordinators during each year's programme. Each year a sample of deaths and survivors will be considered by NCEPOD in a rolling programme to provide an ongoing audit of clinical practice.

5 EXCLUDED CASES

The NCEPOD will **not** consider deaths after:

i) Diagnostic procedures carried out by physicians or other non-surgeons;

ii) Therapeutic procedures carried out by physicians or other non-surgeons;

iii) Radiological procedures performed solely by a radiologist without a surgeon present;

iv) Obstetric operations or delivery;

v) Dental surgery other than that taking place in the hospitals listed in Section 1 above.

6 LITIGATION

The Department of Health has confirmed that it will support the total confidentiality of the NCEPOD.

The Data Protection Act does **not** apply to the information collected on the dead patients since there is no provision for third party access to the data. We intend to request information already in the patient's notes for the **index** and **survivor** cases and no assessment of these cases will be carried out. The information will be collated in an anonymous form and will not be stored as identifiable data.

Extract from Data Protection Act 1984 Section 33(6)

> "Personal data held only for –
> (a) preparing statistics; or
> (b) carrying out research,
> are exempt from the subject access provisions; but it shall be a condition of that exemption that the data are not used or disclosed for any other purpose and that the resulting statistics or the results of the research are not made available in a form which identifies the data subjects or any of them."

The Secretary of State has confirmed that the same support will be provided for the NCEPOD as is already given for the Confidential Enquiry into Maternal Deaths. The Secretary of State is satisfied that disclosure of documents about individual cases prepared for these enquiries would be against the public interest. The courts have always had regard to the overriding public interest as grounds for refusal of requests for disclosure of documents, and Section 35 of the Supreme Court Act 1981, which provides that the Court shall not make an order, under Sections 33 or 34 of that Act, for disclosure "if it considers that compliance with the Order, if made, would be likely to be injurious to the public interests" has provided additional support for such opposition. The Department has been assured that if it should be necessary, the claim for public interest immunity would be pressed vigorously by the Crown.

The Department in addition states that in its opinion a fruitful outcome to this Enquiry will be a major achievement by the medical profession in the field of medical audit/quality assurance. Therefore, the information on the dead patients sent to the National CEPOD is protected from subpoena. However, if any participant takes a photocopy of the form, that photocopy becomes his or her property (the original form remains the property of the NCEPOD) and is open to subpoena by the courts and the NCEPOD cannot protect that copy. It is therefore essential that NO PHOTOCOPIES ARE MADE OF PART OR ALL OF COMPLETED NCEPOD QUESTIONNAIRES. Participants may take copies of the BLANK form but please **DO NOT** keep records other than the patient's notes.

7 LOCAL REPORTING

Arrangements will be made in each district for cases to be reported to the NCEPOD office. An appropriate local reporter will be appointed after discussion with the consultants in each district. The local reporter **must** be a consultant. A pathologist or community physician is recommended. Appropriate delegation of day-to-day duties is, of course, permissible. It is necessary for the local reporter to have a nominated deputy.

The Royal College of Pathologists and the Faculty of Community Medicine are participating in the programme and their members are encouraged to assist data collection.

The reporter's role will be to ensure that **all** deaths in hospital within 30 days of an operation are reported to the NCEPOD office.

The reporter will be asked to provide demographic data **only** on the dead patient, and the names of the consultants in charge. No further information will be sought from the local reporter.

Each hospital has arrangements for the storage of death certificates and other information. We expect each local reporter to organise his/her own method to inform us of all perioperative deaths in hospital. To enable an adequate system to be established we suggest the support of the DMO and the DGM is sought. Printed advice about this task can be obtained from the NCEPOD office.

8   QUESTIONNAIRES

The questionnaires have been developed by the specialist groups to obtain details of particular surgical and anaesthetic procedures. All personal identification of patients and medical staff will be removed before entry of a particular case into the computer.

It is our recommendation that consultants ask their junior staff to complete the questionnaire from the patient's notes. Once the form is completed the consultant and his junior should review it together and it should be returned to the NCEPOD office. It is hoped that this joint completion will act as a training process by reviewing the case on a one-to-one basis. This method could be used to develop a framework of local review of clinical practice. Trainees and consultants may write in total confidentiality to the NCEPOD office under separate cover if they wish.

Consultants *(surgeons and anaesthetists)* will also be asked to complete a small number of questionnaires on patients who have survived surgery. These cases will provide the benchmarks for assessment.

The information you give to us is important. It must be complete and accurate if valid conclusions are to be drawn.

If further information is required we may request the patient's notes be provided.

9   FEEDBACK

The Enquiry recognises the importance of adequate feedback to individual consultants and to the profession as a whole. However, feedback must avoid any likelihood of legal or professional jeopardy to the individual consultant. Therefore the Enquiry will publish an annual report which will present aggregated data but will not allow identification of individual consultants. There will be no assessments provided on individual cases.

10   ACCREDITATION

All the Colleges and Faculties stress the importance of clinical audit for both monitoring clinical standards and as a discipline in the training of junior doctors. NCEPOD is a national audit system. The Colleges and Faculties require audit as a precondition for accreditation for training.

11   PARTICIPANTS

The annual report will include the names of all consultants who have contributed all the index, survivor and dead cases requested for the data base.

12 CLINICAL COORDINATORS

The coordinators appointed by the Steering Group may be contacted by telephone.

        Dr J N Lunn   0222 763601 (direct)
        Mr H B Devlin   0642 603571 (direct)

Assistant to the Coordinators;

        Mr R W Hoile   0634 400677 (direct)

or via the National CEPOD office.

13 FURTHER INFORMATION

Please contact Ms Anne Campling, Administrator, on 01-831 6430 if you require any further information, or write to;

NCEPOD
35-43 Lincoln's Inn Fields
London
WC2A 3PN

*Buck N., Devlin H. B., Lunn J. N. Report of the Confidential Enquiry into Perioperative Deaths. Nuffield Provincial Hospitals Trust and The King Edward's Hospital Fund for London. London 1987.

APPENDIX B
GLOSSARY

ADMISSION

Elective - at a time agreed between the patient and the surgical service.

Urgent - within 48 hours of referral/consultation.

Emergency - immediately following referral/consultation, when admission is unpredictable and at short notice because of clinical need.

AMERICAN SOCIETY OF ANESTHESIOLOGY (ASA) CLASSIFICATION OF PHYSICAL STATUS

Class 1

The patient has no organic, physiological, biochemical or psychiatric disturbance. The pathological process for which operation is to be performed is localised and does not entail a systemic disturbance. Examples: a fit patient with inguinal hernia; fibroid uterus in an otherwise healthy woman.

Class 2

Mild to moderate systemic disturbance or distress caused by either the condition to be treated surgically or by other pathophysiological processes. Examples: non - or only slightly limiting organic heart disease, mild diabetes, essential hypertension, or anaemia. Some might choose to list the extremes of age here, either the neonate or the octogenerian, even though no discernible systemic disease is present. Extreme obesity and chronic bronchitis may be included in this category.

Class 3

Severe systemic disturbance or disease from whatever cause, even though it may not be possible to define the degree of disability with finality. Examples: severely limiting organic heart disease; severe diabetes with vascular complications; moderate to severe degrees of pulmonary insufficiency; angina pectoris or healed myocardial infarction.

Class 4

Severe systemic disorders that are already life threatening, not always correctable by operation. Examples: patients with organic heart disease showing marked signs of cardiac insufficiency, persistent angina, or active myocarditis; advanced degrees of pulmonary, hepatic, renal or endocrine insufficiency.

Class 5

The moribund patient who has little chance of survival but is submitted to operation in desperation. Examples: the burst abdominal aneurysm with profound shock; major cerebral trauma with rapidly increasing intracranial pressure; massive pulmonary embolus. Most of these patients require operation a resuscitative measure with little if any anaesthesia.

CLASSIFICATION OF OPERATION

Emergency

Immediate operation, resuscitation simultaneous with surgical treatment (eg trauma). Operation usually within one hour.

Urgent

Operation as soon as possible resuscitation (eg irreducible hernia, intussusception, intestinal obstruction, perforation, embolism, some forms of haemorrhage, major fractures). Operation usually within 24 hours.

Scheduled

An early operation but not immediately life-saving (eg malignancy, cardiovascular surgery). Operation usually within 3 weeks.

Elective

Operation at a time to suit both patient and surgeon (eg cholecystectomy, hysterectomy, cataract surgery).

DAY CASE

A patient who is admitted for investigation or operation on a planned non-resident basis (i.e. no overnight stay).

GLASGOW COMA SCALE

Eye opening	Pts	Verbal response	Pts	Motor response to pain (best limb)	Pts
Spontaneous	4	Orientated verbal response	5	Obeys commands	5
Eye opening to speech	3	Confused verbal response	4	Localisation	4
Eye opening to pain	2	Inappropriate words	3	Flexion normal/abnormal	3
None	1	Incomprehensible sounds	2	Extension	2
		No verbal response	1	No motor response	1

INDEX CASES

Index cases were a sample of patients on whom a surgical procedure was performed and who survived more than 30 days after surgery. The specified surgical procedures matched those performed on those patients who died (see pages 18 and 19).

HIGH DEPENDENCY UNIT

A high dependency unit (HDU) is an area for patients who require more intensive observation and/or nursing than would be expected on a general ward. Patients who require mechanical ventilation or other organ support would not be admitted to this area.

INTENSIVE CARE UNIT

An intensive care unit (ICU) is an area to which patients are admitted for treatment of actual or impending organ failure who may require technological support (including mechanical ventilation of the lungs and/or invasive monitoring).

RECOVERY AREA

A recovery area is an area to which patients are admitted from an operating room, where they remain until consciousness is regained and ventilated and circulation are stable.

CAUSE OF DEATH - OFFICE OF POPULATION CENSUSES AND SURVEYS FORMAT

The condition thought to be the "Underlying Cause of Death" should appear in the lowest completed line of Part I.

I **(a)**   Disease or condition directly leading to death*

   (b)   Other disease or condition, if any, leading to I (a)

   (c)   Other disease or condition, if any, leading to I (b)

II   Other significant conditions CONTRIBUTING TO THE DEATH but not related to the disease or condition causing it.

* This does not mean the mode of dying, such as heart failure, asphyxia, asthenia, etc: it means the disease, injury, or complication which caused death.

National Confidential Enquiry into Perioperative Deaths
35-43 Lincoln's Inn Fields, London, WC2A 3PN

SURGICAL QUESTIONNAIRE (DEATHS) 1991/2

QUESTIONNAIRE No. **S** ☐☐☐☐☐

DO NOT PHOTOCOPY ANY PART OF THIS QUESTIONNAIRE

QUESTIONNAIRE COMPLETION

The questionnaire should be completed with reference to the last operation before the death of the patient specified by the NCEPOD office. If you feel that this was not the **main** operation in the period before the patient's death, you may give additional information. See question 61.

The whole questionnaire will be shredded when data collection is complete. The information will be filed anonymously.

Neither the questions nor the choices for answers are intended to suggest standards of practice.

Please enclose a copy of all the relevant surgical operation notes, the postmortem reports and the postmortem request form if available. Any identification will be removed in the NCEPOD office.

Many of the questions can be answered by "yes" or "no". **Please insert a tick(✔) in the appropriate box.**

Where multiple choices are given, please insert the tick(s) in the appropriate box(es).

Where more details are requested for an answer, please write in **BLOCK CAPITALS**

If you wish to alter an answer, please "white" out the incorrect answer. Please do not write in amendments, which can not be accepted by the computer.

Consultants or junior staff may write to the NCEPOD office under separate cover, quoting the questionnaire number, offering any additional details which may be relevant to the understanding of the case. All original copies of correspondence will be confidential (but **do not** retain copies of your correspondence).

In case of difficulty, please contact the NCEPOD office on:

071-831-6430

REMINDER

HAVE YOU ENCLOSED COPIES OF THE OPERATION AND POSTMORTEM NOTES ?

1

---

1. Specialty of Consultant Surgeon in charge at time of final operation before death (any additional special interests may be entered under "other" below).

		1
a	General	☐
b	General with special interest in Paediatric Surgery	☐
c	General with special interest in Urology	☐
d	General with special interest in Vascular Surgery	☐
e	General with special interest in Gastroenterology	☐
f	General with special interest in Endocrinology	☐
g	General with special interest in _____	☐
h	Accident and Emergency	☐
i	Cardiac - Paediatric	☐
j	Cardiac - Adult	☐
k	Cardiac - Mixed	☐
l	Thoracic	☐
m	Gynaecology	☐
n	Neurosurgery	☐
o	Ophthalmology	☐
p	Oral/Maxillofacial	☐
q	Orthopaedic	☐
r	Otorhinolaryngology	☐
s	Paediatric	☐
t	Plastic	☐
u	Transplantation	☐
v	Urology	☐
w	Other (Please specify) _____	☐

2

2. In which type of hospital did the last operation take place?

2								
	a	b	c	d	e	f	g	h

a   District General Hospital

b   University/Teaching Hospital

c   Surgical Specialty Hospital

d   Other Acute/Partly Acute Hospital

e   Community Hospital

f   MOD Hospital

g   Independent Hospital

h   Other (Please specify) _____

PATIENT DETAILS

3. Date of birth

D	D	M	M	Y	Y

4. Age at final operation _____

5. Sex

5	
a	b

Male   a

Female   b

6. Main diagnosis:

_____

_____

_____

_____

7. Final operation performed:

_____

_____

_____

8. Established cause of death:

_____

_____

_____

N.B. You may be asked for this information elsewhere on the form. NCEPOD considers it useful to record the details here in order to summarise the case.

9. Was a record of the patient's weight available?

a Yes

b No

9 | a | b |

9A. If **yes**, what was this weight?

_____ kg or _____ st _____ lb

9B. If **no**, please indicate the patient's physique.

a Thin

b Average

c Obese/overweight

d Not recorded

9B | a | b | c | d |

10. Was a record of the patient's height available?

a Yes

b No

10 | a | b |

10A. If **yes**, what was this height?

_____ cm or _____ ft _____ in

10B. If **no**, please indicate the patient's estimated height.

a Short

b Average

c Tall

d Not recorded

10B | a | b | c | d |

5

11. To which ethnic group did the patient belong?

a White

b West Indian/Guyanese

c Indian/Pakistani/Bangladeshi

d Chinese

e African

f Arab

g Mixed Origin

h Other (Please specify)

11 | a | b | c | d | e | f | g | h |

ADMISSION DETAILS

12. Initial admission intention for the last operation performed:

a **Elective** - at a time agreed between patient and surgical service

b **Urgent** - within 48 hours of referral/ consultation

c **Emergency** - immediately following referral/consultation, when admission is unpredictable and at short notice because of clinical need.

12 | a | b | c |

Please specify the following dates:

13. Date of initial referral for condition leading to final operation (eg date on letter of referral):

13 | | | | | | | D D M M Y Y

14. Date of first consultation following referral:

14 | | | | | | | D D M M Y Y

6

15. Decision to operate:

[| | | |] 15   Time [| | |] 15A
D D M M Y Y   (use 24 hour clock)

16. Date of admission to hospital in which final operation took place:

[| | | |] 16   Time [| | |] 16A
D D M M Y Y   (use 24 hour clock)

16A. Admission

[| | |] 16A

a Weekday (ie Monday to Friday)

b Weekend (ie Saturday or Sunday)

c Public Holiday

d Extra-statutory Holiday (NHS)

ELECTIVE ADMISSIONS

If the patient was admitted on an urgent or emergency basis please move straight to Q24.

17. Date placed on waiting list:

[| | | | |] 17
D D M M Y Y

18. Was the patient's category as an elective admission appropriate (bearing in mind subsequent events)?

[|] 18
Yes
No

19. If the patient waited longer than six months, was his/her clinical status reassessed in a pre-admission clinic prior to admission?

[|] 19
a Yes
b No

20. Was this patient initially intended as an elective day case? (see definition below)

[|] 20
Yes
No

Definition

A surgical day case is a patient who is admitted for investigation or operation on a planned non-resident basis (ie no overnight stay).

21. Had this patient's admission ever been cancelled on a previous occasion as a result of a lack of resources (ie not a patient imposed delay)?

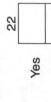

[|] 21
Yes
No

If **yes**, please explain.

_____

_____

22. Was the outcome in this case altered by the time spent on the waiting list?

[|] 22
Yes
No

If **yes**, please explain.

_____

_____

25B. Did this delay affect the outcome?

Yes
No

        25B ☐☐

REFERRAL DETAILS

26. Source of referral:

a General Medical Practitioner
b General Dental Practitioner
c A/E department
d Out-patient follow-up clinic
e Transfer from another hospital
f Other specialty
g Self referral by patient
h Own specialty
i Other (please specify) _____

26 ☐☐☐☐☐☐☐☐☐ a b c d e f g h i

27. Was the patient transferred from another department within the hospital where the operation took place?

Yes
No

27 ☐☐

If **yes**, give date and time of transfer to surgical team:

Date [☐☐☐☐☐☐] 27A   Time [☐☐☐☐] 27B
     D D M M Y Y   (use 24 hour clock)

N.B. If the patient was transferred as an in-patient from another hospital, ie option "e" in Q26, answer Q28 to Q31 below, otherwise go directly to Q32.

---

23. Did any out-patient investigations impose an undesirable delay in setting a date for surgery?

Yes
No

23 ☐☐

If **yes**, please explain.

Now move to Q26.

URGENT AND EMERGENCY ADMISSIONS

If the patient was admitted on an elective basis please move straight to Question 26.

24. Was there any delay in **REFERRAL** on this occasion?

Yes a
No b

24 ☐☐

24A. If **yes**, was the delay:

a Doctor related
b Patient related
c Other (Please specify)

24A ☐☐☐ a b c

25. Was there any delay in **ADMITTING** the patient?

Yes a
No b

25 ☐☐

25A. If **yes**, was the delay due to:

a Lack of resources (Please specify) _____
b Surgical staff committed elsewhere
c Non-medical staff shortages
d Other (Please specify) _____

25A ☐☐☐☐ a b c d

28. Location of referring hospital:

a non-NHS
b same District (or Health Board)
c same Region
d outside Region
e overseas
f other (Please specify)

28	a	b	c	d	e	f

29. Type of referring hospital:

a District General Hospital
b University/Teaching Hospital
c Surgical Specialty Hospital
d Other Acute/Partly Acute Hospital
e Community Hospital
f MOD Hospital
g Independent Hospital
h Other (Please specify)

29	a	b	c	d	e	f	g	h

30. Why was the patient transferred?

_____

_____

31. Did the patient's condition deteriorate during transfer?

Yes / No

31	

32. Was the patient's transfer **to** another hospital ever considered?

Yes / No

32	

33. If transfer was considered desirable, why was it not undertaken?

_____

_____

_____

34. To what type of area was the patient first admitted? (see definitions)

a Medical ward
b Coronary care unit (CCU)
c Geriatric ward
d Surgical ward
e Mixed medical/surgical ward
f Gynaecological/obstetric ward
g Admission ward

h Day unit
i HDU (see definition)
j ICU (see definition)
k A/E holding area (or other emergency admission ward)
l Direct to theatre
m Other (please specify)

34	a	b	c	d	e	f	g		h	i	j	k	l	m

_____

Definitions

A high dependency unit (HDU) is an area for patients who require more intensive observation and/or nursing than would be expected on a general ward. Patients who require mechanical ventilation or other organ support would not be admitted to this area.

An intensive care unit (ICU) is an area to which patients are admitted for treatment of actual or impending organ failure who may require technological support (including mechanical ventilation of the lungs and/or invasive monitoring).

35. Was the patient initially admitted to an adult or paediatric ward?

35 | a |
|---|
| b |

a Adult

b Paediatric

36. Was the site of admission appropriate for the patient's condition?

36 | |
|---|

Yes

No

If **no**, please explain

_____

_____

37. Was care undertaken on a formal shared basis with another specialty?

37 | |
|---|

Yes

No

If **yes**, please specify

_____

_____

_____

13

---

38. Who made the **working diagnosis**? (This can be a multiple entry - please put a tick in **each** appropriate box).

Please tick the second column if a locum.

	Locum
a	
b	
c	
d	
e	38
f	
g	
h	
i	
j	

a General Practitioner (Medical or Dental)

b HO

c SHO

d Registrar

e Senior Registrar

f Consultant

g Staff Grade

h Clinical Assistant

i Associate Specialist

j Other (please specify) _____

39. Which grade of surgeon made the **final decision to operate**?

Please tick the second column if a locum.

	Locum
a	
b	
c	
d	39
e	
f	
g	
h	
i	

a HO

b SHO

c Registrar

d Senior Registrar

e Consultant

f Staff Grade

g Clinical Assistant

h Associate Specialist

i Other (please specify) _____

14

40. What was the grade of the most senior surgeon **consulted** before the operation?

Please tick the second column if a locum.

a HO

b SHO

c Registrar

d Senior Registrar

e Consultant

f Staff Grade

g Clinical Assistant

h Associate Specialist

i Other (please specify) —————————

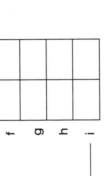

	Locum
a	
b	
c	
d	40
e	
f	
g	
h	
i	

41. Please record all surgical staff who **took history** before operation but after admission (this can be multiple entry).

Please tick the second column if a locum.

a HO

b SHO

c Registrar

d Senior Registrar

e Consultant

f Staff Grade

g Clinical Assistant

h Associate Specialist

i Other (please specify) —————————

	Locum
a	
b	
c	
d	41
e	
f	
g	
h	
i	

42. Please record all surgical staff who **examined** the patient before operation but after admission (this can be multiple entry).

Please tick the second column if a locum.

a HO

b SHO

c Registrar

d Senior Registrar

e Consultant

f Staff Grade

g Clinical Assistant

h Associate Specialist

i Other (please specify) —————————

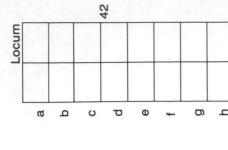

	Locum
a	
b	
c	42
d	
e	
f	
g	
h	
i	

43. Working diagnosis by most senior member of surgical team.

_____

_____

_____

44. What operation was proposed by the most senior member of the surgical team?

_____

_____

_____

45. What was the immediate indication for the proposed operation?

_____

_____

_____

_____

46. Co-existing problems at time of final surgery (specify disorder in space next to category). Please put a tick in each appropriate box.

		46
a Respiratory _____	a	
b Cardiac _____	b	
c Renal _____	c	
d Haematological _____	d	
e Gastrointestinal _____	e	
f Vascular _____	f	
g Sepsis _____	g	
h Neurological _____	h	
i Endocrine (including diabetes mellitus) _____	i	
j Musculoskeletal _____	j	
k Psychiatric _____	k	
l Alcohol-related problems _____	l	
m Drug addiction _____	m	
n Genetic abnormality _____	n	
o Other (Please specify) _____	o	

47. ASA class (see definition below)

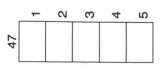

47	
	1
	2
	3
	4
	5

American Society Of Anesthesiology (A.S.A.) Classifications Of Physical Status

Class 1

This patient has no organic, psychological or psychotic disturbance. The pathological process for which operation is to be performed is localised and does not entail a systemic disturbance.

Class 2

Mild to moderate systemic disturbance or distress caused by either the condition to be treated surgically or by other pathophysiological processes.

Class 3

Severe systemic disturbance or disease from whatever cause, even though it may not be possible to define the degree of disability with finality.

Class 4

Severe systemic disorders that are already life threatening, not always correctable by operation.

Class 5

The moribund patient who has little chance of survival but is submitted to operation in desperation.

48. What was the anticipated risk of death related to the proposed operation?

a Not expected

b Small but significant risk

c Definite risk

d Expected

48	
	a
	b
	c
	d

48A. If death was **expected**, specify the anticipated benefit of the operation.

_____

_____

_____

PRE-OPERATIVE PREPARATION

49. What precautions or therapeutic manoeuvres were undertaken pre-operatively (excluding anaesthetic room management) to ensure adequate physiological function?

Enter a tick in each appropriate box.

49 | a | b | c | d | e | f | g | h | i | j | k | l | m | n | o | p | q |

a Pulse rate recording
b Blood pressure recording
c Respiratory rate recording
d Temperature
e Central venous pressure measurement
f Cardiac support drugs or antidysrhythmic agents
g Gastric aspiration
h Intravenous fluids
i Correction of hypovolaemia
j Urinary catheterisation
k Blood transfusion
l Diuretics
m Anticoagulants
n Vitamin K
o Antibiotics (pre or intraoperative)
p Bowel preparation (specify method used) _____
c Chest physiotherapy

continued . . .

r | s | t | u | v | w | x | y | z |

r Oxygen therapy
s Blood gas analysis
t Pulse oximetry
u Airway protection (eg in unconscious patients)
v Tracheal intubation
w Mechanical ventilation
x Nutritional support
y DVT prophylaxis (please specify method used) _____
z Others (please specify) _____

N | | None

50. If no DVT prophylaxis was used, is this your usual policy?

50 | a | b |

Yes a
No b

51. Was emergency radiology (including CT scanning) readily accessible?

51 | | |

Yes
No

If **no**, please explain

52. Did the patient's medication (excluding premedication) influence the outcome?

52 | | |

Yes
No

If **yes**, please explain :

_____

53. Date of start of final operation before death:

D D M M Y Y   53

53A. Please circle day: M   T   W   Th   F   Sa   Sun

53B. Was this,

a Public Holiday

b Extra-statutory Holiday (NHS)

c Neither

53B | a | b | c |

53C. Time of start of operation:
(not including anaesthetic time)

53C

(use 24 hour clock)

53D. Out of hours operations only:
Would this operation have been done during the routine list time if operating theatre space had been available?

53D | a | b |

Yes   No

If **yes**, please specify.

_____

_____

---

54. What was the grade of the most senior operating surgeon? Please tick the second column if a locum.

Locum

54

a HO

b SHO

c Registrar

d Staff Grade

e Senior Registrar

f Clinical Assistant

g Associate Specialist

h Consultant

i Other (please specify) _____

55. How long had this surgeon spent in this grade in this specialty?

_____ yrs   _____ mths

56. How many similar procedures had this surgeon performed in the last year? (If not known, please enter an estimate)

_____ procedures

57. Was a more senior surgeon **immediately** available, ie in the operating room/suite?

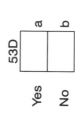

57

Yes

No

If **yes**, please specify grade and location.

Grade _____

Location _____

58. Diagnosis established at operation:

_____

_____

59. Final operation undertaken:

_____

_____

60. If the operation was different to that proposed, please explain.

_____

_____

_____

N.B. **Please include a copy of all operation notes. If the final operation is one of a sequence please send copies of preceding operation notes, numbered in sequence, and include any comments you wish to make about the relevance of these preceding operations to the final outcome. Identification will be removed at the NCEPOD office.**

61. Multiple operations. If this operation was the most recent in a sequence or was preceded by a minor procedure, please list the other procedures.

Operation	Date	Specialty of Operating Surgeon
a		
b		
c		
d		

62. Classify the final operation (see definitions below and choose the category most appropriate to the case).

a Emergency

b Urgent

c Scheduled

d Elective

62 | | a
   | | b
   | | c
   | | d

Definitions

a **Emergency**

Immediate life-saving operation, resuscitation simultaneous with surgical treatment (eg trauma, ruptured aortic aneurysm). Operation usually within one hour.

b **Urgent**

Operation as soon as possible after resuscitation (eg irreducible hernia, intussusception, oesophageal atresia, intestinal obstruction, major fractures). Operation usually within 24 hours.

c **Scheduled**

An early operation but not immediately life saving (eg malignancy). Operation usually within 3 weeks.

d **Elective**

Operation at a time to suit both patient and surgeon (eg cholecystectomy, joint replacement).

63. In view of your answer to Q62, was there any delay due to factors other than clinical?

63 | |
Yes

No

If **yes**, please specify:

_____

64. Duration of operation (not including anaesthetic time)

_____ hrs _____ mins

Cardiac cases only:

Ischaemic Time

_____ hrs _____ mins

65. Was the time taken acceptable?

65 | |
Yes

No

66. Were there any unanticipated intra-operative problems?

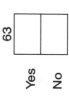

66 | |
Yes

No

If **yes**, please specify.

_____

_____

LOCAL/REGIONAL ANAESTHESIA OR SEDATION

67. Was local/regional anaesthesia or sedation administered by the **operating surgeon** at any time during the procedure?

Yes
No

[box 67]

If **no**, go to Q71

If **yes**, what was the main drug/agent used?

_____

What dosage was administered?

_____

68. Was any other drug administered with the local anaesthetic?

Yes
No

[box 68]

If **yes**, please describe.

_____
_____

69. If the procedure was performed **solely** under local anaesthetic or sedation administered by the surgeon, which of the following were recorded during or immediately after the procedure?

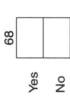

a Blood pressure

b Pulse

c ECG

d Pulse oximetry

e Other (please specify) _____

f None

---

70. Were facilities for resuscitation, including airway management, immediately available during this procedure?

Yes
No

[box 70]

POSTOPERATIVE PROGRESS

71. Which of the following are available in the hospital in which the final operation took place (see definitions below):

a Theatre recovery area

b Adult ICU

c Adult HDU

d Paediatric ICU/HDU

e None of the above

[boxes 71 a b c d e]

Definitions (as used by the Association of Anaesthetists of Great Britain and Ireland)

1. A **recovery area** is an area to which patients are admitted from an operating room, where they remain until consciousness is regained and ventilation and circulation are stable.

2. A **high dependency unit (HDU)** is an area for patients who require more intensive observation and/or nursing care than would normally be expected on a general ward. Patients who require mechanical ventilation or other organ support would not be admitted to this area.

3. An **intensive care unit (ICU)** is an area to which patients are admitted for treatment of actual or impending organ failure who may require technological support (including mechanical ventilation of the lungs and/or invasive monitoring).

72. Was the patient admitted immediately to an ICU or HDU postoperatively?

72 [a | b | c]

- a ICU
- b HDU
- c Neither of the above

73. If **neither**, was the patient admitted to an ICU/HDU after an initial period on a routine postoperative ward ?

73 [a | b]

Yes a

No b

After how many days postoperatively? _____ days

N.B.If the answer to either Q72 or Q73 was negative, then please answer question 74 and then proceed directly to Q79. If the answer to either question was yes, then please answer all the following questions.

74. Were you at any time unable to transfer the patient into an ICU/HDU within the hospital in which the surgery took place?

74 [a | b]

Yes a

No b

If **yes**, why?

_____

75. Were the ICU/HDU facilities adequate?

75 [|]

Yes

No

If **no**, what was inadequate?

_____
_____
_____

76. What were the indications for the admission to ICU/HDU? (This can be multiple entry).

76 [a | b | c | d | e | f | g | h | i | j | k]

- a Specialist nursing
- b Presence of experienced intensivists
- c General monitoring
- d Metabolic monitoring
- e Ventilation
- f Surgical complications
- g Anaesthetic complications
- h Co-incident medical diseases
- i Inadequate nursing on general wards
- j Transfer from hospital without facilities
- k Other (Please specify)

77. Discharge from ICU/HDU was due to:

77 [a | b | c | d]

- a Elective transfer to ward
- b Pressure on beds
- c Death
- d Other (Please specify)

78. Was the patient subsequently readmitted to an ICU/HDU etc?

78 [a | b]

Yes a

No b

If **yes**, please give details.

_____
_____
_____

79. Were there any postoperative complications?

79   a   Yes

      b   No

If **yes**, which of the following?

79A

a Haemorrhage/postoperative bleeding requiring transfusion

b Upper respiratory obstruction

c Respiratory distress

d Generalised sepsis

e Wound infection

f Wound dehiscence

g Anastomotic failure

h Low cardiac output

i Cardiac arrest

j Hepatic failure

k Renal failure

l Endocrine system failure

m Stroke or other neurological problems

n Persistent coma

o Other organ failure (Please specify)

p Problems with analgesia

q DVT and/or pulmonary embolus

r Fat embolus

s Orthopaedic prosthetic complication

t Pressure sores

u Peripheral ischaemia

v Urinary tract infection

w Urinary retention/Catheter blockage

x Ureteric injury/fistula

y Nutritional problems

z Other (Please specify)

80. Was mechanical ventilation employed postoperatively?

80   Yes

     No

80A. Is this your usual practice in this type of procedure?

80A   Yes

      No

80B. If mechanical ventilation was employed, were there any complications with it?

80B   Yes

      No

If **yes**, please explain:

Continued . . . .

DEATH

81. Date of death

D D M M Y Y 81

81A. a Weekday
 b Weekend
 c Public holiday
 d Extra-statutory holiday (NHS)

81A a b c d

82. Time of death. (use 24 hour clock)

83. Place of death

 a Theatre
 b Recovery room
 c Ward
 d ICU/HDU
 e CCU
 f Home
 g Another hospital
 h Other (Please specify) _____

83 a b c d e f g h

84. Was cardiopulmonary resuscitation attempted?

Yes
No

84

If **not**, why not? _____

_____

85. What was the immediate **clinical** cause of death? (This need not be a duplication of the death certificate.)

_____

_____

_____

_____

86. **CAUSE OF DEATH** (this is a facsimile of the death certificate: please complete it accordingly).

I (a) Disease or condition directly leading to death

_____

_____

(b) Other disease or condition, if any, leading to I(a)

_____

_____

(c) Other disease or condition, if any leading to I(b)

_____

_____

II Other significant conditions CONTRIBUTING TO THE DEATH but not related to the disease or condition causing it

_____

_____

_____

_____

---

87. Was the death reported to the coroner?

Yes ▢ No ▢ 87

87A. If **yes**, was an autopsy ordered (and performed) under the coroner's authority?

Yes ▢ No ▢ 87A

88. Was a **hospital** postmortem requested?

Yes ▢ No ▢ 88

If **no**, why not?

_____

88A. If **yes**, who requested the postmortem permission from the relatives?

88A ▢a ▢b ▢c ▢d ▢e ▢f ▢g

a HO
b SHO
c Registrar
d Senior Registrar
e Associate Specialist
f Consultant
g Other (Please specify)

_____

▢ NCEPOD use

89. Was a hospital postmortem refused?

Yes ☐ No ☐ **89**

89A. If **yes**, by whom?

a Relative
b Pathologist
c Other (Please specify)

89A [a ☐] [b ☐] [c ☐]

N.B. If a postmortem was not performed, please move to Q98.

90. Was the surgical team informed of the date and time of postmortem?

Yes ☐ No ☐ **90**

91. Which member of the surgical team attended the postmortem?

a HO
b SHO
c Registrar
d Staff Grade
e Senior Registrar
f Associate Specialist
g Consultant
h Other (please specify)

91 [a][b][c][d][e][f][g][h]

i None of the above [i]

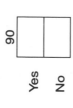

91A. If a surgeon did not attend the postmortem, why not?

_____
_____

92. Did the consultant surgeon and his/her team receive a copy of the postmortem report?

Yes ☐ No ☐ **92**

93. What was the date of the first written information received about any postmortem?

[ ][ ] [ ][ ] [ ][ ] **93**
D D   M M   Y Y

94. Please list what you regard as the relevant findings of the postmortem (not a copy of the death certificate).

_____
_____
_____
_____
_____
_____

PLEASE SEND A COPY OF ALL POSTMORTEM REPORTS AND POSTMORTEM REQUEST FORM IF AVAILABLE

95. Was the pathological information given useful, ie did it contribute additional information to the understanding of the patient's illness?

95 [|] Yes / No

If **not**, why not?

_____

96. Who performed the postmortem?

a Specialist pathologist (e.g. Neuropathologist)

b Consultant pathologist

c Junior pathologist

96 [a | b | c]

97. Are you aware of any other specialty of the pathologist involved? (e.g. Haematology, Microbiology, Biochemistry, etc)

97 [|] Yes / No

If **yes**, please specify:

_____

_____

98. Has this death been considered, (or will it be considered) at a local audit/quality control meeting?

98 [|] Yes / No

99. Was there a shortage of personnel in this case?

99 [|] Yes / No

99A. If **yes**, which?

a Consultant surgeons

b Trainee surgeons

c Consultant anaesthetists

d Trainee anaesthetists

e Skilled assistants

f Nurses

g ODAs

h Porters

i Other (Please specify) _____

99A [a | b | c | d | e | f | g | h | i]

100. Who completed this questionnaire?

a HO

b SHO

c Registrar

d Staff Grade

e Senior Registrar

f Associate Specialist

g Consultant

h Other (please specify) _____

100 [a | b | c | d | e | f | g | h]

101. Did you have any problems in obtaining the patient's notes?

101 [|] Yes / No

If **yes**, how long did they take to reach you? _____

102. Were all the notes available?

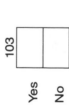

Yes

No

102

102A. If **no**, which part was inadequate/unavailable?

a Pre-operative notes

b Operative notes

c Postoperative notes

d Death certificate book

e Other notes (Please specify) ————————

102A
a
b
c
d
e

103. Were the nursing notes available?

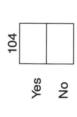

Yes

No

103

104. Has the consultant surgeon seen and agreed this form?

Yes

No

104

105. Date questionnaire completed

D D M M Y Y

THANK YOU FOR TAKING THE TIME TO COMPLETE THIS

QUESTIONNAIRE

<u>**YOU MUST NOT KEEP A COPY OF THIS QUESTIONNAIRE**</u>

Please return it in the reply-paid envelope provided to:

NCEPOD

35-43 Lincoln's Inn Fields

LONDON

WC2A 3PN

THIS QUESTIONNAIRE IS THE PROPERTY OF NCEPOD

If you wish to inform the NCEPOD office of any other details of this case,

please do so here or on a separate sheet.

National Confidential Enquiry Into Perioperative Deaths

35-43 LINCOLN'S INN FIELDS, LONDON WC2A 3PN

ANAESTHETIC QUESTIONNAIRE (DEATHS) 1991-1992

QUESTIONNAIRE No. [A][ ][ ][ ][ ]

DO NOT PHOTOCOPY ANY PART OF THIS QUESTIONNAIRE

QUESTIONNAIRE COMPLETION

The whole questionnaire will be shredded when data collection is complete.

The information you supply is important. It must be accurate if valid conclusions are to be drawn.

Neither the questions nor the choices for answers are intended to suggest standards of practice.

Please **enclose** a copy of the ANAESTHETIC record(s) and of the fluid balance chart(s). Any identification will be removed in the NCEPOD office.

Many of the questions can be answered by "Yes" or "No".
Please insert the relevant number in the appropriate box eg

[1] for Yes

[2] for No

Where multiple choices are given, please insert the relevant letter(s) of your answer in the box(es), and leave the remaining boxes blank.

Eg question 6b

[C][D][ ]

indicates that advice was sought from both a Senior Registrar and a Consultant.

Consultants or junior staff may write to the NCEPOD office under separate cover, quoting the questionnaire number.

All original copies of correspondence will be confidential (**but do not retain copies of your correspondence**).

In case of difficulty, please contact the NCEPOD office on:

071 831 6430

HAVE YOU ENCLOSED COPIES OF THE ANAESTHETIC

HOSPITAL

1. In what type of hospital did the anaesthetic take place?
   - A District General Hospital
   - B University/Teaching Hospital
   - C Surgical Specialty Hospital
   - D Other Acute/Partly Acute Hospital
   - E Community Hospital
   - F MOD Hospital
   - G Independent Hospital
   - H Other (please specify)

   [ ] 1

2. Is this hospital part of, or wholly, an NHS Trust?

   Yes = 1   No = 2

   [ ] 2

PROXY ANAESTHETISTS

3. If you were not involved in any way with this anaesthetic and have filled out this questionnaire on behalf of someone else, please indicate your position.
   - A Chairman of Division
   - B College Tutor
   - C Duty Consultant
   - D Other Consultant
   - E Other (please specify)

   [ ] 3

THE ANAESTHETIST(S)

4. Grade(s) of anaesthetist(s) who were present at this anaesthetic. Enter the appropriate letter for each person present.
   - A SHO
   - B Registrar
   - C Senior Registrar
   - D Consultant
   - E Staff Grade
   - F Associate Specialist
   - G Clinical Assistant
   - H General Practitioner
   - I Hospital Practitioner
   - J Other (please specify)

   [A][B][C][D][E][F][G][H][I][J] 4

...want to know about the experience of the **most senior anaesthetist** in the operating room at the start of this procedure

Questions 8 to 10 inclusive refer to this anaesthetist

8. Year of primary medical qualification ☐☐☐☐ 8a

   and the university (or institution) awarding this qualification: _____ 8b

   If not in UK, please state country: _____ 8c

9. Year of first full-time anaesthetic training post ☐☐☐☐ 9a

   Which higher diploma in anaesthesia is held? 9b

   A none ☐ A
   B FFARCS/FCAnaes/FFARCSI/FFARACS ☐ B
   C DA (ie Part 1 FCAnaes) ☐ C
   D Other (please specify) ☐ D

   Year of award of higher qualification: ☐☐☐☐ 9c

10. If the most senior anaesthetist present was **not** in a training grade, please enter the appropriate letters in the boxes provided if he/she has regular weekly (ie more than 50 operations per year) NHS commitments in anaesthesia for the following: 10

    A cardiac surgery ☐ A
    B children under 3 years old ☐ B
    C neurosurgery ☐ C
    D plastic surgery ☐ D

THE PATIENT

11. Date of patient's birth ☐☐ ☐☐ ☐☐ 11
        D D M M Y Y

12. Age of patient at time of operation _____Y _____M 12

13. Date of admission to hospital in which final operation took place
    eg 05 04 91 (5th April 1991). ☐☐ ☐☐ ☐☐ 13
        D D M M Y Y

Yes = 1   No = 2

☐ 5a

If **yes**, specify grade(s) _____ b

6. Did the anaesthetist (of whatever grade) **seek advice** at any time from another anaesthetist (not mentioned in question 4)?

   Yes = 1   No = 2 ☐ 6a

   If **yes**, grade(s) of anaesthetist(s) from whom advice sought: 6b

   A SHO ☐ A
   B Registrar ☐ B
   C Senior Registrar ☐ C
   D Consultant ☐ D
   E Staff Grade ☐ E
   F Associate Specialist ☐ F
   G Clinical Assistant ☐ G
   H General Practitioner ☐ H
   I Hospital Practitioner ☐ I
   J Other (please specify) ☐ J

7. Did any colleague(s) (not mentioned in question 4) **come to help** at any time?

   Yes = 1   No = 2 ☐ 7a

   If **yes**, grade(s) of anaesthetist(s) who came to help: 7b

   A SHO ☐ A
   B Registrar ☐ B
   C Senior Registrar ☐ C
   D Consultant ☐ D
   E Staff Grade ☐ E
   F Associate Specialist ☐ F
   G Clinical Assistant ☐ G
   H General Practitioner ☐ H
   I Hospital Practitioner ☐ I
   J Other (please specify) ☐ J

14. Time of admission ☐☐☐☐ 14

use 24 hour clock

15. Date of operation ☐☐☐☐☐ 15

D D M M Y Y

16. Date of death ☐☐☐☐☐ 16

D D M M Y Y

17. Was the patient transferred from another hospital? 17 ☐

Yes = 1   No = 2

If **no**, please go to question 26
If **yes**, please answer questions 18 to 25

18. From what type of hospital was the patient transferred? 18 ☐

A   District General Hospital
B   University/Teaching Hospital
C   Surgical Specialty Hospital
D   Other Acute/Partly Acute Hospital
E   Community Hospital
F   MOD Hospital
G   Independent Hospital
H   Other (please specify)
_____

19. Who accompanied the patient during transit? 19 ☐☐☐☐☐☐

A B C D E F

A   ambulance crew

B   relative(s)

C   nurse
      (specify grade) _____

D   anaesthetist
      (specify grade) _____

E   other doctor (please specify)
_____

F   other (please specify)

---

20. Was there any special care of the airway during transfer? 20a ☐

Yes = 1   No = 2

20b ☐☐☐☐☐
A B C D E

if **yes**, which

A   added oxygen
B   pharyngeal airway
C   tracheal tube
D   controlled ventilation
E   other (please specify)
_____

21. Did the patient's condition deteriorate during transfer? 21 ☐

Yes = 1   No = 2   Not known = 3

If **yes**, please explain:
_____
_____

22. What was the patient's clinical circulatory state on arrival? 22 ☐

A   well-perfused and warm
B   cold and vasoconstricted

23. What was the patient's state of clinical oxygenation on arrival? 23 ☐

A   well oxygenated
B   mild hypoxaemia
C   severe hypoxaemia

24. Was cardiorespiratory resuscitation required immediately on arrival? 24 ☐

Yes = 1   No = 2

If **yes**, please explain (eg fluids, inotropes etc) :
_____
_____
_____

25. What was the patient's neurological status at the time of arrival? 25

A Glasgow Coma Scale less than 7
B Glasgow Coma Scale 7 or more

Glasgow Coma Scale

Eye opening	Pts	Verbal response	Pts	Motor response to pain (best limb)	Pts
Spontaneous	4	Orientated verbal response	5	Obeys commands	5
Eye opening to speech	3	Confused verbal response	4	Localisation	4
Eye opening to pain	2	Inappropriate words	3	Flexion normal/abnormal	3
None	1	Incomprehensible sounds	2	Extension	2
		No verbal response	1	No motor response	1

THE OPERATION

26. Primary diagnosis

_____
_____
_____
_____

27. What operation was planned?

_____
_____
_____
_____

28. What operation was performed, if different?

_____
_____
_____
_____

29. If this operation was the most recent in a sequence, please list the previous procedures.

Procedure   Date

_____   _____
_____   _____
_____   _____
_____   _____

Please enclose a copy of all anaesthetic record(s)

30. Classification of operation (last before death). See definitions below. 30

A Emergency
B Urgent
C Scheduled
D Elective

Definitions

A **Emergency**
Immediate life-saving operation, resuscitation simultaneous with surgical treatment (eg trauma, ruptured aortic aneurysm). Operation usually within one hour.

B **Urgent**
Operation as soon as possible after resuscitation (eg irreducible hernia, intussusception, oesophageal atresia, intestinal obstruction, major fractures). Operation within 24 hours.

C **Scheduled**
An early operation, but not immediately life-saving (eg malignancy). Operation usually within 3 weeks.

D **Elective**
Operation at a time to suit both patient and surgeon (eg cholecystectomy, joint replacement).

CONDITION BEFORE OPERATION

31. Was a record of the patient's weight available?

31 ☐

Yes = 1   No = 2

If **yes**, what was this weight? _____ kg

If **no**, the estimated weight was _____ kg

32. Was a record of the patient's height available?

32 ☐

Yes = 1   No = 2

If **yes**, what was this height? _____ cm

If **no**, estimated height was _____ cm

33. Was an anaesthetist **consulted** by the surgeon (as distinct from informed) before the operation?

33 ☐

Yes = 1   No = 2

34. Did an anaesthetist visit the patient before the operation?

34a ☐

Yes = 1   No = 2

If **yes**, was <u>this</u> anaesthetist present at the start of the operation?

34b ☐

Yes = 1   No = 2

35. Were any investigations done before the operation? (Including tests carried out in the referral hospital and available before the operation.)

35a ☐

Yes = 1   No = 2

If **yes**, which of the following?

PLEASE WRITE RESULTS IN THE SPACE NEXT TO THE TEST NAME

INDICATE WHICH TEST(S) BY INSERTION OF THE APPROPRIATE LETTER IN EACH BOX

35b

A ☐   Haemoglobin _____ gm.litre^{-1}

B ☐   Packed cell volume (haematocrit) _____

C ☐   White cell count _____ x10^9.litre^{-1}

D ☐   Sickle cell test (eg Sickledex) _____

E ☐   Coagulation screen _____

F ☐   Plasma electrolytes   Na _____ m mol.litre^{-1}

G ☐   K _____ m mol.litre^{-1}

H ☐   Cl _____ m mol.litre^{-1}

I ☐   HCO$_3$ _____ m mol.litre

J ☐   Blood urea _____ m mol.litre^{-1}

K ☐   Creatinine _____ micro mol.litre^{-1}

L ☐   Serum albumin _____ g.litre^{-1}

M ☐   Bilirubin (total) _____ micro mol.litre^{-1}

N ☐   Glucose _____ m mol.litre

O ☐   Urinalysis (ward or lab)

P ☐   Blood gas analysis

Q ☐   Chest x-ray

R ☐   Electrocardiography

S ☐   Respiratory function tests

Continued

T Echocardiography _____

U Special cardiac investigation
   (eg cardiac catheterization) _____

V Special neurological investigation
   (ie imaging) _____

W Others relevant to anaesthesia (please specify) _____
   _____

35b

T	U	V	W

36. Coexisting medical diagnoses (please enter the appropriate letter in a box, **and** specify the disorder in the space next to the category).

36

A	B	C	D	E	F	G	H	I	J	K

A none _____

B respiratory _____

C cardiac _____

D neurological _____

E endocrine _____

F alimentary _____

G renal _____

H musculoskeletal _____

I haematological _____

J genetic abnormality _____

K other (please specify) _____
   _____
   _____

37. What drug or other therapy was the patient receiving at the time of operation (but excluding premedication or drugs for anaesthesia)?

Please enter each appropriate letter, and specify drugs and doses in the space below each category.

37

A	B	C	D	E	F	G	H	I	J	K	L	M	N	O	P	Q	R	S	T	U	V	W	X

A none _____

B analgesic – aspirin _____

C analgesic – other non-narcotic (specify) _____

D analgesic – narcotic (specify) _____

E anti-angina _____

F anti-arrhythmic _____

G anticoagulant _____

H anticonvulsant _____

I antidepressant _____

J antidiabetic _____

K antihypertensive _____

L anti-infective (antibiotic, antifungal, antiviral etc) _____

M anti-Parkinson's _____

N anxiolytic _____

O benzodiazepines _____

P bronchodilator _____

Q cardio- or vaso-active drug (not otherwise specified) _____

R contraceptive _____

S corticosteroid (including Dexamethasone) _____

T cytotoxic _____

U diuretic _____

V H_2 blockers _____

W psychotropic _____

X other (please specify) _____

38. Was there any history of a drug reaction? Please <u>exclude</u>
minor reactions to penicillin.

Yes = 1   No = 2

38 ☐

If **yes**, specify drug and reaction:

_____

_____

_____

39. ASA Status (enter class number)

39 ☐

Class 1
Class 2
Class 3
Class 4
Class 5   (Note we do not use the E subclassification)

ASA Grades

American Society of Anesthesiology Classification of Physical Status

Class 1

The patient has no organic, physiological, biochemical, or psychiatric disturbance. The pathological process for which the operation is to be performed is localized and does not entail a systemic disturbance.

Examples: a fit patient with inguinal hernia
fibroid uterus in an otherwise healthy woman.

Class 2

Mild to moderate systemic disturbance caused either by the condition to be treated surgically or by other pathophysiological processes.

Examples: non-, or only slightly limiting organic heart disease
mild diabetes
essential hypertension
anaemia.

Some might choose to list the extremes of age here, either the neonate or the octogenarian, even though no discernible systemic disease is present. Extreme obesity and chronic bronchitis may be included in this category.

Class 3

Severe systemic disturbance or disease from whatever cause, even though it may not be possible to define the degree of disability with finality.

Examples: severely limiting organic heart disease
severe diabetes with vascular complications
moderate to severe degrees of pulmonary insufficiency
angina pectoris or healed myocardial infarction.

Class 4

Severe systemic disorders that are already life threatening, not always correctable by operation.

Examples: patients with organic heart disease showing marked signs of
cardiac insufficiency
persistent angina or active myocarditis
advanced degree of pulmonary, hepatic, renal or endocrine
insufficiency.

Class 5

The moribund patient who has little chance of survival but is submitted to operation in desperation.

Examples: burst abdominal aneurysm with profound shock
major cereral trauma with rapidly increasing intracranial
pressure massive pulmonary embolus.

Most of these patients require operation as a resuscitative measure with little if any anaesthesia.

PREPARATION OF PATIENT BEFORE OPERATION

40. When was the last fluid/food given by mouth?

40 ☐

A   more than 6 hours before operation

B   between 4-6 hours before operation

C   less than 4 hours before operation

D   not known/not recorded

Please specify nature and volume if known.

_____

_____

Continued

...indicate measures taken to reduce gastric acidity and volume, as prophylaxis against acid aspiration.

41

A none   ☐ A
B antacids   ☐ B
C H$_2$ antagonists   ☐ C
D metoclopramide   ☐ D
E nasogastric/stomach tube   ☐ E
F other (please specify)   ☐ F

42. Did the patient receive intravenous fluid therapy in the 12 hours before induction?

42

Yes = 1   No = 2   ☐ a

If **yes**, please specify nature and volume in 12 hour pre-induction period.

Fluid (enter letter for each)	Total (mls) given in 12 hours before induction
☐	☐☐☐☐ 42b
☐	☐☐☐☐
☐	☐☐☐☐
☐	☐☐☐☐
☐	☐☐☐☐
☐	☐☐☐☐

A Crystalloid or dextrose
B Colloid
C Whole blood
D Red cell component
E Other components eg. platelets
F Mannitol

43. Was anything added to the above solution(s)?

43

Yes = 1   No = 2   ☐

If **yes**, please specify:

_____
_____

44. Were measures (other than those specified in questions 20 and 24) taken to improve the respiratory system **before** induction of anaesthesia?

44a

Yes = 1   No = 2   ☐

If **yes**, please indicate which measure(s) by entering a letter for each.

44b

☐☐☐☐☐

A antibiotic therapy
B bronchodilators (nature and dose)
C chest physiotherapy
D airway management eg oral airway, tracheostomy
E other (please specify)
_____

45. Were premedicant drugs prescribed?

45a

Yes = 1   No = 2   ☐

If **yes**, please enter the appropriate letter in each box, and specify drugs and dose in the space next to each category.

45b

A Atropine _____ ☐ A

B Chloral hydrate _____ ☐ B

C Diazepam (eg Valium) _____ ☐ C

D Droperidol _____ ☐ D

E Fentanyl _____ ☐ E

F Glycopyrronium (Robinul) _____ ☐ F

G Hyoscine (Scopolamine) _____ ☐ G

H Lorazepam (eg Ativan) _____ ☐ H

I Ketamine _____ ☐ I

J Metoclopramide _____ ☐ J

K Methohexitone _____ ☐ K

L Midazolam (Hypnovel) _____ ☐ L

45b

M Morphine —————————— ☐ M

N Papaveretum (Omnopon) —————————— ☐ N

O Pethidine —————————— ☐ O

P Prochlorperazine (eg Stemetil) —————————— ☐ P

Q Temazepam —————————— ☐ Q

R Promethazine (eg Phenergan) —————————— ☐ R

S Trimeprazine (Vallergan) —————————— ☐ S

T Other (Please specify) —————————— ☐ T

---

46. Was **non-invasive** monitoring established **just before** the induction of anaesthesia?   46a ☐

Yes = 1   No = 2

if **yes**, please indicate whether

A ECG
B BP
C pulse oximetry
D other (please specify)

46b ☐☐☐

If **yes** to question 46 what was the blood pressure immediately before induction?

————— / ————— mmHg

---

47. Was **invasive** monitoring established **before** induction of anaesthesia (eg CVP, arterial line)?   ☐

Yes = 1   No = 2

if **yes**, please specify

---

48. Was it necessary to take measures additional to those specified in questions 24 and 43 to improve the patient's cardiovascular function just before and at the induction of anaesthesia?   48a ☐

Yes = 1   No = 2

If **no**, please go to question 49.

If **yes**, please specify (enter appropriate letter in **each** box below).

B Crystalloid IV fluids (Ringer lactate, 0.9% saline, etc)   48b ☐

Yes = 1   No = 2

Please specify type and amount:

C Colloid IV fluids (Dextran, gelatin, etc)   48c ☐

Yes = 1   No = 2

Please specify type and amount:

D Whole blood transfusion   48d ☐

Yes = 1   No = 2

If **yes**, how many units?

E Blood components (packed cells, FFP, Platelets etc)   48e ☐

Yes = 1   No = 2

Please specify type and volume:

F Antiarrhythmic drugs (Verapamil etc)   48f ☐

Yes = 1   No = 2

Please specify drug and dose:

G Cardiac glycoside   48g ☐

Yes = 1   No = 2

If **yes**, please specify:

H Diuretics 48h

Yes = 1   No = 2 ☐

If **yes**, please specify:

I Vasopressors 48i

Yes = 1   No = 2 ☐

If **yes**, please specify:

J Inotropic drugs by infusion (Dobutamine, adrenaline etc) 48j

Yes = 1   No = 2 ☐

If **yes**, please specify drug and strength, solution and dose:

K Others (please specify) 48k

Yes = 1   No = 2 ☐

49. Was there an inappropriate delay before the start of the operation? 49a

Yes = 1   No = 2 ☐

If **yes**, was this due to non-availability of: 49b ☐☐☐☐☐☐☐☐☐☐☐ A B C D E F G H I J K

A radiology
B haematology
C pathology
D operating theatre
E anaesthetist
F anaesthetist's assistant
G surgeon
H theatre staff
I portering staff
J other staff (please specify) _____
K other (please specify) _____

---

50. Were any measures taken (before, during or after operation) to prevent venous thrombosis? 50a

Yes = 1   No = 2 ☐

If **yes**, please enter letter for each measure taken

Before or during ☐☐☐☐☐☐

After ☐☐☐☐☐☐☐ A B C D E F G

A aspirin
B heparin
C dextran infusion
D leg stockings
E calf compression/stimulation
F Warfarin
G Other (please specify)

THE ANAESTHETIC

51. Time of start of anaesthetic 51 ☐☐☐☐

(enter "X" in boxes if times not recorded)   use 24 hour clock

52. Time of start of surgery 52 ☐☐☐☐

use 24 hour clock

53. Time of transfer out of operating room (ie to recovery, ITU etc) 53 ☐☐☐☐

use 24 hour clock

If you are not able to provide the **times**, please indicate total duration of operation (ie time of start of anaesthetic to time of transfer)

_____ hours _____ mins

54. What was the grade of the most senior **surgeon** in the operating room?

54 ☐

A House Officer
B Senior House Officer
C Registrar
D Senior Registrar
E Associate Specialist
F Clinical Assistant
G Staff Grade
H Consultant
I Other (please specify)

55. Did you have **non-medical** help with anaesthesia?

Yes = 1   No = 2

55a ☐

If **yes**, please specify

55b ☐☐☐☐☐☐☐☐☐ A B C D E F G H I

A trained anaesthetic nurse
B trainee anaesthetic nurse
C theatre nurse
D trained operating department assistant (ODA or SODA)
E trainee ODA
F operating department orderly (ODO)
G ward nurse
H physiological measurement technician
I other (please specify)

56. Is there an anaesthetic record for this operation in the notes?

Yes = 1   No = 2

If **yes**, please send a complete copy of it with this questionnaire to the NCEPOD office. (We will delete/remove identification marks).

If **no**, please give an account of the anaesthetic below. Please include details of anaesthetic agents, drugs, routes of administration, breathing systems, and tube size.

59. Were monitoring devices used during the management of this anaesthetic?

Yes = 1   No = 2   59a ☐

If **yes**, please indicate which monitors were used.

Please enter appropriate letter(s) in boxes:

	Anaesthetic Room	Operating Room
A ECG		59b
B pulse oximeter		
C indirect BP		
D pulse meter		
E oesophageal or precordial (chest wall) stethoscope		
F fresh gas O$_2$ analyser		59c
G inspired gas O$_2$ analyser		
H inspired anaesthetic vapour analyser		
I expired CO$_2$ analyser		
J airway pressure gauge		59d
K ventilation volume		
L ventilator disconnect device		
M peripheral nerve stimulator		59e
N temperature (state site) _____		
O urine output		
P CVP		59f
Q direct arterial BP (invasive)		
R pulmonary arterial pressure		
S intracranial pressure		
T other (please specify)		

60. Was there any malfunction of monitoring equipment?   60 ☐

Yes = 1   No = 2

If **yes**, please specify: _____

_____

---

57. Did the patient receive intravenous fluids DURING the operation?

Yes = 1   No = 2   57a ☐

If yes, please indicate which:

Crystalloid

Fluid (indicate type by inserting appropriate letter)	Total volume during operation (mls)
☐☐☐	☐☐☐☐ 57b

A Dextrose 5%
B Dextrose 4% saline 0.18%
C Dextrose 10%
D Saline 0.9%
E Hartmann's (Compound Sodium Lactate)
F other (please specify)

Colloid

☐☐☐	☐☐☐☐ 57c

A Modified gelatin (Gelofusine, Haemaccel)
B Human Albumin solution
C Starch (HES)
D Dextran
E Mannitol (please specify concentration)
F other (please specify)

Blood

☐☐	☐☐☐☐ 57c

A Whole blood
B Red cell component
C Other component (please specify)

58. What was the assessed blood loss during operation?

☐☐☐☐☐ 58
ml

GENERAL ANAESTHESIA

61. Did anything hinder full monitoring?

Yes = 1   No = 2

If **yes**, please specify: (eg bilteral arm surgery, radiotherapy, skin pigmentation, inaccessibility, non-availability of monitors)

61 ☐

_____

POSITION OF PATIENT

62. What was the position of the patient during surgery?

A   supine
B   lateral
C   prone
D   sitting
E   knee-elbow
F   lithotomy (inc. Lloyd-Davies)
G   jack knife
H   other (please specify)

62 ☐

_____

63. Was the main position changed during the procedure?

Yes = 1   No = 2

If **yes**, please explain

63 ☐

_____

TYPE OF ANAESTHESIA

64. What type of anaesthetic was used?

A   general alone (65-73)
B   local infiltration alone
C   regional alone (74-75, and 77)
D   general and regional (65-75)
E   general and local infiltration (65-73)
F   sedation alone (76-77)
G   sedation and local infiltration (76-77)
H   sedation and regional (74-77)

64 ☐

Please now answer the questions (if any) indicated in brackets, and then continue from question 78.

_____

65. Did you take precautions **at induction** to minimise pulmonary aspiration?

65a ☐

Yes = 1   No = 2

If yes, please indicate which

A   cricoid pressure
B   postural changes – head up
C   postural changes – head down
D   postural changes – lateral
E   pre-oxygenation without inflation of the lungs
F   aspiration of nasogastric tube
G   other (please specify)

65b
A	B	C	D	E	F	G

_____

66. How was the airway established during anaesthesia?

A   face mask (with or without oral airway)
B   laryngeal mask
C   orotracheal intubation
D   nasotracheal intubation
E   tracheostomy
F   other (please specify)

66
A	B	C	D	E	F

_____

67. What was the mode of ventilation during the operation?

A   spontaneous
B   controlled

67
A	B

_____

68. If the trachea was intubated, how was the position of the tube confirmed?

A   tube seen passing through cords
B   chest movement with inflation
C   auscultation
D   expired CO_2 monitoring
E   oesophageal detector device
F   other (please specify)

68
A	B	C	D	E	F

REGIONAL ANAESTHESIA

74. If the anaesthetic included a regional technique, which method was used?

74 [| | | | | | | |] A B C D E F G H I

A   epidural – caudal
             lumbar
             thoracic
B   interpleural
C   intravenous regional
D   peripheral nerve block, eg paravertebral, sciatic, intercostal
E   plexus block (eg brachial, 3-in-1 block)
F   subarachnoid (spinal)
G   surface (eg for bronchoscopy)
H
I

75. Which agent was used? Please specify drug(s) and dosage(s)

75 [| |] A B C

A   local _____
B   narcotic _____
C   other (please specify) _____
_____

SEDATION (as opposed to General Anaesthesia)

76. Which sedative drugs were given for this procedure (excluding premedication)?

76 [| | | |] A B C D E

A   inhalant
B   narcotic analgesic
C   benzodiazepine
D   sub-anaesthetic doses of IV anaesthetic drugs
E   other (please specify)
_____
_____

77. Was oxygen given?

77a [ ]

Yes = 1   No = 2

If **yes**, for **what** reason?

77b [|] A B

A   routine
B   otherwise indicated
    (please specify indications)
_____

---

69. Were muscle relaxants used during the anaesthetic?

69a [ ]

Yes = 1   No = 2

If **yes**, please indicate which

69b [|] A B

A   depolarising
B   non-depolarising

70. How was general anaesthesia maintained?

70 [| | |] A B C D

A   nitrous oxide
B   volatile agent
C   narcotic agent
D   intravenous

71. Were there any problems with airway maintenance or ventilation?

71 [ ]

Yes = 1   No = 2

If **yes**, please specify
_____
_____

72. Was the method of airway management changed during the operation?

72 [ ]

Yes = 1   No = 2

If **yes**, please explain
_____
_____

73. Did you induce hypotension deliberately to aid the surgeon?

73a [ ]

Yes = 1   No = 2

If **yes**, specify lowest systolic pressure achieved

73b [| |] mmHg

RECOVERY FROM ANAESTHESIA

Definitions

(as used by the Association of Anaesthetists of Great Britain and Ireland)

1. A recovery area is an area to which patients are admitted from an operating room, where they remain until consciousness is regained and ventilation and circulation are stable.

2. A high dependency unit (HDU or area A) is an area for patients who require more intensive observation and/or nursing care than would normally be expected on a general ward. Patients who require mechanical ventilation or invasive monitoring would not be admitted to this area.

3. An intensive care unit (ICU) is an area to which patients are admitted for treatment of actual or impending organ failure who may require technological support (including mechanical ventilation of the lungs and/or invasive monitoring).

78. Which special care areas (see definitions above) exist in the hospital in which the operation took place?

78 [ ][ ][ ][ ][ ]
A
B
C
D
E

A recovery area or room equipped and staffed for this purpose
B high dependency unit
C intensive care unit
D other (please specify) _____
E none of the above

79. After leaving the operating room, did the patient go to a specific recovery area or room (ie option "A" in question 78)

79 [ ]

Yes = 1   No = 2

If **yes**, please continue with questions 80 and following.

If **no**, please answer question 80 and then go straight to question 86.

If patient died in theatre go to question 94.

80. Were you unable at any time to transfer the patient into an ICU, HDU, etc?

80a [ ]

Yes = 1   No = 2

If **yes**, why?

80b [ ][ ][ ][ ][ ]
A
B
C
D
E

A closed at night
B closed at weekend
C understaffing
D lack of beds
E other (please specify)

RECOVERY AREA/ROOM

81. Were monitoring devices used during the management of this patient in the recovery room?

81a [ ]

Yes = 1   No = 2

If **yes**, please indicate which monitors were used.

Enter a **letter(s)** in **each** box as follows:

81b [ ][ ][ ][ ][ ]
A
B
C
D
E

A ECG
B pulse oximeter
C indirect BP
D pulse meter
E oesophageal or precordial (chest wall) stethoscope

81c [ ]
F

F inspired gas O_2 analyser

81d [ ][ ][ ][ ]
G
H
I
J

G expired CO_2 analyser
H airway pressure gauge
I ventilation volume
J ventilator disconnect device

81e [ ][ ][ ]
K
L
M

K peripheral nerve stimulator
L temperature (state site) _____
M urine output

N CVP
O direct arterial BP (invasive)
P pulmonary arterial pressure
Q intracranial pressure
R other (please specify)

_____

81f

N
O
P
Q
R

82. Who decided that the patient should be discharged from the recovery room?

82 ☐

A the most senior anaesthetist
B another anaesthetist
C surgeon
D nurse
E other (please specify)

_____

83. Time of leaving recovery area

83 ☐☐☐☐

(enter "X" in boxes if times not recorded)   use 24 hour clock

84. Had this patient recovered protective reflexes before discharge from the recovery area?

84 ☐

Yes = 1   No = 2   Not known = 3

85. Where did this patient go next? (ie after the recovery room)

85 ☐

A ward
B high dependency unit
C intensive care unit
D specialised ICU
E home
F another hospital
G died in recovery area (then go to question 94)
H other (please specify)

_____

86. If the patient was **not admitted to a recovery room**, where did this patient go on leaving theatre?

86 ☐

A ward
B high dependency unit
C intensive care unit
D specialised ICU
E home
F another hospital
G other (please specify)

_____
_____

87. Was controlled ventilation used postoperatively?

87a ☐

Yes = 1   No = 2

If **yes**, why?

87b

A ☐
B ☐
C ☐
D ☐

A respiratory inadequacy
B control of intracranial pressure or other neurosurgical indications
C part of the management of pain
D other reasons (please specify)

_____

CRITICAL INCIDENTS DURING ANAESTHESIA OR RECOVERY

88 Did any of the following events, which required specific treatment, occur
during anaesthesia or recovery (see definition below)?

88a ☐

Yes = 1   No = 2

Definition
**A critical incident is defined as an adverse event, which did cause,
or might have caused if left uncorrected, an adverse outcome.**

If **yes**, please specify nature by insertion of the appropriate letter(s)
in a box.

88b

A	B	C	D	E	F	G	H	J	K	M	N	P	Q	S	T	V	W	X	Y	Z

A air embolus

B airway obstruction

C anaphylaxis

D arrhythmia

E bronchospasm

F cardiac arrest (unintended)

G convulsions

H cyanosis

J disconnection of breathing system

K hyperpyrexia
(greater than 40°C or very rapid increase in temperature)

M hypertension (increase of more than 50% resting systolic)

N hypotension (decrease of more than 50% resting systolic)

P hypoxia

Q misplaced tracheal tube

S pneumothorax

T pulmonary aspiration

V pulmonary oedema

W respiratory arrest (unintended)

X total spinal

Y wrong dose or overdose of drug

Z other (please specify)

Please specify location of patient, treatment and outcome.

_____

_____

_____

_____

89. Was there any mechanical failure of equipment (excluding that for
monitoring)?

89a ☐

Yes = 1   No = 2

If **yes**, please specify:

89b

A	B	C	D	E

A equipment for IPPV
B suction equipment
C syringe drivers
D infusion pump
E other (please specify)

90. Were there **early** (ie up to 7 days) complications or events after this
operation?

90a ☐

NB – excluding death in theatre or recovery area

Yes = 1   No = 2

Please enter a letter for each, and specify in the space below
each category:

90b

A ventilatory problems (eg pneumonia, pulmonary oedema)   A ☐

B cardiac problems   B ☐
(eg acute LVF, intractable arrhythmias, post-cardiac arrest)

_____

C hepatic failure   C ☐

_____

90b

D   septicaemia

E   renal failure

F   central nervous system failure
    (eg failure to recover consciousness)

H   other (please specify)
_____

_____

Please give an account of any adverse events during this period.

_____

_____

_____

91. Were narcotic analgesic drugs given in the first 48 hours after operation?
91 ☐

Yes = 1   No = 2

If **yes**, please specify drug(s), dose(s), frequency and route(s):

_____

_____

_____

92. Did complications occur as a result of these analgesic methods?
92 ☐

Yes = 1   No = 2

If **yes**, please specify:

_____

_____

93. Were other sedative/hypnotic or other analgesic (non-narcotic) drugs given?
93 ☐

Yes = 1   No = 2

If **yes**, please specify drug(s), dose(s), times and routes

_____

DEATH

94. Date of death
☐☐ ☐☐ ☐☐ 94
D D M M Y Y

95. Time of death
☐☐☐☐ 95

use 24 hour clock

96. Place of death
96 ☐

A   theatre
B   recovery area
C   intensive care unit
D   high dependency unit
E   ward
F   home
G   another hospital
H   other (please specify)

_____

97. Do you have morbidity/mortality review meetings in your department?
97a ☐

Yes = 1   No = 2

If **yes**, will this case be, or has it been, discussed at your departmental meeting?
97b ☐

Yes = 1   No = 2

98. Has a consultant anaesthetist seen and agreed this form?
98 ☐

Yes = 1   No = 2

REMINDER

Have you enclosed copies of the anaesthetic record and fluid balance charts?

THANK YOU FOR TAKING THE TIME TO COMPLETE THIS QUESTIONNAIRE

YOU MUST NOT KEEP A COPY OF THIS QUESTIONNAIRE

Please send it to NCEPOD
35-43 LINCOLN'S INN FIELDS
LONDON
WC2A 3PN

in the reply paid envelope provided

THIS FORM IS THE PROPERTY OF THE NCEPOD

If you wish to inform the NCEPOD of any other details of this case, please do so here or on a separate sheet.

APPENDIX E

CONSULTANT SURGEONS and GYNAECOLOGISTS

These Consultants have all returned at least one death or index case questionnaire relating to the period 1 April 1991 to 31 March 1992.

A

P. Abel	D. Alderson	I. Appleyard
G.F. Abercrombie	M.I. Aldoori	J.A. Archbold
S.J. Abramovitch	S. Ali	I.A. Archer
P. Abrams	A. Allan	T.J. Archer
R.R. Acheson	D. Allan	D.G. Arkell
J.S. Ackroyd	D.R. Allen	N.C. Armitage
H.M. Adair	E.D. Allen	T.G. Armitage
A.H. Adam	L.N. Allen	P.R. Armitstead
C.B.T. Adams	N. Allen	R.H. Armour
D.A. Adams	T.R. Allen	C.P. Armstrong
A.K.L. Addison	R.L. Allum	M.J. Armstrong
D.M. Adlam	W.H. Allum	S. Armstrong
P. Adlington	D.J. Almond	G.W. Arthur
F. Afshar	M. Alwitry	E.C. Ashby
P.N. Agarwal	L.A. Amanat	M.H. Ashken
J.L. Aggarwal	N.S. Ambrose	K.F. Ashley
S.P. Aggarwal	A.H. Amery	N.J. Astbury
P.M. Aichroth	A.G. Amias	P. Atkins
D.A. Aiken	C.J. Anders	P.M. Atkinson
R.A. Aiken	G.E. Anderson	R.D. Atlay
D.A.P Ainscow	R.S. Anderson	R. Attard
D.C. Aird	J.M. Anderton	A.I. Attwood
D.W. Aird	B.G. Andrews	A. Aubrey
T. Al-Samarrai	J. Andrews	J.M. Auchincloss
A.R.J. Al-Sheikhli	N. Andrews	W. Aucott
A.B.E. Alaily	J.C. Angel	A. Aukland
D. Albert	G.D. Angelini	P. Aukland
J.S. Albert	P.D. Angus	B.S. Avery
B. Alderman	J.N. Antrobus	R. Avill

B

A.V. Babajews	T.W. Balfour	R.L. Barrington
D. Badenoch	R.M. Ballard	A.A.J. Barros D'Sa
N.J. Badham	D.S. Bamford	J.R. Bartlett
B.M.W. Bailey	P.N. Bamford	R.P.E. Barton
I.C. Bailey	J. Bancewicz	N.J. Barwell
J.S. Bailey	D.K. Banerjee	T. Bashir
M.J. Bailey	A.J. Banks	H.K. Basu
F.B. Bailie	P. Banks	A.J.G. Batch
E.T. Bainbridge	G.C. Bannister	D.E.R. Bateman
P.R.E. Baird	G.S. Banwell	C.P. Bates
R.N. Baird	P.R. Baranyovits	T. Bates
J.G.D. Baker	D. Bardsley	P.G. Bateson
J.L. Baker	C.P.G. Barker	N.R. Batey
R. Baker	J.R. Barker	P.J. Bathard-Smith
R.H. Baker	J.D.W. Barnard	H.C. Batra
W.N.W. Baker	A.D. Barnes	R.D.E. Battersby
D.L. Baldwin	J.M. Barnes	C.D. Baumber
R.P. Balfour	W.W. Barrie	J.D.C. Baxandall

B continued

D.C. Baxter-Smith
C.J.M. Beacock
J.D. Beard
R.C. Beard
R.J. Beard
R.W. Beard
J.M. Beaugie
I. Beck
M. Beck
A.F. Bedford
N.A. Bedford
A.G. Beeden
T. Beedham
H.B. Begg
R. Behl
M. Bell
P.R.F. Bell
R. Bendall
M.S. Benett
J.G. Bennett
M.K. Benson
G. Bentley
P.G. Bentley
R.J. Bentley
L.W. Bernhardt
A.R. Berry
D.A. Berstock
B.G. Best
J.A. Betts
B.F. Beveridge
M.C. Beverly
C.R.A. Bevis
J.L. Beynon
L.L. Beynon
D.R. Bhadreshwar
J.G. Bibby
K.I. Bickerstaff
R.C. Bickerton
K.A. Bidgood
B. Billington
A.S. Binks
M.S. Binns
I.W.L. Bintcliffe
D. Bird
G.G. Bird
C.C.R. Bishop
H.M. Bishop
S. Biswas
R.K. Blach
J.Black
J.B.M. Black
M.J.M. Black
P.D. Black
R.J. Black
R.L. Blackett
H.N. Blackford

P.F. Blacklay
A.R.E. Blacklock
G. Blake
J.R.S. Blake
M.E. Blakemore
C. Blakeway
R.W. Blamey
J.W. Blaxland
B.P. Bliss
P. Bliss
P.G.A. Bloomer
R.J. Blunt
K.P. Boardman
D.L. Boase
S.A. Bober
F. de Boer
R.P. Boggon
A.R. de Bolla
J.P. Bolton
B.G. Bolton-Maggs
A.P. Bond
E.B. Bond
C.D.M. Bone
L.H. Boobis
D.A. Boot
A.E. Booth
D. Booth
J.B. Booth
P.J. Booth
R.C. Bosanquet
J.F. Bostock
P.B. Boulos
J.M. Boulton
D.A. Bowdler
D.I. Bowen
P. Bowen-Simpkins
J.E. Bowerman
T.A. Boxall
I.E. Boyd
N.A. Boyd
P.J.R. Boyd
R.C. Boyd
A.H.W. Boyle
D.D. Boyle
W.J. Boyle
J. Bracegirdle
R.A. Bradbrook
R. Bradford
W.P. Bradford
C.F. Bradish
J.C. Bradley
J.G. Bradley
N. Bradley
P.J. Bradley
R.J. Bradley
R. Bradshaw

A.N. Brain
P.A. Braithwaite
F.J. Bramble
K.G. Brame
R. Brandt
C.J. Bransom
H.A. Brant
S. Brearley
I.M. Breckenridge
A.J. Breeson
M.D. Brennen
J. Brice
J.K. Brigg
M. Briggs
M.V. Bright
A.P. Brightwell
J.B. Bristol
B.J. Britton
D.C. Britton
G. Brocklehurst
A.J.M. Brodribb
G.B. Brookes
R. Brookstein
P.J. Brooman
B.J. Brotherton
F.T. Brough
M.D. Brough
W.A. Brough
A.C. Broughton
A.A. Brown
C. Brown
G.J.A. Brown
M.J.K. Brown
P.M. Brown
P.M. Brown
R. Brown
R. Brown
R.F. Brown
V.A. Brown
M.J. Browne
A.J.F. Browning
N.L. Browse
J.E.F. Bruce
P.A. Bryant
J.R. Bryson
P.C. Buchan
G. Buchanan
J.M. Buchanan
J.A.C. Buckels
M.S. Buckingham
K.G. Buckler
R.J. Buckley
T.E. Bucknall
D.W.G. Budd
G.C. Budden
T.R. Bull

B continued

B.R. Bullen
K.N. Bullock
C.H.W. Bullough
C.H. Bulman
G.A. Bunch
D.M. Burgess

S.P. Burgess
M. Burke
K.G. Burnand
R.G.D. Burr
S.J. Burrough
E.R. Burton

H.M.B. Busfield
C. Butler
L. Butler
J.E.T. Byrne
D.P. Byrnes

C

H.R. Cable
D. Cade
A.T. Calder
I.G. Calder
M.J. Callam
P.J. Callen
K.G. Callum
R.F. Calver
C.H. Calvert
J.P. Calvert
P.T. Calvert
A.E.P. Cameron
C.R. Cameron
D.S. Cameron
M.M. Cameron
A.P. Camilleri
D. Campbell
D.A. Campbell
D.J. Campbell
J. Campbell
J.B. Campbell
J.M. Campbell
R. Campbell
W.B. Campbell
H. Cannell
S.R. Cannon
P. Canty
L.D. Cardozo
A.O.R. Cargill
G.B. Carruthers
R.K. Carruthers
W. Carswell
J.L. Carter
J.E. Carvell
B.D. Case
L.J. Sant Cassia
A.G. Casswell
I.P. Cast
H.C. de Castella
A.A. Castillo
J.E. Castro
A. Catterall
C.J. Chadwick
S. Chadwick
A.N. Chakraborty
J.H. Challis

J.A. Chalmers
G.V.P. Chamberlain
J. Chamberlain
G.M. Chambers
C.J. Chandler
P. Chandra
A.D.B. Chant
J. Chapman
J.A. Chapman
P. Chapman
R.L.K. Chapman
M.J.B. Chare
C.A.C. Charlton
A. Chatterjee
S. Chaturued
R.G. Checketts
S.C. Chen
G.T. Cheney
H. Cheng
J.R. Cherry
R.J. Cherry
J. Chester
C.P. Chilton
I.H. Chisholm
S.K. Choudhuri
S.D. Chowdhury
K.A. Cietak
M.B. Clague
A.D. Clark
A.W. Clark
D.I. Clark
D.R. Clark
D.W. Clark
H.S.G. Clark
J. Clark
R.G. Clark
D. Clarke
D.J. Clarke
J.E. Clarke
J.M.F. Clarke
J.R. Clarke
R.J. Clarke
P.K. Clarkson
A. Clason
N.R. Clay
J.K. Clayton

D.K. Cleak
L.G. Clearkin
J. Clegg
J.F. Clegg
R.T. Clegg
J. Cleland
R.V. Clements
R.P. Clifford
M.A. Clifton
J.C. Clothier
P.R. Clothier
J.R. Clough
W.M. Clow
A.W. Clubb
C.A. Clyne
R.L. Coakes
C.J. Coates
P.M. Coats
A.G. Cobb
N.J. Cobb
J.P.S. Cochrane
G.L. Cohen
M.D. Cole
T.P. Cole
J.F. Colin
J. Collin
R.E.C. Collins
M.R. Colmer
T.M. Coltart
J.D. Common
E.H. Compton
A.P. Condie
R.G. Condie
L.P. Connolly
G. Constantine
M.E. Conybeare
A.I.M. Cook
N.C. Cook
I.D. Cooke
P.H. Cooke
W.M. Cooke
R.J. Cooling
G.B. Coombes
R.R.H. Coombs
H.S. Coonar
J.A. Cooper

C continued

M.J. Cooper
C.R.R. Corbett
W.A. Corbett
A.P. Corfield
M.S. Cornah
A.M. Corrigan
L.M. de Cossart
O.S.T.J. Da Costa
J.G. Corson
C.B. Costello
W.B. Costley
D.G. Cottrell
A.G.A. Cowie
R.A. Cowie
D.J. Cowley
J. Cox
P.J. Cox

R. Cox
S.N. Cox
P.J. Coyle
S.D. Crabtree
B.F. Craig
D.M. Craig
B. Cranley
D.W. Cranston
J.L. Craven
D.J. Crawford
A.D. Craxford
J.C. Crisp
H.A. Crockard
S.G. Crocker
C.B. Croft
R.J. Croft
A.C. Crompton

D.L. Crosby
F.W. Cross
M.C. Crowson
M.K.H. Crumplin
R.B. Cuby
K.W. Cullen
R.J. Cullen
J. Cumming
J.G.R. Cumming
B.H. Cummins
W.J. Cunliffe
J.E. Curphey
R.C. Curry
J.R.N. Curt
R.J. Cuschieri
B. Cvijetic

D

J.C. D'Arcy
V.C. Dalal
R.F. Dale
M.E. Dalton
D.J. Dandy
T.E. Dane
R.J. Daniels
S.G. Darke
C.N. Das
S.N. Das
S.K. Datta
T.J. Davenport
V.C. David
B.R. Davidson
M.J.C. Davidson
C.J. Davies
E.W. Davies
H.L. Davies
J.A.K. Davies
J.S. Davies
M. Davies
R.A.C. Davies
R.M. Davies
R.P. Davies
S.J.M. Davies
W. Tudor Davies
B.R. Davis
C. Davis
P.W. Davis
O.W. Davison
E.G. Daw
A.J. Dawson
J.L. Dawson
J.B. Day
J.B. Day

T.K. Day
K.R. De
P.B. Deacon
A.M. Deane
T.C.B. Dehn
A. Deiraniya
L.J. Deliss
S.N. Deliyannis
D.W. Dempster
R.A. Dendy
A.J.N. Dennison
J.S. Denton
C.D. Derry
A. Desai
S.B. Desai
S.P. Desai
A.D. Desmond
P.B. Deverall
H.B. Devlin
E.P. Dewar
J.P. Dhasmana
J.M. Dhorajiwala
C. Diamond
I.K. Dickinson
K.M. Dickinson
G.H. Dickson
R.A. Dickson
W.A. Dickson
G.R. Dilworth
R.R.J. Dinley
W.J. Dinning
J.H. Dixon
P.W. Docherty
D.R. Donaldson
R.A. Donaldson

P. Donnai
P.K. Donnelly
R.J. Donnelly
A.G. Donovan
R. Donovan
J.F. Dooley
M.M.P. Dooley
J. Doran
R.M. Doran
J.A. Dormandy
E.D. Dorrell
J.H. Dorrell
N.J. Dorricott
D.L. Douglas
E.M. Downes
R.J.G. Downie
R. Downing
P.T. Doyle
A.B. Drake-Lee
N.C. Drew
M.D. Duari
T. Duckworth
T.B. Duff
R.G.M. Duffield
T.J. Duffy
A.C. Dunbar
S. Duncan
D.R. Dunkerley
J.M. Dunlop
P.D.M. Dunlop
W. Dunlop
D.C. Dunn
M. Dunn
T.H. Dunningham
G.D. Dunster

D continued

P. Durdey
P. Durning

J.S. Duthie
T.P. Dutt

D.P. Dyson

E

E.M. Eagling
R.J. Earlam
J.J. Earnshaw
A.C. Eaton
S.R. Ebbs
J.H. Eckersley
J.W. Eddy
A.J. Edge
P.T. Edington
H. Edmondson
A.N. Edwards
D.H. Edwards
J.M. Edwards
M.H. Edwards
P. Edwards
P.W. Edwards
K.F. Edwardson
A.F. El-Kordy
A.R. El-Sayad
J.B. Elder

J.A. Elias
A.R. Elkington
A.J. Elliott
H.R. Elliott
J.R.M. Elliott
B.W. Ellis
D.J. Ellis
F.G. Ellis
P.D.M. Ellis
R.P. Ellis
M. Elstein
C.F. Elsworth
W.K. Eltringham
J.M. Emens
S.J. Emery
P.C. England
R.M. England
T.A.H. English
B.E. Enoch
J. Erian

H.J. Espiner
D.M. Essenhigh
D.E. Etchells
A.G. Evans
A.S. Evans
B.T. Evans
C.M. Evans
D.A. Evans
D.M. Evans
G. Evans
H.J.R. Evans
J.D. Evans
J.C. Evans-Jones
W.G. Everett
N.W. Everson
R. Ewing
J. Eyre
I.A. Eyre-Brook

F

R.G. Faber
B. Fabri
A.M. Fagan
P.S. Fagg
D. Fairbairn
J.C.T. Fairbank
B.J. Fairbrother
J.A. Fairclough
H.D. Fairman
M.G. Falcon
A.D. Falconer
T.F. Fannin
J.R. Farndon
R.G. Farquharson
M.A. Farquharson-Roberts
P.A. Farrands
D.J. Farrar
W.T. Farrington
A.N. Fawcett
D.P. Fawcett
R.D.S. Fawdry
C.B. Fearn
J.G. Feeney
J.G.W. Feggetter
G.J. Fellows
J.E. Felmingham

D.J.C. Felton
A. Fenn
P. Fenn
D.W. Fenton
O.M. Fenton
P.J. Fenton
J.N. Fergus
A.M. Ferguson
J. Ferguson
C.M. Fergusson
B.D. Ferris
T.J. Fetherston
N.J. Fiddian
E.S. Field
C. Fielder
J. Fieldhouse
J.W.L. Fielding
D.G. Fife
S.A. Fillobos
G.M. Filshie
D.R.A. Finch
G.F.G. Findlay
R.D. Finlay
D. Finnis
T.R. Fisher
P.N. Fison

J.A.W. Fitzgerald
D.W. Flanagan
G.M. Flannigan
J.D. Fleet
M.S. Fletcher
T.J. Flew
G. Flint
B.M. Flood
L.M. Flood
A. Flower
A.F. Flowerdew
A. Floyd
J.T. Flynn
C.J. Fontaine
A. Forbes
P.A. Forbes-Smith
D.J. Ford
G.R. Ford
M. Fordham
G.H. Forman
J.F. Forrest
L. Forrest
C. Forrester-Wood
D.M.C. Forster
I.W. Forster
A.T. Forsyth

F continued

J.L.R. Forsythe
M.V.L. Foss
D.P. Fossard
M.E. Foster
J.W. Foulds
J.E.B. Foulkes
S.W. Fountain
C.G. Fowler
G.C. Fox
J.A. Fox
J.N. Fox
J.S. Fox
P. Foy

C.E. Fozzard
J. Frampton
M.C. Frampton
M.A. Frangoulis
H.J. Frank
P. Franks
A.C. Fraser
I. Fraser
I.A. Fraser
I.D. Fraser
I.R. Fraser
J.G. Fraser
M.R. Fraser

R.B. Fraser
A.P. Freeland
M.E. French
J.R. Friend
P. Frecker
E. Freedlander
L.S. Freedman
P.M. Fullman
D.V. Furlong
I.S. Fyfe

G

C.G.C. Gaches
C.S.B. Galasko
P. Gallagher
P. Gallagher
R.B. Galland
J.M.D. Galloway
R.G. Gandhi
A.S. Garden
N.H.N. Gardner
J. Garfield
D.J. Garlick
D.B. Garrioch
J.B. Garston
P.C. Gartell
R.J.N. Garth
M.W. Gartside
N. Garvan
J.C. Gazet
M.W.L. Gear
N.P.J. Geary
C.J.M. Getty
N.N. Ghali
S. Ghazali
D.H. Gibb
G.L.D. Gibbens
K.P. Gibbin
C.P. Gibbons
J.R.P. Gibbons
J.R.M. Gibson
G.A. Gie
J.M. Gilbert
A.D. Giles
R.W.H. Giles
I.E. Gillespie
P.N. Gillibrand
R.F. Gillie
E.L. Gilliland
E.W. Gillison
M.D.G. Gillmer

J.C. Gingell
B. Ginz
D.J. Gladstone
M.M.S. Glasgow
M.R. Glass
M.G. Glasspool
G. Glazer
M.J. Gleeson
D.E.H. Glendinning
B.E. Glenville
S. Glick
L.P. Glossop
G.W. Glover
U.K. Goddard
J.J. Goiti
M.G.S. Golby
M.D. Goldman
W.O. Goldthorp
I.M. Golland
C.R. Gomersall
C.J. Good
A.W. Goode
C.F. Goodfellow
M.R. Gooding
D.P. Goodwin
A.G. Gordon
D. Gordon
E.M. Gordon
A.P. Gordon-Wright
D.C. Gosling
A.L. Gough
I.S. Governor
J.P. Gowar
N.F. Gowland-Hopkins
A.R.H. Grace
D.L. Grace
R.H. Grace
J.M. Graham
N.G. Graham

R.M. Graham
W.J. Grange
C.E.P. Grant
H.R. Grant
D.W.R. Gray
I.C.M. Gray
N. Gray
N. Gray
R.F. Gray
W. Gray
M.G. Greaney
G.H. Greatrex
A.D.L. Green
A.E. Green
G.A. Green
J.P. Green
M. Greenall
J.O. Greenhalf
P.J. Gregg
M.E. Greiss
R.H.B. Grey
S.M. Griffin
G.H. Griffith
C.D.M. Griffith
H.B. Griffith
C.L. Griffiths
D.A. Griffiths
N.J. Griffiths
R.W. Griffiths
W.D. Griffiths
P.M.G. Grimaldi
R.J. Grimer
R.P. Grimley
J.L. Grogono
G.J. Grotte
M.L. Grover
D.M. Gruebel-Lee
M.F.B. Grundy
E.P. Guazzo

G continued

D.H. Gudgeon
J. Guest
T. Guha-Maulik
J.R.W. Gumpert
M.F. Gundry

A. Gunn
A.L. Gunn
R.S. Gunn
A.R. Das Gupta
R. Gupta

P.W.Gurney
L. Guvendik
A.J. Guy
B.R. Gwynn

H

J.I.H. Hadfield
D.A. Hadley
A.D. Haeri
S.J. Haggie
J.F. Haines
M.A. Hakeem
E.G. Hale
J.E. Hale
C.N. Hall
G. Hall
J.H. Hall
R. Hall
R.I. Hall
S.J. Hall
J.P. Hallett
J.A. Halliday
D.S. Halpin
R.J. Ham
D.B. Hamer
A.J. Hamilton
J.R.L. Hamilton
J.D. Hamlett
J.F. Hamlyn
R.C. Hammad
Z. Hammad
R.H. Hammond
J.C. Hammonds
B.D. Hancock
K.W. Hancock
D.J. Hanley
G.S.S. Hanna
G. Hannah
D.R. Hanson
M.A. Haque
J.D. Hardcastle
P.F. Hardcastle
A.F. Harden
M.L. Harding
D. Harding-Jones
M. Hardingham
D.G. Hardy
S.K. Hardy
R. Harfitt
A.W. Hargreaves
R.A. Harlow
D. Harris
P.L. Harris

D.J. Harrison
G.S.M. Harrison
I.D. Harrison
J.M. Harrison
N.W. Harrison
R.A. Harrison
T.A. Harrison
A.J.L. Hart
N.B. Hart
W.G. Hartfall
D. Hartley
R.C. Hartley
R. Hartwell
C.F. Harvey
D.R. Harvey
J.S. Harvey
S.S. Hasan
R. Haskell
J.R. Havers-Strong
M.J.G. Hawe
J.E. Hawkesford
K.S. Haworth
S.M. Haworth
M.R. Hawthorne
A.M. Hay
D.J. Hay
D.M. Hay
B.R. Hayes
I.G. Haynes
P.J. Haynes
S. Haynes
R. Hayward
A.C. Head
M.R. Heal
R.J. Heald
A.R. Hearn
R.N. Heasley
D.V. Heath
B.P. Heather
F.W. Heatley
R. Hedges
A. HedleyBrown
H.P. Henderson
R.R. Henein
A.P.J. Henry
M.M. Henry
R.J.W. Henry

R. Hensher
G.L. Henson
B. Hercules
J. Hermon-Taylor
M.R. Heslip
J.W. Hetherington
T. Heyworth
M. Hickey
K. Hicks
A.F. Higgins
P.M. Higgins
M.J. Higgs
A. Higham
D.I.R. Higton
C.M. Hill
J.G. Hill
N.H. Hills
C.J. Hilton
P. Hilton
A. Hinchliffe
M.O. Hindle
J.R. Hindmarsh
C.P. Hinton
B.L. Hinves
N. Hira
P.J. Hirsch
D. Hirschowitz
E.R. Hitchcock
E.M. Hoare
J.E. Hoare-Nairne
J.H. Hobbiss
K.E.F. Hobbs
J.P. Hodgkinson
R.W. Hoile
M.C. Holbrook
C.E.A. Holden
D. Holden
M.P. Holden
B.J. Holdsworth
J.D. Holdsworth
C.S. Holland
H.W. Holliday
J.P. Hollingdale
R. Hollingsworth
A. Holmes
D. Holmes
F.J. Holmes

H continued

J.T. Holmes
W. Holms
J.B. Holroyd
E.M. Holt
S. Holt
S.D.H. Holt
W.E. Hook
A.A. Hooper
P.W. Hopcroft
G.A. Hope
N.B. Hopkin
D.J. Hopkins
J.S. Hopkins
R.E. Hopkins
B.R. Hopkinson
D.A.W. Hopkinson
I. Hopper
M.S.C. Hopper
D.S. Hopton
F.T. Horan
J. Horner
D.H. Horwell
J. Hoskinson

D.J. Houghton
P.W.J. Houghton
M.C.C. Houlton
M. House
J.K. Houston
E.R. Howard
F.A. Howard
J.M.T. Howat
A.J. Howcroft
C.J. Howell
M.R. Howells
G. Hoyle
M. Hoyle
M.J.S. Hubbard
C.N. Hudson
K.B. Hughes
M.A. Hughes
R.G. Hughes
J. Hughes-Nurse
M.G.R. Hull
N.R. Hulton
W.G. Humphreys
W.V. Humphreys

K.M. Hunt
G. Hunter
I.W.E. Hunter
P.A. Hunter
I.D. Hunter-Craig
R.A. Hurlow
P.A. Hurst
R.P. Husemeyer
I.Y. Hussein
R.B. Hutcheson
C.J. Hutchins
P.M. Hutchins
G.H. Hutchinson
I.F. Hutchinson
I.L. Hutchison
J.D. Hutchison
R.S. Hutchison
D.J.R. Hutchon
J.A. Hutter
P.A.N. Hutton
D.W. Hyatt
I.D. Hyde
J. Hyde

I

R.D. Illingworth
T.C.M. Inglis
C.J.H. Ingoldby
G.Ingram
N.P. Ingram

S.E. Inman
A. Innes
G.K. Ions
J. Ireland
T.T. Irvin

G.H. Irvine
M.H. Irving
B.C. Irwin
S.T. Irwin

J

B.T. Jackson
D.B. Jackson
R.K. Jackson
G. Jacob
J.S. Jacob
P.M. Jacobs
P.H. Jacobsen
J.D. Jagger
R.H. Jago
J. Jakubowski
C.R. James
J.H. James
S.E. James
C.W. Jamieson
N.V. Jamieson
M.H. Jamison
K. Janardhan
P.E.M. Jarrett
A.C. Jarvis
G.J. Jarvis

B.S. Jay
A.F. Jefferis
I.T.A. Jeffery
P.J. Jeffery
R.M. Jeffery
M.N. Jeffrey
R.V. Jeffreys
A. Jenkins
D.H.R. Jenkins
H.M.L. Jenkins
I.L. Jenkins
L.R. Jenkinson
S.D. Jenkinson
R.E. Jenner
K.M. Jennison
K. Jepson
J.D. Jeremiah
K. Jeyasingham
K. Johansen
D.R. John

A.M. Johns
A.N. Johns
D.L. Johns
A.D. Johnson
A.G. Johnson
A.O.B. Johnson
A.P. Johnson
C.D. Johnson
D.A.N. Johnson
I.R. Johnson
J.N. Johnson
J.R. Johnson
M.G. Johnson
P. Johnson
P.M. Johnson
R.H. Johnson
S.R. Johnson
B. Johnston
G.W. Johnston
J.M.S. Johnstone

J continued

A.H. Jones
A.J. Jones
A.S. Jones
C. Jones
C.A. Jones
C.B. Jones
C.K. Jones
D. Jones
D. Jones
D.A. Jones
D.A. Jones
D.J. Jones

D.R.B. Jones
E.R.L. Jones
G.M. Jones
J.B. Jones
J.R. Jones
M. Jones
M.A. Jones
M.B. Jones
N.A.G. Jones
P.A. Jones
R.A.C. Jones
R.B. Jones

R.N. Jones
R.O. Jones
W.A. Jones
W.I. Jones
J.A. Jordan
K. Jordan
M.H. Jourdan
R.L. Jowett
D.N. Joyce
M. Joyce
R. Juniper
W.A. Jurewicz

K

A.V. Kaisary
B.A. Kamdar
P.L. Kander
G.S. Kanegaonkar
C.R. Kapadia
R.D. Kapadia
D. Kaplan
A.K. Kar
H.D. Kaufman
N.J. Kay
N.R.M. Kay
P. Kay
S.P.J. Kay
D.J.M. Keenan
M.H. Keene
S.J. Keightley
J.S. Kenefick
C.R. Kennedy
S.J.S. Kent
J. Kenwright
V.G. Kenyon
A.W. Keogh
B. Keogh
D. Keown
J.G. Kernohan
A.G. Kerr
R.S.C. Kerr
M.G. Kerr-Muir

R. Kerr-Wilson
J. Kersey
W.W. Kershaw
R.C. Kester
M.J. Kettle
A.S. Khambata
I.A.Khan
M.A.A. Khan
M.A.R. Khan
G. Khoury
L.C. Kidd
E.S. Kiff
D. Kilby
J.O. Kilby
S.R. Killick
R.B. Kinder
T. King
J.M. Kingsmill-Moore
A.N. Kingsnorth
R.D. Kingston
J.G. Kinley
R.A. Kipping
R. Kirby
R.M. Kirby
J.S. Kirkham
E.O.G. Kirwan
P. Kirwan
P. Kitchen

J. Kelly
J. Kelly
J.D.C. Kelly
J.M. Kelly
M.J. Kelly
A.A. Kemeny
J.V.H. Kemble
R.W. Kendrick
A.I. Kiwanuka
L. Klenerman
O. Klimach
D.J. Klugman
J.R. Knight
M.J. Knight
S. Knight
D. Knight-Jones
P. Knipe
R.P. Knowlden
J.E.A. Knowles
A.J.S. Knox
R. Knox
A.E.R. Kobbe
E.N.P. Kulatilake
D. Kumar
P.A.V. Kumar
K.M.N. Kunzru

L

K. Lafferty
J.B. Laine
D.N.W. Lake
S.P. Lake
R.C. Lallemand
N. Lalljee
C.E.M. Lamb
M.P. Lamb

W.T. Lamb
D. Lambert
M.E. Lambert
W.G. Lambert
B.G.H. Lamberty
A.J. Lamerton
P. Lamont
R.F. Lamont

J.M. Lancer
I.F. Lane
J. Lane
R.H.S. Lane
J.D. Langdon
S.R. Large
B.M. Laskiewicz
M.A. Lavelle

L continued

R.J. Lavelle
T.A. Lavin
K.P. Law
W.T. Lawrence
I.M. Laws
A.H. Lawson
L.J. Lawson
R.A.M. Lawson
W.R. Lawson
J.O. Lawton
R.E. Lea
R.D. Leach
D.J. Leaper
D. Learmont
P.K. Leaver
G.B. Leckie
J.O. Lee
M.D. Lee
P.W.R. Lee
R.J. Lee
R.D. Leeming
T. Leese
R.J. Leicester
R.J. Lemberger
G.J. Lemon
T.W.J. Lennard
C.M.E. Lennox
J.M. Lennox

M.S. Lennox
P.J. Leopard
B. Levack
M de Leval
S.H. Leveson
I. Levy
H.J.E. Lewi
A.A.M. Lewis
B.V. Lewis
C.T. Lewis
G.J. Lewis
J. Lewis
J.L. Lewis
M.H. Lewis
R.E. Lewis
S.L. Lewis
A. Leyshon
B.A. Lieberman
W.M. Lien
K.B. Lim
D.G. Limb
G. Little
J.T. Little
S. Livesey
R.E. Lloyd
E.R.V. Lloyd-Davies
R.W. Lloyd-Davies
W. Lloyd-Jones

M.O. Lobb
V. Lobo
M. Lock
M.R. Lock
T.J. Locke
F.E. Loeffler
A.M. Logan
C.J.H. Logan
V.S.D. Logan
N. Longrigg
I.J. Lord
J.D. Lorimer
J.C. Lotz
W.G.G. Loughridge
J.A. Lourie
I.M.R. Lowdon
D.S. Lowry
J.C. Lowry
C. Lucas
M.G. Lucas
R.J. Luck
M.J. Lutterloch
R. Lye
C.C.B. Lynch
M.C. Lynch
M.J. Lyons

M

H.N. MacDonald
R.C. MacDonald
J. MacFie
N. MacGillivray
J.C.R. MacHenry
N.N.S. MacKay
I. MacKenzie
W.E. MacKenzie
D.M. MacKinnon
N.A. MacKinnon
I. MacLennan
D.S. MacPherson
G.H. MacPherson
A.L. Macafee
J.J. Maccabe
A.P. Macdonald
H.N. Macdonald
R.R. Macdonald
M.C. Mace
D.G. Machin
G. Mackay
I.S. Mackay
I.W. Mackee
R.P. Mackenney

C.R. Mackie
D.B. Mackie
A.D.W. Maclean
I. Macmichael
G. Macnab
J. Macvicar
S.M. Mady
P.G. Magee
J. Magell
P.A. Magnussen
I.W. Mahady
P.J. Mahaffey
N.A.H. Mahmoud
M. Mahoney
B.J. Main
W.S.J. Mair
O. Maiwand
B. Majumdar
C.A. Makin
G.S. Makin
R.K. Mal
B. Maltby
J. Malvern
A.M. Mander

K.S. Mangat
E.A.D. Manning
R.E. Mansel
S.L. Manuja
R.W. Marcuson
M.J.A. Maresh
D.E. Markham
N.J. Marks
S.M. Marks
D.R. Marsh
C.L. Marx
D.A. Mason
J.R. Mason
R.C. Mason
J.A. Massey
G.M. Masson
M.B.R. Mathalone
D.M. Matheson
D.D. Mathews
D.B. Mathias
H.R. Matthews
J.G. Matthews
P.N. Matthews
R.N. Matthews

M continued

E.J. Mattock
R.S. Maurice-Williams
H.J.D. Mawhinney
R.J. Maxwell
A.R.L. May
P. May
R.E. May
N.K. Maybury
K.D. Fortes Mayer
A.D. Mayer
A.H. McAdam
G. McAdam
W.A.F. McAdam
P.G. McAndrew
O.J. McAnena
P. McArthur
D.O'B McCarthy
C.N. McCollum
M.S. McCormick
G.F. McCoy
C.J. McCullough
G.S. McCune
B.C. McDermott
J.M. McDonnell
A.B. McEwan
R.J. McFarland
H.W. McFarlane
J.N. McGalliard
A. McGeorge
F.P. McGinn
R. McGowan
J.A. McGuigan
M.C. McGurk
J.C. McIlwain
G.S. McIntosh
I.H. McIntosh
J.W. McIntosh
A.J. McIrvine
J.A. McKelvey
S.T.D. McKelvey
D.M. McKenna
B. McKenzie-Gray
A. McKibbin
M.I. McLaren
G. McLatchie
N.R. McLean
D. McLeod
F.N. McLeod
P. McMaster
A.H. McMurray
B.J. McNeela
W.D. McNicoll
J.F. McPartlin
J. McQueen
A.R. McRae
N.A. McWhinney

D.J. McWilliams
T.H. Meadows
A.J. Mearns
B. Measday
W.M. Mee
S.E. Meehan
B.F. Meggitt
J. Meggy
H.K. Mehta
S.B. Mehta
D. Meikle
D.D. Meikle
H.J. Mellows
D.M. Melville
A.D. Mendelow
D. Mendonca
T.J. Menon
N. Menzies-Gow
J.L. Mercer
L.A. Mercurius-Taylor
A.P. Meredith
W.F. Merriam
M.J. Metcalf
C.H.A. Meyer
A. Midwinter
P.J. Milewski
D.R. Millar
R. Millar
A.J. Miller
G.A.B. Miller
G.F. Miller
I.A. Miller
I.M. Miller
I.T. Miller
J.M. Miller
J.M. Miller
S.E.P. Miller
C. Millford
G.F. Milligan
A.W.F. Milling
M.A.P. Milling
J.C. Milner
E.J.G. Milroy
J.E. Milson
P.J.D. Milton
T.M. Milward
A.J. Minchin
A. Mitchell
G.G. Mitchell
V.K. Modgill
C.U. Moisey
R.A.B. Mollan
M.D. Moloney
J.M. Monaghan
P.R.W. Monahan
D. Moncrieff

J.L. Monro
A.C.V. Montgomery
R.J. Montgomery
I.J. Monypenny
A.S. Moolgaoker
A. Moore
B. Moore
C.J. Moore
D.M. Moore
K.T.H. Moore
P.J. Moore
W.K. Moores
G.A. Morewood
B.D.G. Morgan
H. Morgan
L.H. Morgan
M.W.E. Morgan
N. Naunton Morgan
W.E. Morgan
B.T. Morgans
M.T. Morrell
B.D.A. Morris
E.D. Morris
I.R. Morris
M.A. Morris
P.G. Morris
P.J. Morris
W. Morris-Jones
D.L. Morrison
N. Mortensen
C.W. Mortimer
M.E. Morton
V. Moshakis
J.G. Mosley
D. Moss
P.A. Mounfield
H. Moussalli
M.A.S. Mowbray
P.D. Moynagh
D.S. Muckle
D.G. Mudd
B.N. Muddhu
G. Mufti
M.M. Mughal
J.E.T. Mulholland
R.C. Mulholland
P.W.S. Muller
T.O. Mulligan
K.W. Munson
C.G. Munton
A. Murday
R.W.G. Murdoch
F. Murphy
W.M. Murphy
A. Murray
B.J. Murray

M continued

J.M. Murray
K.H. Murray

T.J. Muscroft
B. Musgrove

F. Musumeci

N

A.A. Naftalin
N.J. Naftalin
K.K. Nair
U. Nair
D.S. Nairn
A.G. Nash
E.S. Nash
J.R. Nash
T.G. Nash
D.G. Nasmyth
H.G. Naylor
D.E. Neal
R.W. Neale
P.G. Needham
W.F. Neil
G. Neil-Dwyer

R.W.K. Neill
R.J. Nelson
J.P. Neoptolemos
C.J.R. Newbegin
J.F. Newcombe
M.R.B. Newman
R.J. Newman
J.R. Newton
N.S. Nicholas
J.C. Nicholls
R.J. Nicholls
H.O. Nicholson
R.A. Nicholson
R.W. Nicholson
P.A.R. Niven
J.R. Nixon

A.D. Noble
M.C.B. Noble
H.C. Norcott
R. Norcott
E.A.M. Normington
M.G. Norris
S.H. Norris
M.D. Northmore-Ball
E.R. Norton
R. Norton
M.J. Notaras
R.G. Notley
C. Nsamba
D. Nunn
I.D. Nuttall
A.M. Nysenbaum

O

P. O'Boyle
T.E.B. O'Brien
B.T. O'Connor
M. O'Driscoll
J.N. O'Hara
M.F. O'Hare
H.O.J. O'Kane
S. O'Malley
J.J. O'Neill
J. O'Riordan

S.M. O'Riordan
J.F. O'Sullivan
G.D. Oates
M.L. Obeid
G.W. Odling-Smee
N.J. Odom
A.D.R. Ogborn
J.R. Ogden
H.D. Ogus
E.O. Oji

M. Ormiston
M.M. Orr
N.W.M. Orr
J.E. Osborne
D.G. Ostick
A.E. Owen
A.W.M. Owen
W.J. Owen
M.S. Owen-Smith

P

A.L. Pahor
J.A. Pain
W.G. Paley
A. Palmer
J.G. Palmer
J.H. Palmer
K.J.S. Panesar
A.M.I. Paris
A. Parker
B.C. Parker
D.J. Parker
R.J. Parker
H. Parkhouse
D.C. Parr
D.W. Parsons
S. Parvin

I.M. Paterson
J.M.H. Paterson
M.E.L. Paterson
P.N. Pathak
S.M. Patient
R.W. Paton
J.F. Patrick
J.H. Patrick
P.H. Pattisson
M.R. Paul
J.G. Payne
S.R. Payne
P.K. Peace
B.G.S. Peach
R.M. Pearce
K. Pearman

H.J. Pearson
J.B. Pearson
J.F. Pearson
K.W. Pearson
J.E. Peck
P.R.B. Pedlow
A.L.G. Peel
K.R. Peel
A.W. Pengelly
A.F. Pentecost
J.R. Pepper
S.P. Percival
A.J.L. Percy
E.D. Pereira
P.M. Perry
J.W.R. Peyton

P continued

H.T. Phen
J.J. Phillipps
H. Phillips
J.B. Phillips
J.G. Phillips
R.K.S. Phillips
R.M. Phillips
N.H. Philp
T. Philp
J.M. Pickles
M.C. Pietroni
T.A. Piggot
H.W.S. Pigott
R.W. Pigott
R. Pillai
D.J. Pinto
N.G.J. Pipe
M.R. Pittam
A.M. Platt
A.P. Plumb
P.F. Plumley
L.H. Pobereskin
R.D. Pocock
C.E. Polkey

J.P. Pollard
J. Pollet
D. Pollock
M.D. Poole
H.E. Porte
G.P. Porter
M.F. Porter
R. Porter
R.J. Porter
S.M. Porter
W. Porter
K.R. Poskitt
J.C. Postlethwaite
C.S. Powell
J.M. Powell
P.H. Powell
D.P. Powles
P.H. Powley
P.J. Pownall
J.L. Pozo
T.A. Pozyczka
R.J. Pratt
D.J. Premachamdra
T.R. Preston

A.J. Price
E.C.V. Price
G.F.W. Price
J.D. Price
J.J. Price
N.C. Price
W.J. Primrose
R.G. Pringle
M.G. Prinn
K.D. Printer
A.L. Prior
C.J. Pritchett
D.W. Proops
W.G. Prout
J.V. Psaila
S. Puntambekar
M.C.A. Puntis
L.W. Purnell
J.K. Pye
R. Pyke
P.C. Pyper
R.J.D. Pyper

Q

A.R. Quayle
J.B. Quayle
K.B. Queen

C.R. Quick
R.E. Quiney
M.P. Quinlan

R.C. Quinnell

R

A.G. Radcliffe
G.J. Radcliffe
P.J. Rae
A.T. Raftery
J. Rahamin
A.N. Rahman
A. Railton
G.E.T. Raine
M.F. Raines
A.E.S. Rainey
H.A. Rainey
R.M. Rainsbury
K.S. Raju
D.N.L. Ralphs
P.D. Ramsden
R. Ramsden
N.I. Ramus
R.J. Rand
C.J. Randall
G.H. Randle
R.G. Rangecroft

G.L.S. Rankin
A.O. Ransford
P.N. Rao
A. Rashid
J. Rayne
M.D. Read
J.F. Redden
T.N. Reddy
T.R. Redfern
D.H.A. Redford
H. Reece-Smith
M.F. Reed
A. Rees
B.I. Rees
D.A. Rees
M. Rees
R.W.M. Rees
B.F. Reeves
L. Regan
A.P. Reid
C.A. Reid

D.J. Reid
W. Reid
D.T. Reilly
C.D. Rennie
I.G. Rennie
J.A. Rennie
C.J. Renton
A. Resouly
D.A. Reynolds
J.R. Reynolds
J.R. Rhind
W.J. Ribbans
B.F. Ribeiro
G.J. Rice
J.M. Rice-Edwards
A.J. Rich
W.J. Rich
A.B. Richards
A.E.S. Richards
C.J. Richards
D.J. Richards

R continued

D.R. Richardson
J. Richardson
J.A. Richardson
P.L. Richardson
R.G. Richer
D.H. Richmond
W.D. Richmond
J.W. Rickett
A. Riddle
C.C. Rigby
R.S. Rihan
D. Riley
R.F. Rintoul
A.W.S. Ritchie
R.P. Rivron
A. Roberts
A. Roberts
A.D.G. Roberts
A.H.N. Roberts
C. Roberts
G. Roberts
G.D.D. Roberts
J.K. Roberts
M. Roberts
P.N. Roberts
I.G. Robertson
J. Robertson

P.E. Robin
D.W. Robinson
J.M. Robinson
K.P. Robinson
M.R.G. Robinson
P.M. Robinson
P.P. Robinson
R.E. Robinson
T.J. Rockley
H.S. Rogers
I.M. Rogers
K. Rogers
K. Rolles
J.P. Rood
G.D. Rooker
D.H. Rose
E.S. Rosen
B.C. Rosenberg
D.A. Rosenberg
I.L. Rosenberg
M.D. Rosin
R.D. Rosin
A.H.M. Ross
A.P.J. Ross
B.A. Ross
H.B. Ross
K.R. Ross

L.D. Ross
R.P. Rosswick
C.K. Rostron
P.K.M. Rostron
E. Rouholamin
C.J.F. Rowbotham
P.H. Rowe
C. Rowe-Jones
G.F. Rowland
M. Rowntree
A.D. Rowse
R.R. Roy
G.T. Royle
M.G. Royle
C.M.S. Royston
R.W. Ruckley
J. Rumble
J.S.H. Rundle
C.F. Ruoss
B.A. Ruparelia
G.F. Rushforth
C.F.J. Russell
K.R.P. Rutter
E. Ryall
P.G. Ryan

S

S. Sabanathan
G.R. Sagor
J.R.C. Sainsbury
N. Salama
J.R. Salaman
J.E.L. Sales
M.C.P. Salter
W.N. Samarji
A.W. Samuel
D.R. Sandeman
R. Sanders
J.H. Sandford-Smith
D.P.S. Sandhu
D.G.D. Sandilands
J.R. Sansom
N.J. Sarkies
D. Sarson
N.R. Saunders
P. Sauven
P.E.A. Savage
W.D. Savage
R.S. Sawers
P.J. Saxby
F.A. Schiess
P.E. Schlesinger

I.G. Schraibman
P.J. Schranz
A.V. Scott
I.H.K. Scott
I.V. Scott
J.D. Scott
J.E. Scott
N. Scott
P.J. Scott
T.D. Scott
W.A. Scott
A.J. Sear
G.K. Sefton
S.A. Seligman
M. Selinger
R.A. Sells
B.S. Sengupta
R.P. Sengupta
M.E. Setchell
K.K. Sethia
R.S. Settatree
J.A.D. Settle
P.F.T. Sewell
M. Shafiq
N.S. Shah

B. Shahrad
M.D.G. Shanahan
J.E.G. Shand
W.S. Shand
J.P. Shardlow
P.D. Sharma
S.K. Sharma
V.L. Sharma
D.J. Sharp
D.S. Sharp
F. Sharp
M. Sharp
N.C. Sharp
D.T. Sharpe
J. Shaw
L. Shaw
L.M.A. Shaw
M.D.M. Shaw
N.C. Shaw
N.M. Shaw
P.C. Shaw
E.J. Shaxted
J.G. Shea
J.R. Shearer
R.J. Shearer

C.P. Shearman
J.M. Shennan
B.G.F. Shepheard
J.P. Shepherd
R.J. Shepherd
R.J. Sheridan
W.G. Sheridan
C.L. Shieff
M.D. Shields
R. Shields
G. Shoemaker
G.R. Shone
D.F. Shore
B.A. Shorey
A.J. Shorthouse
R.T.J. Shortridge
N. Shotts
K. Shute
T.P. Shuttleworth
G.N. Sibley
D.E. Sibson
P.R. Sill
S.H. Silverman
A.C. Silverstone
A.J.M. Simison
J.M. Simms
R.B. Simonis
B.A. Simpson
E. Simpson
M.T. Simpson
W. Simpson
C. Sims
P.F. Sims
J.N. Simson
A. Singh
K. Singh
K.P. Singh
M. Singh
M. Siodlak
V. Sivagnanavel
D.W. Skinner
P.W. Skinner
R.W.T. Slack
E.G.W. Slater
J.M. Smail
M. Small
C.J. Smallpeice
C.J. Smallwood
R.A. Smart
G.J.C. Smelt
A. Smith
A.M. Smith
B.D. Smith
D.N. Smith
E.E.J. Smith
E.K. Smith

G.H. Smith
G.M. Smith
H.D. Smith
H.M. Smith
J.A.R. Smith
J.C. Smith
M.A. Smith
M.R. Smith
P. Smith
P.A. Smith
P.H. Smith
P.L.C. Smith
R.B. Smith
R.J. Smith
R.P.S. Smith
S.K. Smith
S.L. Smith
S.R. Smith
T.W.D. Smith
M.E. Snell
C.A. Snodgrass
S.J. Snooks
G. Sockett
G.S. Sokhi
M.J. Solan
G.M. Sole
A.W. Sollom
D.W. Somerville
J.J.F. Somerville
K.G. Soni
A.S. Soorae
R.G. Souter
L.M. South
J.A. Southam
R. Southcott
O.C. Sparrow
E.H. Speck
B. Speculand
R.A. Spence
J.D. Spencer
P.J. Spencer
T.S. Spencer
R.N. Spencer-Gregson
A.D. Spigelman
J. Spivey
J.E. Spring
R.G. Springall
W.B. Sproule
T. Spyt
R. Srinivason
P.G. Stableforth
W.G. Staff
J. Stafford
G.D. Stainsby
M.C. Stallard
J.D. Stamatakis

P. Staniforth
K.P. Stannard
P.J. Stannard
J.M. Stansbie
M.B. Stanton
S.L.R. Stanton
P.A. Stanworth
L.F.A. Stassen
W.S.L. Stebbings
W.M. Steel
A.D. Steele
R.J.C. Steele
S.J. Steele
P.J. Steer
R.F. Steingold
P.M. Stell
I.B.M. Stephen
J.G. Stephen
A.G. Stevenson
C.R. Stewart
D.J. Stewart
G.J. Stewart
H.D. Stewart
J.D.M. Stewart
J.S.S. Stewart
M. Stewart
P. Stewart
P.A.H. Stewart
R.D. Stewart
T.J. Stewart
H.M. Stibbe
J.H. Stilwell
W.J.I. Stirling
G.M. Stirrat
C.J. Stoddard
T.A.M. Stoker
I.M. Stokes
G.E. Stollard
B.J. Stoodley
J. Stothard
M.A. Stott
A.T. Stotter
M.J. Stower
C.J.L. Strachan
J.R. Strachan
W.E. Strachan
J. Strahan
F.A. Strang
J.R. Strong
J. Studley
D.W. Sturdee
D.E. Sturdy
H.G. Sturzaker
A.P. Su
A.W. Sugar
M.F. Sullivan

S continued

B.N. Summers
D. Sumner
M. Sutcliffe
K. Sutherns

J. Sutherst
C.J.G. Sutton
M. Swann
A.C. Swift

G. Swingler
P.A. Sykes
E.M. Symonds

T

W. Tait
V.R. Talati
R.W. Talbot
C.J. Tallents
S.C. Tang
T.P.B. Tasker
M. Taube
A.B.W. Taylor
A.R. Taylor
B.A. Taylor
D.S. Taylor
G.J. Taylor
I. Taylor
K.M. Taylor
L. Taylor
M.C. Taylor
P. Taylor
P.H. Taylor
R.M.R. Taylor
S.A. Taylor
T.C. Taylor
T.V. Taylor
C. Teasdale
I.H. Tebbutt
P.J. Teddy
J.G. Temple
T.R. Terry
C.R. Thacker
A.E.G. Themen
N. Theodorou
C.M.H. Thom
A.K. Thomas
A.M.C. Thomas
A.P. Thomas
D.J. Thomas
D.M. Thomas
D.R. Thomas

E.J. Thomas
G. Thomas
G.E.M. Thomas
H.O. Thomas
I.H. Thomas
J. Meyrick Thomas
M.H. Thomas
P.A. Thomas
R.S.A. Thomas
T.L. Thomas
W.E.G. Thomas
J. Thomlinson
A.G. Thompson
C.E.R. Thompson
H.H. Thompson
J. Thompson
M.H. Thompson
M.R. Thompson
P.M. Thompson
S.M. Thompson
W. Thompson
R.G. Thomson
R.W. Thomson
W.H.F. Thomson
J.A.C. Thorpe
M.J. Timmons
M.S. Timms
S.F. Tindall
V.R. Tindall
S.S. To
C. Tomlins
A.H. Tooley
P.G. Toon
K. Toop
E.A. Tooth
J.H. Topham
P.J. Toplis

S.R. Tosson
J.R. Totten
J.M. Towler
G. Towns
A.S. Townsend
E.R. Townsend
P.T. Townsend
A.I. Traub
J.P. Travers
J. Travlos
T. Treasure
N.J. Treble
J.C. Tresadern
J. Tricker
N.R.A. Trickey
N.P. Trimmings
P.M. Tromans
C.S. Tuck
S.M. Tuck
A.G. Tucker
L.A. Tuckwell
J.D. Tuite
C.J. Tulloch
G.A. Turnbull
T.J. Turnbull
A. Turner
A.G. Turner
D.T.L. Turner
G.M. Turner
K.W.R. Tuson
M.K. Tutton
C.W. Twiston-Davies
J.M. Twomey
A.G. Tyers
S.N. Tyrrell

U

C. Ubhi
H.C. Umpleby

G.H. Urwin
M.M. Usherwood

D. Uttley

V

B.S. Vadanan

G.C. Vafidis

J. Vafidis

Appendix E - Participants

V continued

D. Valerio
D.P. Vasey
A.C.R. Vass
R. Vaughan
T. Vaughan-Lane
K.C. Vaughton
K.D. Vellacott

C.W. Venables
G.E. Venn
M. Vere
S.G. Vesey
C.M. Vickery
G. Victoratos
R.N. Villar

J.R.L. Vincent-Townend
J. Vinnicombe
C. Viva
P.R. Vlies
J.C. Voigt
P. Vowden

W

R.T. Waddington
T.I. Wagstaff
M.J.C. Wake
P.N. Wake
A.P. Walby
R.K. Walesby
A.P. Walker
C.J. Walker
D.R. Walker
E.M. Walker
J.E.G. Walker
K.A. Walker
M.G. Walker
P.G. Walker
S.M. Walker
R.J. Wallace
W.A. Wallace
J. Wallwork
B.H. Walmsley
T.H. Walsh
G.P. Walsh-Waring
N.W. Walshaw
P. Walter
H. Walters
S.M. Walton
P. Wanambwa
M.K. Wang
A.S. Ward
D.C. Ward
G.D. Ward
J.K. Ward
J.P. Ward
M.W. Ward
M.W.N. Ward
P.J. Ward
P. Ward-Booth
D.W. Warrell
R.C. Warren
A.J. Warrington
G. Warrington
N.P. Warwick-Brown
C. Wastell
N.B. Waterfall
A.H. Waterfield
A. Waters

J.S. Waters
M.W. Waterworth
T.A. Waterworth
D.F.L. Watkin
G.T. Watkin
R.M. Watkins
D.C.T. Watson
D.J. Watson
G.M. Watson
M.E. Watson
P.G. Watson
R. Watson
J. Watson-Farrar
P.G. Watts
B.G. Way
P.C. Weaver
R.M. Weaver
A.J. Webb
J.B. Webb
J.K. Webb
P.J. Webb
D.J.T. Webster
J.H.H. Webster
D. Wedgwood
D. Weeden
A.R.L. Weekes
R.D. Weeks
G.M. Weidmann
F.J. Weighill
J.S. Weighill
P.E. Weir
W.I. Weir
C.C. Welch
R.A. Welham
P. Weller
A. Wells
F.C. Wells
M.D. Wells
S.C. Wells
J.M. Wellwood
C.L. Welsh
R.J.J. Wenger
C.L. Wengraf
P.W. Wenham
C.G.H. West

S. Westaby
G.A. Westmore
C.A. Westwood
M.H. Wheeler
P. Whelan
B. Whitaker
E.B. Whitby
A. White
C.M. White
P.R. White
S.M. Whitehead
P.F. Whiteley
M. Whittaker
M.G. Whittaker
M.H. Wickham
J.A.K. Wightman
G.P. Wilde
D.J.W. Wilkin
J.L. Wilkins
M.H. Wilkins
A.J. Wilkinson
A.R. Wilkinson
G.A.L. Wilkinson
J.M. Wilkinson
M.J.S. Wilkinson
D.J. Willatt
G.S. Willetts
A. Williams
B. Williams
B.T. Williams
C.B. Williams
C.R. Williams
D.J. Williams
G. Williams
G.T. Williams
H.T. Williams
J.L. Williams
J.P.R. Williams
M.D. Williams
R. Williams
R.H.P. Williams
R.J. Williams
W.G. Williams
E.P.M. Williamson
J.R.W. Williamson

W continued

R.C.N. Williamson
R.G. Willis
H.E. Willshaw
A.J. Wilson
M. Cooper Wilson
D. Wilson
J.K. Wilson
K.W. Wilson
P.C. Wilson
P.J.E. Wilson
R.G. Wilson
R.G. Wilson
R.Y. Wilson
R. Windle
C.W.O. Windsor
J.G. Wingfield
H.S. Winsey

I.G. Winson
R.M.L. Winston
K.S.H. Wise
M. Wise
R.O.N. Witherow
R.L. Wolverson
D. Wong
C.M. Wood
G.A. Wood
G.D. Wood
P.L. Wood
P.L.R. Wood
S.K. Wood
C.R.J. Woodhouse
W. Woods
D.A.K. Woodward
A.B. Woodyer

J. Woolfson
D. Worgan
P.H. Worlock
T. Worstmann
R.W. Worth
A.R. Wray
J.D. Wright
N.L. Wright
P. Wright
P.D. Wright
B.M. Wroblewski
A. Wu
A.P. Wyatt
G.A.M. Wyllie
J.S. Wynn
E.J.C. Wynne

Y

M.H. Yacoub
C. Yates
A.J. Yates-Bell
H.A. Yeates
R. Yeo
C.K. Yeung
A.E. Young

A.H. Young
C.H. Young
C.P. Young
H.L. Young
J.R. Young
K.R. Young
M.H. Young

N.J. Young
R.A.L. Young
T.W. Young
R.P. Youngs
M.W. Yung
H. Yusuf

Z

A.G. Zahir
M.S.Z. Zaklama

M.R. Zeiderman
D.K. Zutshi

CONSULTANT ANAESTHETISTS

These Consultants have returned at least one death or index case questionnaire. We are not able to name all of the Consultants who have done so as their names are not known to us.

A

M.A. Abbott	D.J. Allan	D.F.J. Appleton
C.N. Adams	L. Allan	T.N. Appleyard
H. Adams	M.W.B. Allan	C. Aps
M. Adhikary	P.R. Allen	M. Archer
R. Adley	T.G. Allum	P.L. Archer
K. Aggarwal	S.J. Almond	E.N. Armitage
R.S. Ahearn	T.A.A. Ammar	J. Armstrong
M.V. Ahmed	I. Anderson	R. Armstrong
N. Ahmed	J.D. Anderson	A.E. Arrowsmith
A.R. Aitkenhead	J.M. Anderton	K. Arunasalam
K.A. Alagesan	D.S. Andrew	D.W. Atherley
J.I. Alexander	C.J.H. Andrews	T.R. Austin
J.P. Alexander	J.I. Andrews	A.F. Avery

B

I. Baguley	C.I. Beeton	D.J. Bowen
D.F. Baigent	S.P. Behl	B.J.M. Bowles
P. Bailey	J.K. Bell	C.J. Bowley
P.W. Bailey	P.F. Bell	R.A. Bowman
J.R. Baker	J.M. Bellin	V. Boyd
P.M. Baker	M. Bellman	A.S. Boyle
A. Bala	M. Bembridge	B.G. Bradburn
P.H. Balakrishnan	J.A. Bennett	H.G.C. Bradfield
J. Baldasera	N.R. Bennett	M.M. Brady
I.M. Bali	M. Berry	W.J. Brampton
J. Ballance	D.W. Bethune	R.G.B. Bramwell
P.G. Ballance	M. Bexton	K.G. Branch
P.K. Ballard	D.G. Beynon	P. Brass
P.A. Bamber	B.B. Bhala	A.P. Bray
P. Banerjee	D. Bhar	B.M. Bray
A.J. Barclay	S. Bhattacharya	M. Bray
J. Barcroft	P.J. Bickford-Smith	S.A. Brayshaw
D.M.M. Bardgett	M. Biggart	J.L. Breckenridge
I. Barker	J.F. Bion	C. Breeze
P.K. Barnes	K.J. Bird	J.E. Brett
A.M. Barr	T.M. Bird	M.D. Brewin
P. Barrett	R.J.S. Birks	D.D. Brice
M. Barrowcliffe	D.M. Birley	D. Brighouse
N.A. Barry	D.G.M. Bishop	V.B. Brim
P. Barry	M. Biswas	J. Broadfield
P.M. Bashir	T.D. Biswas	P.J. Brock
H.L.R. Bastiaenen	A. Black	P.M. Brodrick
D.B. Basu	I.H.C. Black	J. Brookes
S. Basu	I. Blacker	R.C. Brookes
S.N. Basu	E. Bland	R.J. Brooks
T.K. Basu	M.D. Blundell	C. Brown
R.C.H. Baxter	G.F. Bond	J.J. Brown
A.V. Beaugie	M.E. Bone	J.M. Brown
G.P. Beck	C.V. Bonnici	L.A. Brown
C.P. Beeby	M.D. Boobyer	P.M. Brown
M.J. Beech	R.A. Botha	C.H.W. Browne

B continued

D.R.G. Browne
M.T.T. Bryant
K. Budd
R. Buist
M.D.G. Bukht
T.M. Bull
R.E. Bullock

J.N. Bulmer
M. Burbidge
N.J. Burbridge
K.R. Burchett
A.N. Burlingham
J.C. Burnell
S. Burnley

P.M. Burridge
J. Butler
B.J. Buxton
A.J. Byrne
W.F. Byrne

C

J.M. Caddy
P.A. Cain
C. Callender
B. Cameron
F.N. Campbell
W.I. Campbell
J.L. Canton
W.D.J. Cantrell
R. Carley
F. Carli
R.J.T. Carlisle
J.C.G. Carmichael
J.C. Carnie
C.A. Carr
L.E. Carrie
I.W. Carson
J. Carter
N.P. Carter
R.F. Carter
D.P. Cartwright
P.D. Cartwright
T.I. Cash
J.N. Cashman
J.S. Catling
R. Cattermole
P. Cauchi
J.A. Caunt
A.G. Chaffe
S.K. Chakraborty
R. Chakrapani
M.E. Chamberlain
J.J. Chambers
P.H. Chambers
J.M. Chandy
J.M. Chapman
A.J. Charlton
P. Charters
C.L. Charway
S.N. Chater
R.R. Chatrath
S.C. Chatterjee
C.K. Cherian

W.N. Chestnutt
D. Childs
A.T. Chmielewski
M.A. Choksi
A. Choudhry
D. Christmas
N. Chung
A.B. Church
J.J. Church
M.D. Churcher
M. Clapham
G. Clark
G.P.M. Clark
J.M. Clark
K. Clark
R.M. Clark
W.G.B. Clark
H.L. Clarke
J.A.C. Clarke
J.T. Clarke
R.S.J. Clarke
T.N.S. Clarke
W.B. Clarkson
A.J. Clement
J.A. Clement
E.A.F. Clements
N.W.B. Clowes
R.W.D. Clunie
A.B. Coach
D. Coates
M.B. Coates
V.A. Codman
J.C. Coghill
A.T. Cohen
D.G. Cohen
M. Cohen
R.J.H. Colback
A. Cole
A.J. Coleman
P. Coleman
S. Coley
B.J. Collett

I.F. Collier
C. Collins
K.M. Collins
M.P. Colvin
I. Conacher
S.W. Coniam
A.G. Conn
P.T. Conroy
H.B. Contractor
M.C. Conway
A.B. Conyers
M.H. Cook
P.R. Cook
R.A. Cooke
A.M.C. Cooper
J. Cooper
J.B. Cooper
P.D. Cooper
W.G. Cooper
M.J.A. Coote
P.F. Copeland
D.L. Coppel
I.M. Corall
G.C. Corser
C.E. Cory
P.S. Cossham
J. Cotter
D. Counsell
H.J.L. Craig
J.F. Craig
D.C. Crawford
P.M. Crean
R. Cross
M.M. Crosse
A.W.A. Crossley
S.G.H. Cruickshank
R.C. Cruikshank
J.M. Cundy
J.P. Curran
P.G. Cutler

D

J.A. Dako
J.G. Dalgleish
J.S. Dallimore
P.E. Daly
W.L. Dann
J.E. Danziger
C. Dark
M. Darowski
A.J. Davey
A.C. David
D.G.D. Davidson
J.P. Davie
D. Davies
G. Davies
G.K. Davies
J.R. Davies
K.H. Davies
K.J. Davies
M.H. Davies
N.J.H. Davies
P.A. Davies
S. Davies
S.D. Davies

B.L. Davis
I. Davis
M. Davis
A.D.G. Dawson
J.C. Dawson
C.D. Day
S. Day
V.H. Daya
W.W. Deacon
B.M. Dempsey
N.M. Denny
H.D. Dervos
H.C. Desai
J.P. Desborough
R.C. Desborough
D. Desgrand
W.R. Desira
M.J. Desmond
A.K. Dewar
J.A. Dewar
J.E. Dickenson
D. Dickson
T.J. Digger

H.R. Dingle
A.E. Dingwall
A.M. Dixon
J. Dixon
M.B. Dobson
P. Dodd
C. Dodds
M.E. Dodson
B.R.H. Doran
R.M. Doshi
J.W. Dowdall
J. Downer
R.S. Drummond
J.E. Duggan
N.H. Duncan
P.W. Duncan
S.R. Dunn
M.A.P. Durkin
D. Dutton
D.J. Dye
A. Dyson
A.D. Dyson

E

P. Eadsforth
C. Earlam
R.J. Eastley
D. Eastwood
C.R. Eatock
D.L. Edbrooke
W.G. Edge
J. Edmonds-Seal
A. Edwards
A.E. Edwards
G. Edwards
H. Edwards

J.C. Edwards
R. Edwards
M.J. Egginton
P.S. Eleersley
D.J. Elliott
M.E. Eltoft
F.M. Emery
E.R. Emmanuel
C. Emmett
D.H. Enderby
E.M.C. Ernst
D.C. Erwin

C.S. Evans
D. Evans
D.H.C. Evans
J.M. Evans
J.M. Evans
M. Evans
M. Evans
P. Evans
R.D. Evans
C.D.G. Evans-Prosser
M.C. Ewart

F

E. Facer
M.J. Fairbrass
M. Fanning
P.A. Farling
G. Farnsworth
D. Faulkner
J.P.H. Fee
D. Fell
J.A. Fenwick
A. Ferguson
B. Ferguson
M.R. Ferguson
N.V. Fergusson
C.J. Ferres

I. Findley
S. Finfer
S. Firn
H.B.J. Fischer
A. Fisher
A.P. Fisher
M.F. Fisher
N. Fletcher
A.M. Florence
G.D. Flowerdew
M.J. Flynn
R.P. Foo
P. Ford
R.M.M. Fordham

D.M. Forster
B. Foster
J. Fox
M.A. Fox
R.M. Foxell
J.M. Foy
G.A. Francis
I. Francis
J.G. Francis
R.N. Francis
C.B. Franklin
A.C.L. Fraser
J.M. Frayne
J. Freeman

F continued

J.W. Freeman
R.M. Freeman
R.M. Frew
J. Friend

A.R. Frost
D.I. Fry
J.M. Fryer
M.E. Fryer

C.A. Fuge
P. Furniss
G.J.J. Fuzzey

G

M. Gabrielczyk
P.S. Gadgil
L.B.S. Gallagher
A. Gallimore
D.W. Galloway
J.E. Galway
J.A.S. Gamble
G.W. Gamlen
A. Ganado
A.S. Gardiner
C.A. Gauci
I. Gauntlett
R. Gautam
R. Gautum
D. Gaylard
M. Geadah
I.R. Gell
K.A. George
T.G. George
I.F. Geraghty
S.P. Gerrish
R.G. Ghaly
F.M. Ghandour
P.C. Ghosh
R.M. Ghosh
F.M. Gibson

J.A. Gil-Rodriguez
K.J. Gill
S.S. Gill
I.A. Gillespie
G.B. Gillett
M. Girgis
C.B. Girvan
J.A. Glass
M. Glavina
C. Glazebrook
T.V. Gnanadurai
P. Goldberg
D. Goldhill
N. Goodman
D.T. Goodrum
J.E. Goodwin
J.E. Goold
S. Gooneratine
P.W. Gorman
J.W.W. Gothard
M.B. Gough
P. Goulden
I.F.M. Graham
R.F. Graham
E.S. Le Grange
D.J. Grainger

I.C. Grant
I.G. Grant
N.H. Graveston
A.J.G. Gray
G.G. Grayling
J.D. Greaves
C.R. Grebenik
B. Green
B. Green
D.L. Greenhalgh
B.K. Greenwood
M.A. Gregory
R.W. Griffin
F.J. Griffiths
J. Griffiths
R.B. Griffiths
M. Grounds
L.H. Grove
N.D. Groves
A.L. Gruneberg
N. Guirguis
K.E.J. Gunning
R.K. Gupta
B.P. Guratsky
C.L. Gwinnutt

H

H. Hackett
E.G. Hadaway
R.M. Haden
D.R. Haines
G. Hall
G.M. Hall
J.P. Hall
P.J. Hall
R.M. Hall
G. Hall-Davies
I. Hallack
M.S. Hamer
J.N. Hamilton
M.R. Hamilton-Farrell
G.W. Hamlin
J.E. Hammond
J.L. Handy
M. Hanna
I. Hardy

S.A. Hargrave
R. Hargreaves
R.L. Hargrove
D.H. Harley
N. Harley
N.F. Harley
M. Harmer
K.W. Harper
N.J.N. Harper
S.J. Harper
G. Harris
P.H.P. Harris
R.W. Harris
S.J. Harris
T.J.B. Harris
A.R. Harrison
C.A. Harrison
G.R. Harrison
J.F. Harrison

K.M. Harrison
R.A. Harrison
A.W. Harrop-Griffiths
I.K. Hartopp
C.R. Harvey
D.C. Harvey
P.B. Harvey
C.R. Hasbury
W.H.K. Haslett
R. Hatts
T.J. Hawkins
B. Hayes
C.M. Heal
D.G. Heap
P.J. Heath
R. Hebblethwaite
J.E. Hegarty
R.T. Hegde
N.M. Heggie

H continued

M.P.D. Heining
J. Hellewell
P.A.L. Henderson
C.P.H. Heneghan
J.G. Henly
J.D. Henville
S.K. Hepton
I.H. Herrema
M.J. Herrick
J.B. Hester
P.B. Hewitt
A. Hewlett
K.C. Hickmott
O. Hifzi
B.D. Higgs
D.J. Hill
H. Hill
M.M. Hills
J. Hindmarsh
I.P. Hine
W. Hinton
G.M. Hitchings
A. Hobbs

R.M.H. Hodgson
S. Holgate
N. Hollis
J.W.L. Holmes
W. Holmes
G. Hood
R.J. Hope
R.B. Hopkinson
E.L. Horsman
B.C. Hovell
E.C. Howard
R.P. Howard
R.M. Howard-Griffin
J.P. Howe
C.W. Howell
P.J. Howell
R.H. Howell
S. Howlin
R.H.A. Hoyal
J.R. Hoyle
N. Huddy
M.C. Hudson
R.B.S. Hudson

D.G. Hughes
D.R. Hughes
T.J. Hughes
V.G. Hughes
D.I. Hughes-Davies
C.J. Hull
M.G. Hulse
J.E. Hunsley
P.C.W. Hunt
T.M. Hunt
J.M. Hunter
J. Hurdley
J.E. Hurley
J. Hurst
D.S. Hurwitz
B.K.D. Huss
A. Hussain
P.J.G. Hutchings
A. Hutchinson
H.T. Hutchinson
J. Hutchinson
C. Hutter

I

G.S. Ingram
M.T. Inman

C.N. Isherwood
M. Islam

D. Iyer

J

A.P.F. Jackson
A.S. Jackson
D.G. Jackson
D.M. Jackson
I.J.B. Jackson
P.W. Jackson
R. Jackson
S. Jacobs
S.V. Jagadeesh
R.H. Jago
I. James
J. James
M.L. James
P. James
P.D. James
R.H. James
A.D. Jardine
E.B. Javed
B. Jayaratne

L.A.G. Jayasekera
D.W. Jayson
V. Jeevananthan
J.D.M. Jeffery
N.G. Jeffs
J.A. Jellicoe
B.J. Jenkins
I.A. Jenkins
J.G. Jenkins
J.R. Jenkins
G. Jephcott
R.J. Johns
C.J.H. Johnson
M.K. Johnson
R.C. Johnson
R.W. Johnson
C.G. Johnston
H.M.L. Johnston
I.G. Johnston

R.D. Johnstone
B.C. Jones
D.F. Jones
D.F. Jones
I.W. Jones
J.A. Jones
J.E. Jones
J.G. Jones
M.J. Jones
M.J.T. Jones
N.O. Jones
P.L. Jones
R.E. Jones
R.M. Jones
M.J. Jordan
S. Jothilingam
D.M. Justins

K

N.S. Kaduskar

B.S.K. Kamath

M.B. Kamath

K continued

G.M. Kane
L.D. Karalliedde
N.H. Kay
P.M. Kay
G.A. Kazi
P. Keeling
P.J. Keep
D.R. Kelly
E.P. Kelly
J.M. Kelly
D.J. Kennedy
J.H. Kerr
I. Kestin
I.A. Khan

T. Khanam
R.M. Kipling
I.J. Kirby
T. Kirwan
R. Kishen
J. Kneeshaw
A.A. Knibb
C.J. Knickenberg
C.L. Knight
P.F. Knight
M.K. Kocan
R.L.J. Kohn
K. Konieczko
V.K. Khanna

A.A. Khawaja
S.M. Kilpatrick
A. Kimberley
N.W. King
R. King
T.A. King
G. Kings
J.D. Kinnell
J.R. Krapez
A.J. Kuipers
B. Kumar
C.M. Kumar
G.W. Kuvelker

L

M. Laban
J.A. Lack
D.A. Laffey
D. Laird
R. Laishley
A.P.J. Lake
S. Lakhani
A.S.T. Lamb
J. Lamberty
P.R.W. Lanham
D. Lassey
P.D. Lassey
B.V. Latham
R.D. Latimer
I.P. Latto
E. Lawes
S.L. Lawrence
A.G.P. Laxton
D. Laycock
D.J. Layfield
A.B. Leach
D.E. Lee
K.G. Lee
P. Lee
P.F.S. Lee
J.D. Leece

J.F. Lees
S.V. Lees
J. Lehane
R.J. Lenz
A. Leslie
P.J.A. Lesser
V. Levack
D.G. Lewis
G.A. Lewis
J.R. Lewis
M.A. Lewis
M.A.H. Lewis
P. Lewis
R.B. Lewis
R.N. Lewis
B. Liban
J.P. Lilley
M. Lim
E.S. Lin
M.J. Lindop
K.G. Lindsay
R.G. Lindsay
W.A. Lindsay
S. Ling
S.P.K. Linter
D.J. Lintin

R.A.F. Linton
A. Lloyd-Thomas
A.B. Loach
A.S. Lockhart
A.D. Logan
L. Loh
T.M.W. Long
M.A. Longan
R.T. Longbottom
M. Lord
M. Lothian
B. Loughnan
P.G. Loughran
W.J. Love
S.S. Lowe
C.F. Loyden
T. Ludgrove
G. Lundil
F.E. Luscombe
M. Lutton
C.G.M. Lynch
M. Lynch
G.R. Lyons
S.M. Lyons

M

J.T. MacBeath
R.G. MacDonald
S. MacDonald
D.H. MacDougall
D.W. MacFarlane
K.C. Macintosh
I.R. Mackay
L.J. Mackay
A.A. Mackenzie

S. Mackenzie
I.M.J. Mair
C.T. Major
E. Major
C.G. Male
L.G. Male
A.F. Malins
A. Manara
P.E. Mann

R.A.M. Mann
A.G. Marshall
F.P.F. Marshall
R.D. Marshall
A.J. Martin
D.G. Martin
J.L. Martin
J.W. Martin
V. Martin

M continued

S.A. Masey
G.F. Macleod
K.G.A. Macleod
D.I.M. Macnair
T.H. Madej
A.M. Hahgoub
O. Mahmoud
C.J.D. Maile
R. Mannar
J.J. Margary
J.S. Mark
K. Markham
S.J. Markham
R.J. Marks
A.M. Marsh
R.H.K. Marsh
J.S. Mason
N.J.A. Massey
J.S. Mather
S.P. Mather
H.A. Matheson
K.H. Matheson
I.M.J. Mathias
J.A. Mathias
N.K. Mathur
A.J. Matthews
N.H. Matthews
P.J. Matthews
R.F.J. Matthews
A.E. May
A.J. May
J.R. May
R.M. Mayall
J.K. Mazumder
R.J. McBride
I.J. McCallum
W. McCaughey
W.N.C. McCleery
I.P. McEwan
J. McFeachie
J.F. McGeachie

T.D. McGhee
I. McInnes
A.C. McKay
P. McKenzie
E.P. McKiernan
C.K. McKnight
I. McLellan
T.J. McMurray
W.T. McNeil
H.G. McNeill
J.J. McPherson
M. McTwohig
R. Mcerlane
D.P. Meadows
G.A. Meadows
M. Mehta
S. Mehta
F. Melikian
L. Mendel
L.M. Mendonca
W.K. Merifield
M.N.A. Messih
V.F. Metias
J. Millar
S.W. Millar
J.S. Miller
R.I. Miller
C.M.H. Miller-Jones
K.R. Milligan
N.S. Milligan
J.P. Millns
B.R. Milne
I.S. Milne
L.A. Milne
M.D. Milne
T.J. Mimpriss
R.K. Mirakhur
P.L. Misra
J.C. Missen
M.D. Mitchell
R.G. Mitchell

R.W.D. Mitchell
K.A. Mobley
S.P. Moffett
A. Mollah
A.H.M. Mollah
C. Monk
R.A. Moody
C. Moon
C.A. Moore
K.C. Moore
M.R. Moore
P. Moore
W.E. Morcos
C. Morgan
G.A.R. Morgan
R.J.M. Morgan
R.N.W. Morgan
J.O. Morgan-Hughes
P.J. Morris
R. Morris
G.W. Morriss
A.J. Mortimer
A.K. Morton
E. Moss
P. Moss
S.M. Mostafa
A. Motom
G. van Mourik
S. Mousdale
M. Mowbray
M.A. Moxon
L.L. Mudie
F.J. Mukasa
D.K. Mukerji
J.V.B. Mundy
J. Murphy
F.P. Murray
J.F. Murray
D.K. Mwanje
K.R. Myerson
H. Myint

N

R. Nalliah
M.L. Nancekievill
K. Nandi
N.H. Naqvi
P.J. Nash
T.P. Nash
K.M. Natrajan
A. Naunton
M.N. Navaratnarajah
H.C. Naylor
T. Neal
A.E. Nesling

S. Nethesinghe
H. Newbegin
J.M. Newbery
D.M. Newby
J.P. Newell
W.S. Ng
M. Nichol
M.P. Nicholas
A.D.J. Nicholl
P. Nichols
A. Nicol
M.S. Nielsen

J.J. Nightingale
K.W. Nightingale
S. Nithianandan
J. Noble
W.A. Noble
J. Norman
J.P. Normandale
P.E. North
A.C. Norton
P.M. Norton
W.G. Notcutt
M.R. Nott

O

A.C. O'Callaghan
J.F. O'Dea
B. O'Donoghue
N.P. O'Donovan

H. O'Dwyer
M.P. O'Neill
P.J. O'Shea
G.M. O'Sullivan

A. Oduro
J. Ormrod
I.A. Orr
J.K. Orton

P

R.N. Packham
N.L. Padfield
H. Padmanabhan
M.L. Paes
J.M. Page
R.J.E. Page
W.A. Pais
P.H. Palin
N. Palmer
C. Pantin
J.C. Pappin
W.G. Park
J.R. Parker
T.F.J. Parker
C.J. Parnell
H. Parry
R.S. Parsons
A. Patel
H.T. Patel
G.M.C. Paterson
D. Pathirana
M.R. Patrick
S. Paul
N.J. Paymaster
M. Payne
T. Peachey
J.E. Peacock
A.J. Pearce

R.M.G. Pearson
D.J. Peebles
M.S. Pegg
C.J. Pemberton
N. Penfold
V.W. Penning-Rowsell
M.L. Pepperman
D. Perks
B.W. Perriss
C.G. Peters
A.C. Peterson
H.V. Petts
P.M. Pfeifer
D.C. Phillips
D.M. Phillips
G. Phillips
G.H. Phillips
K.A. Phillips
M.L. Phillips
P.D. Phillips
F.J. Pickford
R.M.E. Pinchin
C. Pinnock
G.M. Pitt
P.E. Plowman
R.B. Plummer
F.S. Plumpton
A.G. Pocklington

B.J. Pollard
C.G. Pollock
J.C. Ponte
J. Porter
A.J. Porterfield
C.J.F. Potter
D. Potter
D. Powell
D.R. Powell
J.N. Powell
A.B. Powles
C.I. Pratt
E.M. Preston
K.A. Price
A. Pride
A.K. Pridie
V.J. Prior
E.A. Proctor
J.A. Prosser
D.T. Protheroe
B.R. Puddy
V. Punchihewa
G. Purdy
R.J. Purnell
E.A. Putnam
A. Pyne

R

R. Radford
D.G. Raitt
T. Rajasekeran
V.S. Ram
A.J. Rampton
W.N. Ramsden
N.P.C. Randall
P.J. Randall
W.S. Rao
J.M. Raper
R.M.H. Ratcliffe
D.A. Ratliff
S. Ratnavel
P.J. Ravenscroft
S.B. Rawal
E. Rawlings

W.A.L. Rawlinson
A.K. Ray
P.R. Rayner
A. Razak
P. Razis
D. Read
S.E. Rebstein
D.R.O. Redman
P.N. Reed
S. Rehor
M.F. Reid
C.S. Reilly
S.A.M. Remington
A.J.N. Renshaw
R. Rhind
D.C. Richards

D. Richardson
J. Richardson
M.E. Richardson
M.N. Richmond
W.J.K. Rickford
G.S. Riddell
P.L. Riddell
I.F. Riddle
P.J. Rimell
M. Rimmer
P. Ritchie
P.A. Ritchie
F.L. Roberts
J.C. Roberts
M.G. Roberts
W.O. Roberts

R continued

D.S. Robertson
J.A. Robertson
J.E. Robinson
P.N. Robinson
Q.L.A. Robinson
G.E.W. Robson
D. Rogerson
B. Roscoe
A. Rose

M. Rosen
D.M. Ross
M.T. Ross
J.M. Rouse
J. Roylance
A.P. Rubin
M.A. Rucklidge
S.J. Ruff
E. Rush

G.B. Rushman
I.F. Russell
D.V. Rutter
C.R. Ryan
D.A. Ryan
J.P. Ryan
T.D.R. Ryan
W. Ryder

S

B.B. Sahal
L. St John-Jones
J.P. Sale
M.G.D. Salem
N.P. Salmon
P.J. Salt
R.V. Samak
A. Samsome
T.A. Samuels
R.S. Sanders
S. Sanghera
A. Sansome
B. Sarangi
V. Sarma
T.M. Savege
S.N. Saxena
N.M. Schofield
A.C. Scott
J.G. Scott
R. Scott
W.E. Scott
S.J. Seager
M.M. Sealey
J. Sear
J.F. Searle
S.J. Seddon
H.F. Seeley
K. Seethalakshmi
W.F.S. Sellers
W.G. Sellwood
P. Sengupta
A. Seth
R.K. Shah
R.N.N. Shah
Z.P. Shah
A.B. Shanks
C.J. Shannon
L.A.M. Sharaf
T.D.E. Sharpe
E.A. Shaw
I. Shaw
J. Shaw
T.C. Shaw
T.J.I. Shaw

B.J. Sheerin
J.H. Sheldrake
M.P. Shelly
M.P. Shenoy
K.M. Sherry
U.H. Shiyia
S. Short
A.J. Shribman
L.E. Shutt
W.J. Siddall
S.A. Siddiqui
C.A. Sides
J.M. Silk
J. Silver
M.E. Simpson
P.J. Simpson
A.J. Sims
J.R. Sinclair
M. Sinclair
T. Siva
T. Sivalingam
D.G. Skewes
M.A. Skivington
R. Slater
I.P. Slee
C. Smales
J.R. Smethurst
B.A.C. Smith
B.L. Smith
G. Smith
H.S. Smith
J.B. Smith
J.E. Smith
M. Smith
M.B. Smith
N.J. Smith
P. Smith
P.A. Smith
S.P. Smith
S.S. Smith
U.G.C. Smith
W.D. Smith
P.R.F. Smyth
R. Smyth

R.G. Snow
I.D. Somerville
G.R. Sowden
C.C. Spanswick
H.M.S. Speedy
I. Spencer
P.L. Spreadbury
J.S. Sprigge
S. Srivastava
R.K. Stacey
M.A. Stafford
A.F. Stakes
B.J. Stanford
J.C. Stanley
I.K. Stanley-Jones
J.M. Stanton
C. Starkey
P.A. Steane
B. Steer
C.M. Steven
A.J. Stevens
J. Stevens
R.W. Stevens
J.M. Stevenson
A.I. Stewart
P. Stewart
E. Stielow
J.G.L. Stock
J. Stonham
P.J. Stow
S.K. Strachan
C.M. Stray
M. Street
J.E. Strong
P. Strube
J.F. Stubbing
J.T. Styles
M. Styles
M. Suchak
R.J. Summerfield
E. Sumner
A. Sutcliffe
I.A. Sutherland
I.C. Sutherland

S continued

B.G. Swales
D. Swallow

P.T. Sweet
A. Syed

G.V. Symons

T

R.M. Tackley
P.C.M. Taggart
D.B.B. Talwatte
D. Tandon
P.G. Tannett
A. Tappin
T.J. Tarr
M.P. Tattersall
E.A. Taylor
G. Taylor
I.H. Taylor
P.A. Taylor
R.H. Taylor
S. Taylor
V. Taylor
G. Teturswamy
S. Thas
C. Thomas
D.A. Thomas
D.A. Thomas
D.W. Thomas
G.W. Thomas

J.B. Thomas
J.L. Thomas
J.S. Thomas
R.C. Thomas
W.A. Thomas
E.E.M. Thompson
G.R. Thompson
I.D. Thompson
J.F.W. Thompson
M.C. Thompson
R.J. Thompson
J. Thomson
K.D. Thomson
J.L. Thorn
A. Thornberry
A. Thorniley
B. Thornley
T.A.S. Thorp
M.H. Thorpe
P.M. Thorpe
A.C. Thurlow
A.D. Thurlow

S.Q.M. Tighe
S. Tinloi
T.R. Tipping
M.A. Tobias
C.L. Tolhurst-Cleaver
A.A. Tomlinson
J.H. Tomlinson
J.T. Tomlinson
M.J. Tomlinson
M.D. Trask
I.C. Tring
A.P. Triscott
D.J. Turner
J.M. Turner
M.A. Turner
N.M. Turner
R.J.N. Turner
M.J. Turtle
A.J. Twigley
M.M. Twohig
C.K.G. Tyler
M.F. Tyrrell

U

I. Ulyett
S. Underhill

S. Underwood
V.K.N. Unni

H. Utting

V

A. Valijan
C.J. Vallis
J.P. Van Besouw
G.K. Vanner
B.Q. Varley
M. Vater

R.S. Vaughan
L.M. Vella
A.M. Veness
C. Verghese
R. Verma
I.R. Verner

M.S. Vernon
P. Verrill
A.P. Vickers
R.G. Vindlacheruvu

W

T. Waddell
M.J. Wade
A.J. Wadon
C.A. Wadon
E.J. Wadon
A. Wainwright
A.C. Wainwright
C.M. Wait
D. Wakely

B.G. Waldon
A. Walker
A.K.Y. Walker
H.A.C. Walker
J.A. Walker
M.A. Walker
A.J. Walmsley
D.A. Walmsley
E. Walsh

D. Walters
F. Walters
B. Walton
M. Walton
J.G. Wandless
H.M. Wanninayake
M.E. Ward
R.M. Ward
S. Ward

W continued

I. Warnell
J.B. Warren
T.D. Waterhouse
H.R. Waters
J.H. Waters
T.G. Watkins
A.N. Watson
D.A. Watson
D.M. Watson
J.M. Watt
J.W.H. Watt
T.D. Wauchob
T.B. Webb
J.L. Webster
N.R.W. Webster
J.R. Wedley
E.A. Welchew
B. Weldon
O.G.W. Weldon
R. Weller
J.K.G. Wells
J.G.K. Wells
M.J. Wellstood-Eason
B.E. Welsh
P.B. Wemyss-Gorman
D. West
K.J. West
G.A. Weston
R.G. Wheatley
D.K. Whitaker
R. Whitburn
D.G. White

D.J.K. White
J.B. White
P.O. White
W.D. White
M.J. Whitehead
J.H.W. Whitford
J.A. Whitlock
M.P. Whitten
R.T. Whitty
K. Wickremasinghe
A.K. Wielogorski
P.C. Wiener
A.B.S. Wijetilleka
J. Wilkes
R.G. Wilkes
A.D. Wilkey
B.R. Wilkey
D.G. Wilkins
K. Wilkinson
R. Will
D.G. Willatts
S. Willatts
B.R. Wilkey
D.G. Wilkins
K. Wilkinson
R. Will
D.G. Willatts
S. Willatts
A.C. Williams
A.W. Williams
J.G. Williams
J.H. Williams

L.J. Williams
P.A.D. Williams
T.I.R. Williams
A.M. Wilson
J.U. Wilson
M. Wilson
T.J. Wilson
H.J. Wilton
D.P. Winder
J.H. Winder
C.C. Wise
R.T. Witty
M.J. Wolfe
D.W. Wood
N.M. Woodall
T.E. Woodcock
I. Woods
J.M. Woods
P.V. Woodsford
C.H.M. Woollam
W.J.W. Wraight
G. Wray
C.J. Wright
D. Wright
E. Wright
I.G. Wright
J.H. Wright
M.M. Wright
R.M. Bowen Wright
R. Wyatt

X

G.P. Xifaras

Y

B. Yate
P. Yate
J.E.J. Yates

D.A. Young
E. Young
J.R.B. Young

P.N. Young
M.S. Youssef
Y.F. Law Chin Yung

Z

M.A. Zaki
D.A. Zideman

S.L. de Zoysa
Z. Zych

APPENDIX F

LOCAL REPORTERS

The reporters named below are those who are currently (July 1993) reporting to the Enquiry. We greatly appreciate the work of these reporters and of those who preceded them.

Northern

Dr M K Bennett
Consultant Pathologist
Freeman Hospital
Newcastle upon Tyne

Dr C M Dobson
Consultant Histopathologist
Shotley Bridge General Hospital
Consett

Dr A G Hastings
Consultant Histopathologist
Wansbeck General Hospital
Ashington

Dr J D Hemming
Consultant Pathologist
Hexham General Hospital

Dr J Hoffman
Consultant Pathologist
North Tees General Hospital
Stockton-on-Tees

Dr K A Jasim
Consultant Histopathologist
Bishop Auckland General Hospital

Dr V M Joglekar
Consultant Pathologist
Furness General Hospital
Barrow-in-Furness

Dr F Johri
Consultant Histopathologist
North Tyneside General Hospital
North Shields

Dr R A Jones
Consultant Pathologist
Middlesbrough General Hospital

Dr D Laird
Consultant Anaesthetist
Dryburn Hospital
Durham

Dr E D Long
Consultant Histopathologist
Cumberland Infirmary
Carlisle

Dr I M J Mathias
Consultant Anaesthetist
Queen Elizabeth Hospital
Gateshead

Dr A R Morley
Consultant Histopathologist
Royal Victoria Infirmary
Newcastle upon Tyne

Dr K P Pollard
Consultant Histopathologist
South Tyneside District Hospital
South Shields

Dr D Smith
Consultant Histopathologist
West Cumberland Hospital
Whitehaven

Dr D Scott
Consultant Pathologist
Newcastle General Hospital

Dr C Williams
Consultant Histopathologist
Memorial Hospital
Darlington

Mr C P L Wood
Consultant Surgeon
Hartlepool General Hospital

Yorkshire

Dr C Abbott
Consultant Histopathologist
The University of Leeds

Dr H H Ali
Consultant Histopathologist
Huddersfield Royal Infirmary

Dr S Aparicio
Consultant Histopathologist
St James's University Hospital
Leeds

Dr P Evans
Consultant Anaesthetist
Castle Hill Hospital
Cottingham

Dr S Gill
Consultant Anaesthetist
Pinderfields General Hospital
Wakefield

Mr R J R Goodall
Consultant Surgeon
Royal Halifax Infirmary

Dr P Gudgeon
Consultant Histopathologist
Dewsbury District Hospital

Dr D C Henderson
Consultant Histopathologist
Friarage Hospital
Northallerton

Dr J M Hopkinson
Consultant Histopathologist
York District Hospital

Dr D S Hutton
Consultant Anaesthetist
Scunthorpe General Hospital
(for Goole General Hospital)

Dr A M Jackson
Consultant Pathologist
Scarborough Hospital

Dr S Knott
Consultant Microbiologist
Wharfedale General Hospital
Otley

Yorkshire continued

Dr G Kurien
Consultant Pathologist
Scunthorpe General Hospital

Miss A H Lawson
Consultant Surgeon
Harrogate District Hospital

Dr I W C MacDonald
Consultant Histopathologist
Pontefract General Infirmary

Dr B Naylor
Consultant Histopathologist
Bradford Royal Infirmary

Dr R D Pyrah
Consultant Histopathologist
Airedale General Hospital
Keighley

Dr M R F Reynolds
Specialist in Community Medicine
Hull Health Authority

Trent

Dr C A Angel
Senior Lecturer
Department of Pathology
University of Sheffield Medical School

Dr D C S Durrant
Consultant Histopathologist
Pilgrim Hospital
Boston

Dr J Finbow
Consultant Pathologist
Doncaster Royal Infirmary

Dr A Fletcher
Consultant Histopathologist
Leicester Royal Infirmary

Dr J M Frayne
Consultant Anaesthetist
Barnsley District General Hospital

Dr P B Gray
Consultant Histopathologist
Chesterfield & North Derbyshire
Royal Hospital

Dr J Harvey
Consultant Histopathologist
Lincoln County Hospital

Dr J Heaton
Consultant Pathologist
Victoria Hospital
Worksop

Mr R B Jones
Consultant Surgeon
Rotherham District General Hospital

Dr E H MacKay
Consultant Histopathologist
Leicester General Hospital

Dr A A Mousley
Director of Public Health
North Nottinghamshire HA

Dr S Muller
Consultant Pathologist
Glenfield General Hospital
Leicester

Mr J R Nash
Consultant Surgeon
Derbyshire Royal Infirmary

Professor D R Turner
Professor of Pathology
University Hospital
Nottingham

East Anglia

Dr N J Ball
Consultant Histopathologist
James Paget Hospital
Great Yarmouth

Dr T Biedrzycki
Consultant Histopathologist
West Suffolk Hospital

Dr N Cary
Consultant Histopathologist
Papworth Hospital

Dr P M Dennis
Consultant Pathologist
Peterborough District Hospital

Dr D Eakins
Consultant Histopathologist
The Queen Elizabeth Hospital
King's Lynn

Professor G A Gresham
Professor of Histopathology
Addenbrooke's Hospital
Cambridge

Dr B G McCann
Consultant Histopathologist
Norfolk and Norwich Hospital

Mrs G Skillicorn
Director of Information
Ipswich Hospital

Dr A L Whitehead
Consultant Histopathologist
Hinchingbrooke Hospital
Huntingdon

North West Thames

Dr C A Amerasinghe
Consultant Histopathologist
Central Middlesex Hospital

Dr W K Blenkinsopp
Consultant Pathologist
Watford General Hospital

Dr S Boyle
Consultant Histopathologist
Northwick Park Hospital
Harrow

Dr J Dawson
Consultant Anaesthetist
Ashford Hospital
Middlesex

Dr A T Davey
Consultant Pathologist
Hillingdon Hospital

Dr A Fattah
Consultant Histopathologist
Queen Elizabeth II Hospital
Welwyn Garden City

Dr R D Goldin
Senior Lecturer
Department of Histopathology
St Mary's Hospital
W2

Dr S Hill
Consultant Histopathologist
St Albans City Hospital

Dr G Hughes
Consultant Haematologist
West Middlesex University Hospital
Isleworth

Dr D A S Lawrence
Consultant Histopathologist
Luton & Dunstable Hospital

Dr I Lindsay
Consultant Histopathologist
Charing Cross Hospital
W6

Dr D J Madders
Consultant Histopathologist
Lister Hospital
Stevenage

Dr J C McAlpine
Consultant Histopathologist
Edgware General Hospital

Dr A P O'Reilly
Consultant Histopathologist
St Alban's City Hospital
(for Hemel Hempstead Hospital)

Dr R Owen
Consultant Anaesthetist
Ealing Hospital

Dr D Shove
Consultant Histopathologist
Barnet General Hospital

Dr M Walker
Senior Lecturer
Department of Histopathology
St Charles' Hospital
W10

Mr N Waterfall
Consultant Surgeon
Bedford General Hospital

North East Thames

Dr A Atherton
Medical Audit Coordinator
Southend Hospital

Dr S I Baithun
Consultant Histopathologist
St Andrews Hospital
E3

Dr P C Conn
Consultant Pathologist
Severalls Hospital
Colchester

Dr J Dyson
Consultant Histopathologist
Whittington Hospital
N19

Dr P Ellis
Consultant Pathologist
Oldchurch Hospital
Romford

Dr P J Flynn
Consultant Anaethetist
The Royal London Hospital
E1

Dr W J Harrison
Consultant Histopathologist
North Middlesex Hospital
N18

Dr R G M Letcher
Consultant Histopathologist
St Margaret's Hospital
Epping

Dr D Lowe
Consultant Histopathologist
St Bartholomew's Hospital
EC1

Dr J E McLaughlin
Consultant Histopathologist
The Royal Free Hospital
NW3

Dr H A S Reid
Consultant Histopathologist
Chase Farm Hospital
Enfield

Mr A H M Ross
Consultant Surgeon
Broomfield Hospital
Chelmsford

North East Thames continued

Dr S G Subbuswamy
Consultant Histopathologist
St Andrew's Hospital
Billericay

Dr P Tanner
Consultant Histopathologist
King George Hospital
Ilford

Dr D A Thomas
Consultant Anaesthetist
Harold Wood Hospital
Romford

Dr K M Thomas
Consultant Histopathologist
Whipps Cross Hospital
E11

Dr J Secker Walker
Consultant Anaesthetist
University College Hospital
WC1

South East Thames

Dr E J A Aps
Consultant Histopathologist
Queen Mary's Hospital
Sidcup

Dr J Bennett
Consultant in Public Health Medicine
Brighton Health Authority

Dr M E Boxer
Consultant Histopathologist
Conquest Hospital
St Leonard's-on-Sea

Dr D R Davies
Consultant Histopathologist
St Thomas' Hospital
SE1

Dr M H Elmahallawy
Consultant Histopathologist
Orpington Hospital

Dr V K Hochuli
Consultant in Communicable Disease
Maidstone Health Authority

Dr S Humphreys
Consultant Histopathologist
King's College Hospital
SE5

Dr C Keen
Consultant Pathologist
Lewisham Hospital

Dr C W Lawson
Consultant Histopathologist
William Harvey Hospital
Ashford

Professor D A Levinson
Professor of Microbiology
Guy's Hospital
SE1

Dr A E Limentani
Director of Public Health
Canterbury & Thanet Health Authority

Dr G G Menon
Consultant Pathologist
Brook General Hospital
SE18

Dr A Palmer
Director of Public Health
Medway Health Authority

Dr Pinto
Consultant Pathologist
Greenwich District Hospital

Dr A T M Rashid
Consultant Pathologist
Joyce Green Hospital
Dartford

Mr T G Reilly
Medical Records Manager
Eastbourne District General Hospital

Dr G A Russell
Consultant Histopathologist
Kent and Sussex Hospital
Tunbridge Wells

South West Thames

Dr A Berresford
Consultant Histopathologist
Princess Royal Hospital
Hayward's Heath

Dr S Dilly
Consultant Histopathologist
St George's Hospital
SW17

Dr G F Goddard
Consultant Anaesthetist
Frimley Park Hospital
Camberley

Mr J E Hale
Consultant Surgeon
East Surrey Hospital
Redhill

Dr M Hall
Consultant Pathologist
St Peter's Hospital
Chertsey

Mr R D Leach
Consultant Surgeon
Kingston Hospital

South West Thames continued

Dr B Manners
Consultant Histopathologist
Royal Surrey County Hospital
Guildford

Dr T Matthews
Consultant Histopathologist
Epsom District Hospital

Mr E R T Owen
Consultant Surgeon
Crawley Hospital

Dr E H Rang
Consultant in Public Health Medicine
Wilson Hospital
Mitcham

Mr M J Rymer
Consultant Gynaecologist
Worthing Hospital

Dr K Schafler
Consultant Histopathologist
Queen Mary's University Hospital
Roehampton

Mr J N L Simson
Consultant Surgeon
St Richard's Hospital
Chichester

Dr S M Thomas
Consultant Histopathologist
Mayday Hospital
Croydon

Wessex

Dr B J Addis
Consultant Histopathologist
Salisbury District Hospital

Dr A Anscombe
Consultant Pathologist
West Dorset Hospital
Dorchester

Dr E W Hall
Consultant Pathologist
Royal United Hospital
Bath

Dr E M Husband
Consultant Histopathologist
Basingstoke District Hospital

Dr M Lesna
Consultant Pathologist
The Royal Bournemouth Hospital

Dr N J E Marley
Consultant Pathologist
St Mary's Hospital
Portsmouth

Dr I E Moore
Consultant Histopathologist
Southampton General Hospital

Dr J S Nichols
Consultant Histopathologist
Poole General Hospital

Dr A C Vincenti
Consultant Pathologist
Royal Hampshire County Hospital
Winchester

Miss J A Wales
Business Manager
Surgical Directorate
Princess Margaret Hospital
Swindon

Mr P Wellington
Consultant A & E Surgeon
Royal Isle of Wight County Hospital

Oxford

Dr M H Ali
Consultant Histopathologist
Wexham Park Hospital
Slough

Dr J V Clark
Consultant Histopathologist
Northampton General Hospital

Dr K Fleming
Consultant Histopathologist
John Radcliffe Hospital
Oxford

Dr B E Gostelow
Consultant Histopathologist
Kettering General Hospital

Dr S S Jalloh
Consultant Histopathologist
Milton Keynes General Hospital

Dr N J Mahy
Consultant Histopathologist
Horton General Hospital
Banbury

Dr A F Padel
Consultant Histopathologist
Stoke Mandeville Hospital
Aylesbury

Dr M J Turner
Consultant Histopathologist
Wycombe General Hospital

Dr R Menai Williams
Consultant Histopathologist
Royal Berkshire Hospital
Reading

South Western

Dr B Codling
Consultant Pathologist
Gloucestershire Royal Hospital

Dr D W Day
Consultant Histopathologist
Torbay Hospital

Mr I Eyre-Brook
Consultant Surgeon
Musgrove Park Hospital
Taunton

Dr N B N Ibrahim
Consultant Histopathologist
Frenchay Hospital
Bristol

Dr M F Lott
Consultant Pathologist
Weston General Hospital

Dr C B A Lyons
Consultant Pathologist
Derriford General Hospital

Dr R Pitcher
Consultant Histopathologist
Royal Cornwall Hospital
Truro

Dr G Purcell
Consultant Anaesthetist
Yeovil District Hospital

Dr C M D Ross
Consultant Histopathologist
North Devon District Hospital
Barnstaple

Dr E A Sheffield
Consultant Pathologist
Bristol Royal Infirmary

Dr H W Simpson
Consultant Histopathologist
Royal Devon & Exeter Hospital

Dr H White
Consultant Pathologist
Southmead General Hospital
Bristol

Dr P N Young
Consultant Anaesthetist
Cheltenham General Hospital

West Midlands

Dr S M Abraham
Consultant Histopathologist
Dudley Road Hospital
Birmingham

Dr T G Ashworth
Consultant Histopathologist
Walsgrave General Hospital
Coventry

Dr N Bajallan
Consultant Histopathologist
George Eliot Hospital
Nuneaton

Dr G H Eeles
Consultant Histopathologist
Kidderminster General Hospital

Dr R A Fraser
Consultant Pathologist
Royal Shrewsbury Hospital

Dr T A French
Consultant Pathologist
Central Pathology Labarotory
Stoke on Trent

Dr S Ghosh
Consultant Histopathologist
Russells Hall Hospital
Dudley

Dr A R Goldsmith
Consultant Pathologist
Manor Hospital
Walsall

Dr K A James
Consultant Histopathologist
Solihull Hospital

Dr B Jones
Consultant Histopathologist
Selly Oak Hospital
Birmingham

Professor E L Jones
Head of Pathology
The Medical School
University of Birmingham

Dr N Kasthuri
Consultant Histopathologist
Burton General Hospital

Dr A M Light
Consultant Pathologist
Good Hope Hospital
Sutton Coldfield

Dr J C Macartney
Consultant Histopathologist
The Alexandra Hospital
Redditch

Dr F McGinty
Consultant Pathologist
Hereford County Hospital

Dr B McCloskey
Director of Public Health
Worcester and District
Health Authority

Dr J Nottingham
Consultant Histopathologist
Hospital of St Cross
Rugby

Dr F Raafat
Consultant Pathologist
Birmingham Children's Hospital

West Midlands continued

Dr D I Rushton
Senior Lecturer in Pathology
The Birmingham Maternity Hospital

Mr J Shanahan
Surgical Services Manager
Birmingham Heartlands Hospital

Dr J Simon
Consultant Histopathologist
Sandwell District General Hospital

Dr V Suarez
Consultant Histopathologist
Staffordshire General Infirmary

Dr H Thompson
Reader in Pathology
Birmingham General Hospital

Dr J Tomlinson
Consultant Anaesthetist
New Cross Hospital
Wolverhampton

Dr E J Vella
Consultant Pathologist
South Warwickshire Hospital

Dr H Whitwell
Consultant Pathologist
Midland Centre for Neurosurgery and
Neurology

Mersey

Dr M S Al-Jafari
Consultant Histopathologist
Warrington District General Hospital

Dr J Burns
Senior Lecturer
Department of Forensic Pathology
Royal Liverpool University Hospital

Dr C T Burrow
Consultant Histopathologist
Walton Hospital
Liverpool

Dr S A C Dundas
Consultant Pathologist
Southport General Infirmary

Dr G M Edwards
Consultant Anaesthetist
Whiston Hospital
Prescot

Dr M Gillett
Consultant Histopathologist
Arrowe Park Hospital

Dr W E Kenyon
Consultant Histopathologist
Broadgreen Hospital
Liverpool

Dr M J Peaston
Medical Director
Chester City Hospital

Mr G B Rawsthorne
Consultant Surgeon
Leighton Hospital
Crewe

Dr W Taylor
Consultant Histopathologist
Fazakerley Hospital

Professor D van Velzen
Institute of Child Health
Royal Liverpool Children's Hospital

Dr A R Williams
Consultant Histopathologist
Macclesfield District General Hospital

Dr H D Zakhour
Consultant Histopathologist
Clatterbridge Hospital

North Western

Dr E W Benbow
Consultant Pathologist
Department of Pathological Sciences
University of Manchester

Dr J Coyne
Consultant Pathologist
Withington Hospital
Manchester

Dr A S Day
Consultant Pathologist
Tameside General Hospital
Ashton-under-Lyne

Mr M Duari
Consultant Surgeon
Burnley General Hospital

Dr I Gupta
Consultant Histopathologist
Royal Albert Edward Infirmary
Wigan

Dr B N A Hamid
Consultant Histopathologist
Trafford General Hospital
Manchester

Dr I K Hartopp
Consultant Anaesthetist
North Manchester General Hospital

Dr P S Hasleton
Consultant Pathologist
Wythenshawe Hospital
Manchester

Dr E Herd
Consultant Pathologist
Bury General Hospital

North Western continued

Mr A D Johnson
Consultant Surgeon
Ormskirk & District General Hospital

Dr A W Jones
Consultant Histopathologist
Hope Hospital
Salford

Dr M Lendon
Senior Lecturer in Paed. Pathology
Royal Manchester Children's Hosptial

Dr D P Meadows
Consultant Anaesthetist
Stepping Hill Hospital
Stockport

Dr A Mene
Consultant Histopathologist
Blackburn Royal Infirmary

Dr J A Morris
Consultant Histopathologist
Lancaster Moor Hospital

Dr C M Nicholson
Consultant Histopathologist
Royal Preston Hospital

Dr I Seddon
Consultant Histopathologist
The Royal Oldham Hospital

Mr D Stewart
Consultant Surgeon
Chorley and District Hospital

Dr K S Vasudev
Consultant Histopathologist
Victoria Hospital
Blackpool

Dr S Wells
Consultant Histopathologist
Bolton General Hospital

Special Health Authorities

Professor B Corrin
Department of Histopathology
Royal Brompton Hospital

Professor A Garner
Director of Pathology
Institute of Ophthalmology
University of London

Dr D A Jewkes
Consultant Anaesthetist
The National Hospital for Neurology
and Neurosurgery

Professor R A Risdon
Consultant Histopathologist
The Hospital for Sick Children

Mr R J Shearer
Chairman of Surgical Division
Royal Marsden Hospital

Dr G Stamp
Consultant Histopathologist
Hammersmith Hospital

Dr T E McEwan
Consultant Anaesthetist
Eastman Dental Hospital

Mr J Wright
Medical Committee Chairman
The London Chest Hospital

Wales

Dr R B Denholm
Consultant Histopathologist
West Wales General Hospital
Carmarthen

Dr A G Douglas-Jones
Consultant Pathologist
University Hospital of Wales
Cardiff

Dr J Gough
Consultant Pathologist
Llandough Hospital
Penarth

Dr M Hughes
Consultant Histopathologist
Ysbyty Gwynedd
Bangor

Dr R J Kellett
Consultant Pathologist
Nevill Hall Hospital
Abergavenny

Professor B Knight
Forensic Pathologist
Cardiff Royal Infirmary

Dr G R Melville Jones
Consultant Histopathologist
Withybush General Hospital
Haverfordwest

Dr L A Murray
Consultant Pathologist
Prince Philip Hospital
Llanelli

Dr P R G Needham
Consultant Histopathologist
Glan Clwyd Hospital
Rhyl

Wales continued

Dr A M Rees
Consultant Histopathologist
Princess of Wales Hospital
Bridgend

Dr R C Ryder
Consultant Pathologist
Prince Charles Hospital
Merthyr Tydfil

Dr C G B Simpson
Consultant Pathologist
Bronglais General Hospital
Aberystwyth

Dr D Stock
Consultant Histopathologist
East Glamorgan General Hospital
Pontypridd

Dr R B Williams
Consultant Histopathologist
Wrexham Maelor Hospital

Dr S Williams
Consultant Pathologist
Singleton Hospital
Swansea

Northern Ireland

Dr J P Alexander
Consultant Anaethetist
Musgrave Park Hospital
Belfast

Mr B Cranley
Consultant Surgeon
Daisy Hill Hospital
Newry

Dr J N Hamilton
Chairman
Division of Anaesthesia
Altnagelvin Hospital
Londonderry

Dr W H K Haslett
Consultant Anaesthetist
Ulster Hospital
Belfast

Dr W Holmes
Consultant Anaesthetist
Erne Hospital
Enniskillen

Dr B Huss
Consultant Anaesthetist
Lagan Valley Hospital
Lisburn

Mr S T Irwin
Consultant Surgeon
Belfast City Hospital

Dr J McLoughlin
Department of Radiology
Mater Infirmorum Hospital
Belfast

Mr D G Mudd
Consultant Surgeon
Waveney Hospital
Ballymena

Mr P C Pyper
Consultant Surgeon
Mid-Ulster Hospital
Magherafelt

Dr F Robinson
Consultant Anaesthetist
Tyrone County Hospital
Omagh

Dr J Sloan
Senior Lecturer in Pathology
Royal Victoria Hospital
Belfast

Dr M Thompson
Consultant Radiologist
Downe Hospital
Downpatrick

Dr C Watters
Consultant Anaesthetist
Coleraine Hospital

Jersey

Dr D Spencer
Consultant Histopathologist
General Hospital

Guernsey

Dr B Gunton-Bunn
Consultant Pathologist
Princess Elizabeth Hospital

Isle of Man

Dr J M Deguara
Consultant Pathologist
Noble's Isle of Man Hospital

ISBN 0 9522069 0 0